# Business, the State and Economic Policy

Italy has one of the world's most complex and fascinating political systems. The controversial rise of Silvio Berlusconi and the state of contemporary Italy can be better understood with an examination of the recent past of this intriguing country.

Grant Amyot casts his critical eye upon the Italian business world, setting it in the context of the international economy. He then traces the close, but chequered, relationship between capital, the state, and the political parties up to the election of one of the country's major business magnates, Silvio Berlusconi, as Prime Minister. The book compares Italy with the USA, Germany and Japan and explores the influence of economic realities, organized interests, and political institutions on the formation of policy in Italy.

This interesting, readable and important book gives the reader an insight into the sources and workings of power in a major advanced industrial state. It will be appreciated by students and researchers with an interest in European politics, comparative politics, and political economy. It will also be a good tool for policy-makers and professionals with an interest in Italian business, economics and politics.

**Grant Amyot** is Associate Professor of Political Studies at Queen's University, Kingston, Canada. Another of his books, *The Italian Communist Party: the Crisis of the Popular Front Strategy*, is also published by Routledge.

# Routledge advances in European politics

# Business, the State and Economic Policy
## The case of Italy

**Grant Amyot**

Routledge
Taylor & Francis Group

LONDON AND NEW YORK

Published 2004 by Routledge
2 Park Square, Milton Park, Abingdon, Oxon, OX14 4RN

Simultaneously published in the USA and Canada
by Routledge
52 Vanderbilt Avenue, New York, NY 10017

First issued in paperback 2018

*Routledge is an imprint of the Taylor & Francis Group, an informa business*

*British Library Cataloguing in Publication Data*
A catalogue record for this book is available from the British Library

*Library of Congress Cataloging in Publication Data*
A catalog record for this book has been requested

Typeset in Baskerville by Wearset Ltd, Boldon, Tyne and Wear

ISBN 13: 978-1-138-96523-2 (pbk)
ISBN 13: 978-0-415-04722-7 (hbk)

For D. and V., with thanks

# Contents

# Tables

# Note on currency values

**Value of 1000 lire (annual averages):**

| Year | US$ | UK£ |
|------|------|------|
| 1980 | 1.17 | 0.50 |
| 1985 | 0.52 | 0.40 |
| 1990 | 0.83 | 0.47 |
| 1995 | 0.61 | 0.39 |
| 1998 | 0.58 | 0.35 |

Source: IMF, *International Financial Statistics*

# 1 Introduction

## Capital and the state

This book starts from the basic intuition that the key to understanding the state in capitalism is to understand capital, its forms, its development, and its imperatives. While political struggles have their autonomous role, and institutions and ideological traditions shape political actors' decisions, nonetheless economic forces are the basis upon which these factors operate. In spite of the strong Marxist political and intellectual tradition in Italy, this sort of analysis of Italian politics and policy-making has seldom been attempted. By beginning to fill this lacuna, we hope to provide the kind of confrontation with actual cases that is so necessary as a test of the many competing theoretical perspectives on the state and the determinants of policy-making. Marxist theories, in particular, have often suffered from their abstract character. And, while Marxists have always recognized the global character of the capitalist economy, its increasing internationalization makes it impossible to consider a national case in isolation, and requires an updating of the first generation of Marxist state theories to take full account of the insertion of both capital and the state in the international system.

To start from capital and its development means to accept one of the key insights of the German derivationist school of Marxist state theory;[1] however, this does not mean that the interests of capital or the consequent actions of the state can be read off directly from the economic situation of capitalists. Firms' accounts and balance sheets can indeed point out problems for capitalists;[2] they do not dictate solutions or point out opportunities. How capitalists perceive the objective situations they find themselves in depends on their own mental framework or ideological perspective; how they respond to them depends on the accepted rules of the game, many of them embodied in institutions,[3] and on the strategies they adopt within the context of those rules.[4] Of course, the strategies that capitalists adopt are not the expression of an indeterminate 'agency', but are themselves the products of a series of political, ideological, and other conditions. Hence any suggestion that either the logic of capital accumulation or the rational choices of self-interested economic actors can explain in themselves the political goals which capitalists pursue, much less the policies of the capitalist state, is very wide of the mark. But in beginning with the economic situation of capitalists, we are not only following the *leitmotiv* of Marxist scholarship, but also adopting an approach consistent with that of scholars like Peter Gourevitch, who, in his *Politics in Hard Times*,[5] gives explanatory priority to actors' production profiles, by which he means their objective economic situations.

The German derivationists' approach grew out of a critical reflection on the work of one of the pioneers of Marxist political science, Nicos Poulantzas.[6] Poulantzas' early work, in particular, was based on the political writings of Marx, Engels, and later Marxists, and conceived of the functions of the capitalist state in strictly political terms: to ensure the survival of the capitalist mode of production by unifying the capitalist class and disorganizing or dividing the other classes. The derivationists instead used *Capital* and Marx's other economic texts to argue that the state's primary role is economic: to facilitate the accumulation of capital. Given what we have said above about the role of ideologies and institutions, any attempt to read off the function of the political sphere from the economic along these lines would be mistaken, and this danger was recognized by the historical derivationists such as Joachim Hirsch.[7] Claus Offe went further and suggested that the capitalist state is attempting to fulfil several functions – in particular, promoting the accumulation of capital and at the same time maintaining its own legitimacy – in an inherently contradictory endeavour that is ultimately doomed to fail.[8] In this way, Poulantzas' valuable insight that the capitalist state must organize the consent of both the capitalists and the subordinate classes, especially the workers, can be retained. At the same time, the functionalist tendency of the early Poulantzas – the unspoken assumption that all the activities of the capitalist state contribute to the maintenance of the mode of production, and that revolution is a thaumaturgic act that can come only from outside the framework of the theory[9] – can be overcome.

The increasing importance of the international dimension requires a re-examination of these earlier contributions to the theory of the state. Many of them, including Poulantzas', while devoting much effort to accounting for the existence and nature of the state in the abstract, presuppose that capitalism develops in the context of a plurality of states. Much Marxist thinking on international relations starts from the writings of Hilferding and Lenin, who similarly presuppose a plurality of competing imperialist powers. Karl Kautsky was one of the few to suggest that this inter-state competition was not an essential feature of capitalist development, and that a cartel of imperialists could emerge from World War I.[10] A writer who has problematized the so-called 'Westphalian' system of independent, sovereign states in recent years is Claudia von Braunmühl, who approaches it from a derivationist perspective.[11] While recognizing that this state system pre-dated the rise of industrial capitalism, she also points out that the uneven development of capitalism and the enlisting of the aid of the state in primitive accumulation and the competition between capitals made a multi-state system functional to its growth.[12]

While it can thus account for the plurality of states in the age of capitalism, derivationism is also the framework that can best explain changes in the most recent period, when the powers of the nation-state have been limited by international financial and commercial pressures emanating from the development of global financial markets and trading links. As the centre of political influence appears to be shifting from domestic political to international economic forces, not only Poulantzas' approach seems unable to grasp any given situation as a totality: neo-institutionalism, a competing theory which grew out of a reflection on the Marxist interpretation of history, likewise is at its strongest in explaining the differences between nations, which it attributes to institutional factors. Even Theda Skocpol's state-centred historical institutionalism presupposes competition for power between a plurality of states: while she argues that 'social revolutions cannot be explained without systematic reference to *inter*national developments and world-historical structures',[13] in practice her analyses remain at the level of the individual states, without any systematic discussion of the dynamics of international relations.

While international institutions are of increasing importance, and several writers have traced the influence of ideologies and economic theories at the international level,[14] these have tended hitherto to shape behaviour principally, though not exclusively, at the élite level. They have done this by influencing the behaviour of political leaders or market actors, as when a government deficit undermines the market's confidence in a currency because foreign exchange traders believe economists and commentators who theorize that sound money demands balanced budgets. Institutions, ideologies, and class coalitions, on the other hand, profoundly shape the way in which a national polity responds to the pressures of the international economy; but they cannot fully account for those pressures themselves. For the last quarter of the twentieth century, this requires an analysis of the long-term decline in the rate of profit and the consequent search by capitalists for higher returns through internationalization of their activities and investment portfolios, in the context of a neo-liberal restructuring of the capitalist system that has vastly increased the power of financial capital.[15]

As mentioned above, the real test of these abstract theories is their ability to account for actual events in concrete cases. Italy is of particular interest as a case study, for its economy is often depicted as *sui generis* among capitalist economies, as is its political system.[16] Hence a theoretical approach that can successfully encompass it will have passed a significant test. In the twentieth century, Italian capital underwent several significant transformations: the advent of Fascism marked the triumph of a bank-led heavy industrial complex – a classic case of 'finance capital'.[17] However, the financial crisis of the Depression led to the absorption of almost the entire banking system by the state, allowing for the economic dominance of industrial capital, first in the shape of the large electrical and chemical firms. From the political point of view, the middle classes – the self-employed and the professional and white-collar bourgeoisie – assumed a key role as the mass base, first of the Fascist Party, then, in the post-war Republic, of the Christian Democrats.[18]

With their passive support, the Christian Democrats facilitated the rise of the Fordist bloc of industries, led by Fiat and the other firms of the automotive cycle, such as Pirelli, which eventually supplanted the electrical and chemical monopolies to become the dominant fraction of Italian capital. In the period since the first oil crisis, this fraction has been at the forefront of the internationalization of the Italian economy;[19] at the same time it has faced political competition from the middle classes, reinforced by significant elements of small and medium industry, and by some of the leaders of the newer economic sectors. The best known of these is Silvio Berlusconi, head of the media giant Fininvest and currently Prime Minister.[20] Opting for an international strategy, the dominant fraction has been able to rely on the legitimacy of international institutions and internationally dominant ideologies, as well as the power of global market forces. However, this strategy has also led to increasing exposure to international competition, and to the re-emergence of a private banking sector and the revitalization of financial markets that could threaten the position of the 'good salon' of major industrial capitalists.

This account is incomplete without recognition of the central role of the struggle between capital and labour; indeed, Hirsch, among the state derivationists, laid stress on the role of the capitalist state in the class struggle,[21] and Poulantzas views the state as acting above all to preserve capitalism from the political threat which the working class at least latently always posess. That we can even sketch an account of recent developments without mentioning the class struggle in the first instance is due to the fact that the Italian working class, while displaying remarkable power, class consciousness, and militancy, especially after the culmination of the post-war boom in the Hot Autumn of 1969, has never posed a truly revolutionary threat to the capitalist order. Even during the Cold War era, the Communist Party's strategy was aimed at forming a democratic, anti-monopoly coalition; in any case, it was consigned to political isolation. In the 1970s, when it benefitted from the upsurge in militancy of 1968–70, it pursued the same type of policy in a yet more defensive key, thoroughly frightened as it was by the example of the Chilean *coup d'état* against Salvador Allende.[22] Since that time, the Italian working class and the union movement have retained a formidable defensive strength, which the dominant fraction of capital has had to accommodate, while other capitalist fractions have generally favoured more confrontational strategies.[23]

The left-wing parties, after the transformation and splitting of the Communist Party in 1991, have demonstrated that arguably they can support

and implement the policies the dominant fraction of capital deems necessary better than the parties of the right: the centre-left Prodi government's
success in bringing Italy into the European Monetary Union with the first
group of countries is the best example of the left's ability in this regard.[24]
Even the left-wing offshoot of the former Communist Party, Communist
Refoundation, provided parliamentary support during this crucial phase.

The internationalizing strategy of the dominant fraction of Italian
capital was successful in the 1990s in the face of opposition from the traditional middle-class and protectionist elements grouped around the Christian Democratic regime. Other factors, such as the corruption scandals
unveiled by the *Tangentopoli* investigations and the emergence of the
Northern League, which divided the bloc of petty bourgeois and small
industry, also contributed to the Christian Democrats' demise. The end of
the Cold War not only removed anti-communism as a *raison d'être* for the
DC, but also freed the more moderate segment of the PCI (refounded as
the *Democratici di sinistra*) to promote and implement some of the major
policies of the dominant fraction of capital, such as EMU. This valuable
surrogate role of the political left (well summed up by the term 'Bonapartism'[25]) necessitated a series of compromises on the part of the dominant fraction: while espousing a neo-liberal position on international
economic policy, it has taken a more flexible stance on issues related to
industrial relations, the labour market, and social policy, demonstrating a
willingness to contemplate corporatist-style accommodations with labour.
In striking contrast, the smaller employers and middle strata have pursued
a more rigidly neo-liberal line domestically, while demonstrating far less
interest in deepening the international integration of the Italian
economy. Even the large firms have not been eager to see the complete
opening of capital markets, or the exposure of their own holdings to
foreign take-over bids.

In this book, the framework sketched in very broad outline above will
be utilized to explain the relationship between the state and capital in
Italy, as well as some of the major directions taken by the state in macroeconomic policy – in particular, monetary and fiscal policy[26] – and industrial relations.[27] These policy areas encompass both Italy's entry into the
EMU in 1999 and the July accords of 1993 between the unions, the
employers, and the state, two outcomes among others which surprised
many observers and led to a re-thinking of conventional wisdom. If the
approach outlined here can account successfully for unexpected outcomes in a polity such as Italy's, it will have proved its worth as a theoretical account of the state in capitalism.

# 2   The growth and development of Italian capitalism

The weight of historical legacies can be heavy, indeed crushing, in the contemporary politics of advanced capitalist states. That weight, however, varies considerably from country to country. In Great Britain, for instance, the predominance of financial capital, represented by the City of London, is rooted in centuries of economic and political development which has given the City a privileged position within the state that has continued to bolster its economic role. In Japan, the national culture formed in the country's feudal era is often cited as an explanation of the spirit of co-operation and dedication to work demonstrated by capitalists and workers alike.[1] Italy's history has been much less linear than Britain's or even Japan's, and its legacies are correspondingly less important in explaining the current power of capital within the political system: the *Risorgimento*, rapid industrial and political development, the two world wars, Fascism, and the tumultuous post-war boom broke down many entrenched positions and brought new actors, economic and political, to the fore

Nevertheless, history can still contribute a great deal, even in the Italian case, to our understanding of the current scene; certain seemingly intractable facts, such as the Southern Question, are deeply rooted in the past. Most importantly, throughout Italy's historical development the bourgeoisie have been relatively weak in the political sphere, and bourgeois ideas and attitudes have similarly been weak in the field of ideology. As a 'late-follower' industrializer, like Russia and Japan, Italy fostered capitalist economic development before capitalist ideas or capitalist political representatives had become ascendant. The relative political and ideological weakness of the bourgeoisie persists to this day, in spite of the vicissitudes of twentieth-century history, the business renaissance of the 1980s, and the rise of global neo-liberalism. This has in turn given the state a particularly autonomous role *vis-à-vis* the capitalist class, and political factors a particularly significant role in shaping the development of Italian capitalism.

## Mediaeval and Renaissance Italy: precocious capitalism?

The backward and underdeveloped condition of Italy and Italian capitalism at the time of Unification in 1860 seems especially difficult to explain when we compare it to the vigorous growth of trade and industry in the high Middle Ages and Renaissance. At that time, the Italian city-states, along with those of Flanders, were undergoing what seemed to be a precocious 'bourgeois revolution': international trade flourished, large-scale manufacturing and a numerous urban proletariat grew up, a distinct merchant and entrepreneurial class appeared and took political power from the feudal magnates. Feudal laws and institutions were replaced by more modern Roman-based law and the 'bourgeois' democracy of the guildsmen. Italy and Flanders appeared, from the standpoint of the year 1300, destined to be the first European countries to complete the transition from feudalism to capitalism.

Yet, in spite of this head start, by the mid-seventeenth century Italy had become an economic backwater, on the 'semi-periphery' of Europe, while England and the Netherlands had surged ahead and taken the lead in capitalist development. The reasons for this failed transition to capitalism have been the subject of considerable historical debate.[2] The traditional explanation that trade routes shifted from the Mediterranean to the Atlantic seaboard with the voyages of discovery cannot be considered satisfactory, as the germs of decline were present in Italy long before 1492, and the revival of Mediterranean trade in the mid-sixteenth century did not reverse the process.

A first group of explanations focuses on the limits of the changes accomplished in the Italian city-states from the eleventh to the fourteenth centuries. Feudal law, custom, and manners were by no means abolished entirely; and, in spite of the many ordinances limiting the rights and privileges of the 'magnates' and the broadened, 'democratic' constitutions of many city-states, the nobility remained the dominant element in political life.[3] The introduction of more advanced techniques and, above all, of capitalist forms of organization of work (the formal and real subsumption of labour under capital) occurred only in certain relatively restricted parts of the country. As Gramsci points out,[4] the democracy of the city-states was limited to the minority who belonged to guilds (and in practice the richest burghers and the nobility had the lion's share of power and office), and totally excluded the inhabitants of the surrounding countryside (*contado*), who were economically exploited by the towns. These limits of the mediaeval bourgeoisie, which made it incapable of generating broad popular support, Gramsci linked to its failure to develop a distinctive ideology, along the lines of the French revolutionary ideas of 1789 or even the English of 1649. It remained enveloped within the ideology of the mediaeval Church, which did not embody or serve the goals of a nascent capitalism, and, later on, the humanism of the Renaissance similarly provided no support or impetus to capitalism, idealizing as it did the leisured scholar-gentleman engaged in the study of dead languages and literatures.

In this context, the 'refeudalization' of the later fifteenth and sixteenth centuries is less a radical break with the previous period than a strengthening of tendencies that had always been significant in the Italian city-states. Nevertheless, the growing ascendancy of aristocratic manners as well as of the aristocracy itself is evident. The nobility forged close alliances with the tyrants or 'lords' (*signori*) who replaced the democratic governments in one city-state after another; the always significant movement of wealthy burghers into the ranks of the aristocracy continued apace, and increasingly they chose to invest their profits in the purchase of landed estates or in luxury goods, rather than in trade or industry. This shift in society and the economy contributed to Italy's economic decline.

The development of the towns as political centres also prevented the formation of a national state in Italy; therefore, it did not benefit from the assistance of such a state in economic development, through war and conquest, exploration, the establishment of colonies, or mercantilist policies. The feudalistic mentality of the ruling strata of the city-states promoted division rather than national unity, and, as Gramsci charged,[5] the presence of the papacy and the Empire had made Italian intellectuals cosmopolitan rather than national in character. In fact, the conflicts between the Italian states were a standing invitation to foreign intervention, and the French invasion of 1494 marked the beginning of a long period of foreign political hegemony, first French, then Spanish.

Another type of explanation starts from an analysis of the economic structure of Renaissance and early modern Italy; it had been the most successful economy of the previous era, and was therefore slow to change and adapt.[6] It had based its success on the production and/or exchange of high-quality goods for a narrow, affluent market. This model made eminent sense in the fourteenth and fifteenth centuries, when there was little mass market for consumer goods of any kind: for all but the richest, clothing was produced at home, and many other products (e.g. spices) were not used at all by peasants or the mass of townspeople. Italy's fine cloths, metal wares, etc., were produced for an international market of nobles and wealthy burghers. This economic model continued to stand the country in good stead through the sixteenth century, but by 1600 markets were slowly widening and Italy's goods and processes could not satisfy their demand for cheaper goods. The persistence of this 'Renaissance' economic model is also responsible for the lack of technical progress that would have allowed the Italian economy to take a qualitative step forward.

Finally, Italy did not see a general move towards commercial agriculture of the type that played such an important part in England's transition to capitalism, first with the wool trade in the late Middle Ages, then with the development of high farming in the eighteenth century. Both the lack of markets for its products and the lack of capital investment, especially in livestock, lay behind the relative stagnation of Italian agriculture. (The irrigated plains of Lombardy were a partial exception, but even there progress was limited by the failure to invest sufficiently). However, more specific factors were also at work: the sharecropping system, widely introduced in Central Italy in the fourteenth century, as the fall in population gave the peasants increased bargaining power, discouraged labour-intensive crops and stock-raising.[7] Faced with a fairly united bourgeois-aristocratic bloc, and without the protection of a strong national monarchy, the peasants themselves had little political power or ability to resist possible attempts to undermine their rights to cultivate the land; however, the landlords did not feel, in most parts of the country, any strong impulse to engage in commercial agriculture. Both the movement to refeudalization and the rise in the price of grain, which discouraged experiments with other crops, contributed to this relative immobilism on the part of the landed class.[8]

While in the eighteenth century there was an agricultural revival, and various cash crops and industrial raw materials came to be cultivated more extensively (raw silk, olive oil, etc.), Italian agriculture as a whole remained of a subsistence type. The peasantry were not driven from the land, as in parts of England, nor did they increase their rights on it, as in France, nor were they part of a labour-repressive system of commercial agriculture, as in East Prussia. While the reforming movements of the courts of the Enlightenment in the late eighteenth century sought to eliminate both the residues of feudalism and the peasants' rights on the land, the countryside remained largely stagnant, in a transitional phase which was no longer feudal in its relations of production, but where the commercial relations more typical of capitalism were dominant only in limited areas. These factors account for the weakness of the bourgeois impulse in Italy in the eighteenth and early nineteenth centuries, and hence for the relatively conservative nature of the unification movement (known as the *Risorgimento*) and the relatively feeble drive towards capital accumulation in united Italy prior to the state's decision to promote it as part of a policy of national prestige.

## Unification

There has been considerable debate about the character of the Risorgimento: many, believing they were following Gramsci, called it a bourgeois revolution, others held that it could not be, for the bourgeoisie and capitalism had triumphed long before.[9] In the sense that it carried out some of the tasks of a bourgeois revolution – i.e. it created the conditions for the further development of capitalism – the Risorgimento can be called one, but it was of an incomplete and belated type. It created a national state, eliminated internal tariff barriers, and completed the work of the anti-feudal reformers. However, it was belated because the relations of production and, in some measure, the laws of motion of the Italian economy were already no longer feudal but in part capitalist.[10] And it was carried out by a 'bourgeoisie' that was still closely related to the landowning aristocracy.

Because it was relatively belated as a bourgeois revolution, the Risorgimento had an 'incomplete' character in several ways. The upper classes who led the movement for unification were careful to control the pressures for radical social as well as political change. While the Third Estate in France had gained overwhelming popular support by giving the peasants full property rights in their land, Cavour and the other 'moderates' who led the Risorgimento would not take such a step; the Italian peasants were not as close to true independence as the French had been in 1789, and in any case the moderates were too closely connected to the landowning strata themselves to contemplate such a step – the titled Cavour, like many of his supporters, was an improving Piedmontese landlord. Moreover, the revolutionary upheavals of the previous seventy years had made the bourgeoisie as well as the aristocracy very wary of the common people. The social character of the Risorgimento was therefore more conservative than that of the French Revolution, and the Italian bourgeoisie missed the chance to forge an alliance with the peasantry and the urban poor. This is the burden of Gramsci's writing on the subject, which acutely notes the failures of the more radical democratic leaders, like Giuseppe Mazzini, and the astute policy of Cavour and the moderates, centred in the Kingdom of Piedmont.[11]

Because of the moderate leadership of the Risorgimento, the ruling class of the new Kingdom of Italy lacked ideological hegemony, to use Gramsci's term: the mass of the people, who were still overwhelmingly peasants, were not involved in the movement, and often scarcely understood it. Those who tried to turn the unification movement into a social movement that would finally give them ownership of the land were savagely repressed (as the peasant revolt in the town of Brontë in Sicily in 1860 was put down). In fact, the unification of Italy ushered in a decline in the peasants' conditions: in the South, it was followed by attacks on their customary rights, e.g. to use common lands, and a further concentration of landed property in the hands of *nouveaux riches* and the old nobility; everywhere, taxes were increased to crushing levels to pay off the debts incurred during the wars of unification. It is scarcely surprising that pro-Bourbon brigands gained widespread support from the Southern peasantry in the 1860s, and could be put down only by sending 120,000 troops to the region.[12] The peasantry, particularly in the South, were therefore alienated from the new state and its leaders.

Furthermore, the new state also alienated the Church and devout Catholics. The leadership of the Risorgimento were secular in orientation, and, under the reactionary Pius IX, the Church set itself against the unification movement which threatened its temporal power. After the Italian occupation of Rome in 1870, the Pope retired into the Vatican and issued the *non expedit*, prohibiting Catholics from even voting in Italian elections. This rift between Church and state was not fully healed until the Concordat of 1929.

Liberal Italy, then, had a very narrow base of support: the liberal, secular members of the propertied classes, and even among these there were widespread regional jealousies and resentments, especially in the South. In recognition of this narrow base, the electoral law enfranchised only 8 per cent of adult males, and even among this limited electorate, turnout was as low as 45.5 per cent (1870), an index of both Catholic and regional disaffection.[13] Whatever else it meant, the Risorgimento did not lead to the spread of bourgeois or capitalist ideas; while the moderates were, by and large, devotees of Manchesterian free-trade, *laissez-faire* economics, and liberal constitutional politics, unification did nothing to bring these ideas to the masses of the people but if anything generated hostility to them.

From 1860 to 1876, politicians of the 'historic Right', the heirs of the Cavourian moderates, steered the country on a path of cautious liberal orthodoxy. They saw little industrial future for Italy, except in textiles; indeed, many of them feared industrialization, which they thought would endanger social stability. In keeping with their free-trade ideology, they lowered tariffs. Because of their preoccupation with paying off the debt, they were unwilling to finance large economic development schemes. Like the rural elites of many contemporary Latin American countries, they were prepared to assume a subordinate place in the liberal world order dominated by Great Britain. Thus railway construction, for instance, was undertaken in this period with foreign financing (principally French) and foreign capital goods; it was not used to provide a stimulus to industrial growth, as in so many other late-following industrializing countries. In class terms, the historic Right represented the prevailing opinion of the majority of the ruling class, with their strong ties to the land.

## Industrial growth

The so-called 'parliamentary revolution' brought down the historic Right in 1876; their defeat was due more than anything else to their overly rigorous fiscal policies, which led to widespread discontent at the tax burden. Their successors of the Left were predominantly Southern-based; they saw themselves as the heirs of the more radical, Garibaldian tradition of the Risorgimento, but in practice they did not favour agrarian reform any more than the Right. With their Southern roots, they were less representative of modern industrial and commercial interests; however, their traditions made them more nationalistic in outlook than the Right.

Furthermore, the international situation was changing, the brief era of free trade was coming to an end, and the scramble for colonial empire was about to intensify. As a result, the Left began a somewhat more vigorous policy of economic development, closely linked to a programme of national prestige and military preparedness.[14] In 1878 it introduced a relatively modest tariff; starting in 1881, it began a large naval construction programme, and in 1884 promoted the creation of the Terni steel mill, which was located inland to protect it from attack and guaranteed orders from the navy. In 1885, it extended subsidies and legal preferences to the Italian merchant marine. Italy's entry into the Triple Alliance in 1882 gave a further impetus to military and naval expansion.

The imperialist policy begun in the 1880s, which included the acquisition of Eritrea and Somalia, was not, as that of the more advanced states may have been, a consequence of cartelization and a surplus of capital.[15] Rather, the state here played an autonomous role, as it often would later in Italian history, in giving industry and finance a start. In keeping with the suggestions of Skocpol and others, external factors were significant causes of the state's decision to promote industrial growth. It is true that growth in the 1880s was slow compared to other 'late-follower' industrializing economies, and really sustained increases in production occurred only in the period 1896–1908,[16] by which time Italy was also a capital exporter, but the foundation for future growth was laid in the earlier decade.

The *pièce de résistance* of the Left's economic policy was the tariff of 1887; while that of 1878 could be defended as a revenue measure, the new tariff was strongly protectionist, in fact the second highest in Europe, after France's. It protected not only industry, but also agriculture, which now demanded tariffs because of the competition of American grain, which had provoked a serious agricultural crisis. In Gourevitch's terminology, the 'production profile' of Italian agriculture was shifted by this new competition, and a high-tariff alliance between grain producers and domestically oriented, subsidized industry, similar to the 'marriage of iron and rye' in Bismarck's Germany, resulted.[17] It can hardly be argued that the tariff had a beneficial effect on Italy's economic growth: the industries that received the strongest protection were those that were already strong – textiles and iron and steel – rather than the newer, dynamic branches with the greatest growth potential, such as engineering and chemicals. Furthermore, iron and steel production was a poor choice of speciality for Italy, which had to import virtually all its coal, but it was considered essential to a modern economy in this era. The agricultural tariff encouraged the sowing of grain rather than the more profitable Southern export crops, such as wine and citrus fruits, and by provoking a trade war with France it further restricted the market for these products. It also raised wage costs for industry. Furthermore, it widened the gap between North and South by protecting not only Northern industry, but the typical Northern crops, such as rice, beet sugar, and hemp.

From the point of view of the political interests of the dominant class, however, the tariff of 1887 was more successful. As Gramsci wrote in the Lyons Theses, it finally unified the Northern industrialists and the Southern landowners in a single ruling bloc.[18] More generally, it overcame the regional particularism of the capitalist class and created a firmer basis for its dominance. And, in spite of its limitations, it did allow for industrial growth, even if this growth was not as rapid or efficient as it might have been.

One reason for the relatively disappointing growth of the 1880s was the character of the banking system: founded on the French model, the banks engaged in only a limited amount of longer-term industrial investment, preferring short-term speculation, particularly in real estate and construction.[19] The government attempted to prop up ailing banks, but in 1893 the whole system collapsed with the failure of the Credito Mobiliare and Banca Generale. In 1894 the Banca Commerciale Italiana was founded with the participation of German capital, and it brought to Italy the German model of the 'mixed bank', taking deposits from the public and investing them for long terms in industry. It developed interests in the textile industry in particular, though it had a role in many other sectors of the economy. The Credito Italiano, founded the same year, developed a particular interest in the electrical sector.[20] In Italy, as in Germany, finance capital in Hilferding's sense – the linking of banking and industrial capital[21] – took shape, at the same time as the economy embarked on the most rapid expansion it had ever known.

However, in spite of its stronger economic position, thanks to the tariff, the development of finance capital, and the boom conditions of the turn of the century, Italian capital was unable to conquer political hegemony. In the 1890s, first under Francesco Crispi, a leader of the historic Left (Prime Minister 1887–91 and 1893–96), then under a succession of conservative figures, the government attempted to continue along the 'Prussian road' it had begun with the tariff of 1887. Crispi pursued a policy of repression at home and imperial expansion abroad that could be justly labelled 'proto-fascist'. The defeat of Italian forces at Adowa by the Ethiopians led to his fall, and the repression of riots in Milan in 1898 with fifty deaths convinced his successor Antonio Rudinì that an authoritarian policy was impractical. In 1900, the Zanardelli-Giolitti government inaugurated a new era of liberalism. Under the skilful leadership of Giovanni Giolitti, the next fifteen years saw a policy of accommodation of the rising socialist movement and of the trade unions. The government ceased to intervene against strikes, and positively favoured the socialist co-operatives of the North with contracts and concessions. While accepting Italian capitalism as it had developed and the policies which underpinned its growth, such as the tariff, Giolitti was no friend of monopolies: he opposed the shipping monopoly, supported by the Banca Commerciale, and eventually nationalized the insurance monopoly.[22]

The relative political weakness of capital was due in the first place to its own divisions. In spite of the unifying role of the banks, there were fundamental differences of interest between the trust industries, dependent on the state and on tariff protection, and the more dynamic, export-oriented sectors. The former included iron and steel and shipbuilding, while the latter embraced the small speciality steel producers of the North and the machinery, automobile, and rail industries. This division was itself due to the intervention of the state, which had fostered the trust industries; it was to play a significant part in the rise of Fascism after the war. Furthermore, both capitalism and the state lacked ideological hegemony over the masses of the people, as the riots and demonstrations of the 1890s had amply demonstrated. Giolitti believed the only rational course was to conciliate the workers; at the same time, he kept the South in subjection by means of electoral fraud, coercion, and the corruption of the Southern political class.[23] Indeed, his parliamentary majority was drawn largely from the South, where he could most fully use the government's influence to secure the election of his supporters. This Giolittian system did not take into account the Southern peasants, whose interests were sacrificed (e.g. by the tariff), but it nevertheless involved significant compromises with the subordinate classes (the workers) and with allied and supporting classes (the Southern petty bourgeoisie, in particular).

Giolitti's governments were, then, quite autonomous with respect to the immediate interests of the capitalist class, but he did not perceive that the working out of the economic trends set in motion as early as the 1880s was strengthening the trusts and finance capital and leading to the formation of sectoral consortia to control prices and regulate wages, very much along the lines described by Hilferding. By 1911, the trusts were strong enough to mount a challenge to Giolitti, promoting a more aggressive foreign policy, particularly in the Balkans, the Near East and North Africa.[24] Both the trust industries and the banks were especially interested in imperialist expansion: the former could benefit from military contracts and the construction of ships for colonial trade and public works in the colonies, while the Bank of Rome, for example, was eager to finance an Adriatic-Danube railroad. Reluctantly, Giolitti declared war on Turkey to obtain Libya (September 1911). This act lost him the Socialists' good will; in fact they mounted a vigorous anti-war campaign. In the same year he felt constrained to introduce universal male suffrage, thereby tripling the electorate. This measure demonstrated the need of the state to seek support from the subordinate classes, another source of its autonomy from capitalist interests. In particular, Giolitti 'changed his rifle from one shoulder to the other' by seeking the support of the Catholic electorate to counterbalance the loss of the Socialists' sympathy. This policy eventually led to his defeat in 1914 by an anti-clerical majority in parliament.

Finally, in 1915 the trust industries and their allies, with the organized support of the nationalist movement, were successful in pushing Italy into

World War I on the side of the Entente. The King and the foreign minister negotiated a secret treaty with the Entente, then virtually imposed the declaration of war on parliament, where the majority would have been willing to follow the neutralist course favoured by Giolitti. In many ways, Italy's entry into the war was more 'a domestic political action' than anything else, for conservative politicians hoped it would bring a return of authoritarian government and end the growing social unrest.[25] The trust industries, the 'military-industrial' fraction of capital, were able in this particular conjuncture to prevail, because other strong reasons stemming from the need to control the subordinate classes also militated in favour of the same course. At the same time, other elements of capital, such as the Banca Commerciale, were neutralist.

## The advent of Fascism

In the post-war situation, the differences between the military-industrial fraction of capital and the export-oriented sectors became even more acute. The former had grown tremendously during the war, and now faced an inevitable contraction of their activities. They depended again on the state to save them. When Giolitti returned to power in 1920 and resumed his earlier line of mediation between capital and labour, and his successor, Bonomi, refused to save the Banca di Sconto, linked to the huge Ansaldo armaments and shipbuilding firm, the trust industries became impatient with constitutional government. At the same time, the capitalist class as a whole was thoroughly frightened by the working-class agitation of the 'two red years', 1919 and 1920, culminating in the factory occupations of September 1920. The advent of Fascism, then, was not only a 'posthumous and preventive counter-revolution' by the bourgeoisie as a whole, but also a moment in the struggle of one fraction of capital for more complete control over the state, in opposition to other fractions (and to the landowners, who were cool to industrial protectionism in general).[26] In the immediate post-war years, it seemed as if the compromise of 1887 might be overthrown by a new liberal, free-trade coalition, including agriculture and the exporting industries; the victory of Fascism prevented this outcome, and stabilized the position of the steel-armaments complex.

Although it did restore the position of the previously hegemonic fraction of capital, Fascism exercised sufficient autonomy to be called a truly 'Bonapartist' regime. This margin of autonomy was derived in part from the bourgeoisie's need of Fascism in its struggle to control the workers and peasants, and in part from the divisions within the bourgeoisie itself. In its first years, although it did salvage Ansaldo and the Bank of Rome, the regime pursued a generally 'liberal' economic policy. It was only in 1925, in concomitance with the consolidation of its power, that it turned in a more autarchic direction. It raised tariffs, including those on wheat and sugar, and in 1926–27 carried out a massive deflationary operation by increasing the exchange value of the lira by two thirds (to 'quota 90', i.e. 90 lire to the pound sterling). This measure won the wholehearted approval of petty bourgeois savers and rentiers, who provided an important part of Fascism's social base, but was strongly opposed by exporting industry. Even the banks were generally opposed. However, the regime felt it could ignore the immediate interests of these elements of capital. On the other hand, basic industries like iron and steel welcomed the lowering of raw material prices. The deflationary package also induced a series of mergers, furthering the concentration of capital.

Throughout the 1930s, Fascism continued to ignore the interests and suggestions of the export-oriented sector of capital. Its deflationary policies worsened the impact of the Depression. The regime refused to take even a timid step in the direction of a 'Fordist'[27] solution: in 1932, it chose to respond to the crisis with wage cuts rather than simply reducing hours, as Fiat proposed. The regime's colonial policy and pro-German foreign policy were also opposed by Fiat, which favoured closer ties with the USA. However, while the steel-armaments complex (including the military side of Fiat, for instance) gained from these policies, the major beneficiaries were the relatively new electrical and chemical sectors, aluminium, rubber goods, and the aircraft industry. The Montecatini chemical giant enjoyed considerable state patronage, and the five large regional electrical companies, led by Edison of Milan, reaped large, guaranteed profits from their monopoly position. Many of these industries were promoted because the regime wanted to achieve self-sufficiency in strategic goods; others, like the electrical firms, were also favoured because they were preferred vehicles for the savings of the petty bourgeoisie.

The financial crisis induced by the Depression further increased the relative weight of the electrical and chemical sectors. While not as badly hit as some of the more developed economies, Italy suffered serious reductions in sales and production in many branches of industry. The banks, which, as 'mixed banks', held large portfolios of industrial shares, found their assets considerably reduced. The devaluation of the pound in 1931 led to a crisis of confidence, and the state was obliged to step in and rescue the Banca Commerciale, the Credito Italiano, and the Bank of Rome.[28] It thereby acquired their stock portfolios, and with them a controlling interest in the major steel, shipping, and shipbuilding companies. In 1933 it created the holding company IRI (Institute for Industrial Reconstruction) to manage these holdings, naming as President Alberto Beneduce, who already managed two long-term credit institutions set up by the state to assist the electric and telephone industries and others involved in public works. The greater part of the old dominant fraction of capital, the steel-armaments complex, thus passed into the hands of the state, leaving the electric monopolies as the hegemonic sector of private industry.

At the same time, the largest section of banking also came under state control, and a new banking law in 1936 forbade banks to engage in long-term financing of industry. Hence both the political and economic weight of the banks was also reduced, and the structure of the credit market fundamentally altered, with the state and its agencies becoming the chief sources of long-term finance.

It is difficult to present the creation of IRI as a major instance of state autonomy, since the salvage operation was absolutely necessary to private capital to prevent a complete collapse of investor confidence and the total failure of many firms. As Grifone writes,

> Italian finance capital, tainted by incurable organic weaknesses, convinced itself, in the darkest hours of the crisis, that it was its specific, fundamental interest to entrust directly to the State the regulation of the chief national economic activities, beginning with credit. It was too interpenetrated with the State itself, too commingled with it to have to fear its economic omnipotence. It knew it had it completely under its control.[29]

Nevertheless, the action of the state brought about a significant alteration in the configuration of private capital. This was to have serious consequences in the post-war period. And in creating IRI, it gave birth to a new and distinctive fraction of capital, state capital, which was also to play a very significant role after the war.

Under Fascism, as many scholars have pointed out, economic growth was slow,[30] but nonetheless significant structural modifications of the Italian economy took place. The regime encouraged the concentration of capital as well as the formation of cartels, or consortia. It also promoted the growth of new sectors, while taking over much of the traditional heavy industrial complex. These developments only confirmed two of the original characteristics of Italian capital: its highly concentrated character and its dependence on the state.

## Industry from 1945 to 1962: the hegemony of the old oligarchy

In the early post-war period, from 1945 to 1962, the general make-up of Italian capital appeared on the surface only slightly changed from what it had been under Fascism; yet, economic and political developments were afoot that would revolutionize it. The electric monopolies retained an apparently dominant position. They depended on the state for their monopoly position, but, precisely because they feared nationalization, they adopted a strongly *laissez-faire*, anti-statist position. They were tendentially protectionist and willing to accept a limited, subordinate position for Italy within the international division of labour. They had absorbed in many ways the rentier outlook of their small shareholders, who regarded electrical shares as safe 'blue chip' investments, providing a steady income.[31]

The five electric companies were linked to many of the other centres of economic power, which were their shareholders or customers, or both. While often management-controlled (e.g. Edison), their boards of directors and shareholders' meetings resembled salons for the leading lights of Italian business. For instance, Pirelli held a significant share of the Centrale, the company which served Central Italy, and Pirelli, the Falck family, owners of the largest private steel firm, and Carlo Pesenti, who was involved in cement, insurance, and finance, were connected to the Milanese Edison company. Together with these allies, Edison dominated Assolombarda, the Lombard regional industrialists' association, and through it the national association, Confindustria.[32] Even though some of these firms, such as Pirelli, were linked to the auto industry and therefore objectively interested in openings to external markets and a policy quite different from the electric companies', Edison and its co-monopolists were able to hegemonize them throughout the 1950s. Only Fiat stood apart and pursued a largely independent policy, cultivating its own direct contacts with the government in Rome.

The chemical industry, the other major beneficiary of Fascist policy, was also part of this dominant bloc. Montecatini, the largest chemical firm, enjoyed a quasi-monopoly of several products, such as fertilizers, 'comparable only to that of the electric companies'.[33] It was therefore also not much interested in a more open economy. Furthermore, in the 1950s it had for the first time to face serious competitors: ANIC, owned by the state holding company ENI, and Edison itself, which was beginning to diversify as a form of insurance against the nationalization of electric power. Montecatini was anti-state because it suffered what it saw as unfair competition backed up by the state's bottomless coffers and because it feared state action disturbing its hitherto tranquil enjoyment of monopoly rents.

A brief examination of this dominant bloc lends some credence to the contemporary Communist denunciations of 'monopoly capitalism', whose control of markets and key inputs such as electric power throttled economic growth. The dominant firms, furthermore, seemed content to accept American economic hegemony. In this context, it is understandable that the Socialists demanded the nationalization of electric power as part of their price for entering the centre-left coalition government in 1963. This was not simply a matter of taking over a natural monopoly which belonged in the public sector; it was a structural reform which struck at the heart of the dominant conservative bloc within Italian capital.

At the same time, the forces of economic as well as political change were undermining the traditional dominant groups. The driving force of the economic boom of the 1950s and early 1960s, the 'economic miracle', was the so-called 'automobile cycle', the complex of industries and firms that contributed to automobile production and served the growing number of vehicles on Italy's roads. These included large segments of the steel and rubber industries, the tyre industry, the oil industry, the public companies which constructed and managed the *autostrade*, the automakers themselves, and the myriad of smaller suppliers of these firms. As Salvati has pointed out,[34] a series of political and economic conditions favoured this model of development. The gradual opening of Italy to international trade allowed auto firms, especially Fiat, to capture export markets. The South and other rural regions furnished a large supply of prime labour (young, male, and mobile) so that wage increases lagged productivity throughout the boom.

The Christian Democratic political regime, as we shall see, ensured consent in the regions of the country, particularly the South, which did not benefit directly from growth; it also acted to keep the unions and the labour movement in the industrial North as weak as possible. Furthermore, the rapid expansion of state industry in the 1950s took place primarily in sectors which promoted and assisted the development of the auto industry: oil, steel, and motorways in particular. ENI's gasoline company, AGIP, was able to continually lower its prices throughout the 1950s; state-owned steel works supplied a large part of Fiat's raw material (it produced much of its own steel as well); and the construction of the network of *autostrade* to supplement an antiquated and inadequate highway system made car ownership that much more attractive.

The boom, in other words, strengthened the industries of the auto cycle and weakened the traditionally dominant ones.[35] These developments, which were the 'natural' product of economic growth, were also, as we have already noted, promoted and furthered by the state. This may seem paradoxical, given the dominant position of the electrical-chemical complex and its allies within Confindustria, and the great influence wielded by Confindustria over the state.[36] The explanation of this situation lies in the fact that, while the electrical-chemical group hegemonized the capitalist class, the capitalist class in turn did not exercise direct control over the state, which, as in previous eras, enjoyed a considerable degree of autonomy. The Christian Democratic regime derived its autonomy in the first place from the fact that the capitalist class, as we have seen, did not exercise intellectual and moral hegemony over Italy as a whole. Bourgeois liberal ideology was a poor third to Catholicism and Marxism in terms of mass influence. Therefore, the DC had to perform the function of legitimating the state and its policies, using Catholicism and clientelism, as well as anti-Communism and generic conservatism. It therefore had considerable freedom of manoeuvre, particularly in the management of the state and its spending.

A prime example of the autonomous role of the state was the growth of the state holding company ENI (Ente Nazionale Idrocarburi: National

Hydrocarbons Administration).[37] In the climate of consensus around the Confindustria's line in the 1950s, ENI was the only major economic force in opposition to the business establishment. Its president, Enrico Mattei, had been put in charge of AGIP in 1945 with instructions to liquidate it as a residue of Fascism. Instead, he developed it into a powerful national oil and gas firm. The crucial event in AGIP's rise was the oil and gas discovery at Cortemaggiore in the Po Valley in 1949; while the oil reserves proved insignificant, Mattei recognized the value of the gas and rapidly built a network of gas pipelines to serve Northern Italy. Setting the price of the gas with reference to that of fuel oil, he was able to reap substantial profits that permitted the company to diversify and also to finance newspapers and politicians. This expansion led to the creation in 1953 of ENI, with interests in chemicals, nuclear energy, engineering and construction, textiles, and publishing (to list only its principal activities).

A former Catholic partisan and active Christian Democrat, Mattei was in the first place a political actor, and saw his business activities as essentially a means to his political ends, which were to secure Italy the cheap and reliable energy supplies it needed for its growth and to modernize the economic structure of the country, which he viewed as sclerotic and dominated by a provincial, oligarchic, and backward-looking clique. While AGIP and ENI owed their existence to the state, under Mattei's leadership they soon began to influence the state in turn; they enjoyed autonomy, while Mattei financed parties and factions of the DC in order to pursue his own goals. His actions were in part defensive, as ENI was exposed to a constant barrage of criticism from the right-wing and business-oriented press, which was hostile to the idea of a state oil company, and even more to some of ENI's initiatives, such as the barter arrangement for oil it concluded with the Soviet Union. In part, though, they were intended to further his own plans for Italy's economic and political development.

Mattei was on good terms with Vittorio Valletta, the President of Fiat, and his view of Adriano Olivetti, president of the business machine firm, is best described as one of 'admiration'.[38] However, he was implacably opposed to the dominant powers of Italian capitalism, Edison, Montecatini, and Confindustria. He campaigned in favour of the nationalization of the electric companies, which he believed restricted the economy with their economic rents, and in 1956 succeeded in taking all public-sector firms out of Confindustria and organizing them separately in a new grouping, Intersind. Intersind pursued a less reactionary and anti-union line than Confindustria. He was critical of IRI, the other major public holding company, for not taking a sufficiently independent line *vis-à-vis* the giants of private industry. Mattei also entered into direct competition with Edison and Montecatini in the chemical field, through ANIC, ENI's chemical affiliate.

Moreover, Mattei challenged the American- and British-owned oil majors, the 'seven sisters', in numerous ways, offering the producer countries more favourable royalties, supporting Mossadeq's government in

Iran, and initiating a gasoline price war in Italy in 1959. His moves provoked an angry reaction from the American Ambassador in Rome, Clare Booth Luce, and the hostility of the Italian business establishment, which was unwilling to challenge US hegemony. Mattei was accused of pursuing his own foreign policy in contradiction to Italy's official position; it would be more accurate to say that he set Italian foreign policy in his spheres of interest, and the government was forced to follow his lead. Mattei's autonomy from the dominant industrial interests of the day can be explained in part by his political position and in part by the economic strength of his firm and its key role in the emerging model of development.

Another field in which Confindustria and its leading backers were not successful was trade policy. The leading group was protectionist, and Italy had among the highest tariffs in the industrialized world. Nevertheless, it could not prevent Italy's entry into the European Coal and Steel Community in 1952, even though Confindustria voiced its opposition publicly.[39] By the time the Treaty of Rome was signed in 1957, the organization had resigned itself to the inevitable, and even saw in European integration a possible escape from the threat of more state regulation in Italy. On the European issue as a whole, however, foreign policy considerations of a distinctly political sort had overridden the most powerful economic interest group.

Throughout the period 1945–62 the influence of the capitalist class was strong; it was by and large united, and the political regime, one of whose bases was anti-communism, was fundamentally in harmony with its goals. The government's broad background policies were labour-repressive and favoured industry in many other ways as well, through subsidies, monopoly concessions, etc. The political climate was clerical and conservative. Nevertheless, even in this period significant instances of state autonomy are evident.

From the perspective of the regulation school,[40] the Italian economy in the 1950s had not yet completed the transition to a Fordist regime of accumulation. The predominant sectors of the economy were not the consumer durables and associated capital-goods industries, though these were growing rapidly throughout the boom. Instead, they were relatively capital-intensive firms which either supplied other firms or furnished consumers with necessities (e.g. electricity) for which the demand was relatively inelastic. Unlike the typical Fordist industries, they were not interested in increasing workers' purchasing power, and in fact wages in Italy trailed productivity throughout the boom, as unions remained divided, cowed by government hostility, and weak in the factories. The welfare state also was woefully underdeveloped, while Keynesian economics was eschewed in favour of fiscal and monetary orthodoxy. In only one major respect Italian industry conformed to the Fordist model: the organization of work, especially in the consumer-goods sector, was being Taylorized and becoming extremely productive. However, the domestic market was still insufficient to absorb this production, as wages remained low, so that Italian automobiles and appliances had to rely on export markets. The boom was to a large extent, then, export-led. Fiat, for example, did attempt to adjust its product line in a Fordist direction, introducing the economical 'utilitaria', the 600, in 1955,[41] followed by the even cheaper 500 in 1957. At first, however, these cars were within the reach only of the lower middle class.

The regulation school hypothesizes a natural correspondence between a 'regime of accumulation', such as Fordism, and a 'mode of regulation', the political and social framework. However, it holds that this correspondence is not guaranteed, but depends on political factors and relations of force. Fordism is characterized by the mass production of consumer durables by Taylorist methods, and a mass market of consumers with sufficient purchasing power to absorb these products – i.e. a relatively high-wage economy. The latter, in particular, requires a mode of regulation that will ensure its continuance – for instance, a corporatist-type system of collective bargaining, one in which national-level wage agreements between peak organizations of business and labour are the norm, as well as full-employment policies and a modern welfare state to maintain the purchasing power of workers facing temporary loss of wages. The state derivationist perspective can account for the development of the mode of regulation required by a regime of accumulation; for historical derivationists, as for the regulation school, this development is not guaranteed, but the result of class struggles and the relations of force in the political system; hence causation does not go simply from the economy to the political system. The early development of industrial capitalism in the 1880s can be seen as a particularly clear instance in which the requirements of capitalist accumulation were created in large part by the state, and Fascist economic policy involved a choice between different paths of capitalist development.

In this context, the reasons for the non-Fordist character of the Italian economy as a whole in the 1950s are more evident in the light of the nature of the political regime. The DC's principal political base was the self-employed or state-employed petty bourgeoisie, which was hostile to the working-class movement and which would have been threatened by a thorough-going modernization of the state and the economy. A modern welfare state would have eliminated many of its sources of income. The entire South, with over a third of the population of the country, was a depressed area with even lower incomes than the average, where modern industry had scarcely penetrated at all. The Italian economy, then, was not Fordist in the 1945–62 period; the most one could argue is that it was economically part of a European 'Fordist circuit' in which it produced the consumer durables for other markets, while Germany specialized in capital goods.

## The struggle for hegemony: 1963–76

The nationalization of the electric industry in 1962 fundamentally altered the constellation of forces within Italian capital. The companies, rather than their shareholders, received the compensation paid by the state (a considerable lobbying success for the firms), and therefore survived as holding companies, but they had lost their principal source of profits. Now the industries connected to the 'auto cycle' were relatively more important, and Fiat had an opportunity to seize hegemony over Italian capital as head of a 'Fordist' bloc. However, it did not do so, and instead took a hard line against the unions during the 1962 strikes and supported the conservative attempts to dilute the centre-left's reform programme.[42]

Meanwhile, the 1960s saw a further expansion of the state sector, but a change in its political stance. State firms, such as the newly created electric company, ENEL, floated large bond issues, which attracted savers and crowded out new stock issues by private firms. State industry also had access to special credit institutions. This situation permitted the state sector to grow, while damaging small and medium private companies in particular. While presiding over this expansion of ENI, Mattei's successor, Eugenio Cefis, also moved towards an accommodation with the oil majors, with IRI, and above all with the ruling faction of the Christian Democrats, the *dorotei*, and later with the *fanfaniani* faction as well. In 1968, with a bold campaign of stock purchases, Cefis acquired control of Montedison, the firm formed by the merger of Montecatini and the Edison holding company in 1966. This moved marked the consolidation, under the aegis of the state sector, of a new non-Fordist bloc.

This bloc incorporated some of the major elements of the old business oligarchy, but its strategy was somewhat more modern.[43] It included industries, such as chemicals and oil, which employed relatively few workers. Financial operations were also a significant source of profit. Therefore, labour relations were not as crucial as for the Fordist firms. Furthermore, these industries did not produce consumer durables and therefore did not rely on the expansion of domestic purchasing power. For these reasons, they supported a strong anti-union stance. On the other hand, they were largely state industries, in which clientelistic practices aimed at the generation of political consent were widespread; their leaders, such as Cefis, were aware of the need for such consent. But they aimed to ensure consent through clientelism, swelling the bureaucracy, and welfare measures channelled preferentially to political supporters. Since their industries employed relatively few, they envisaged that the bulk of the work force would have to be absorbed by the tertiary sector of the economy. Furthermore, their industries were heavily dependent on exports (e.g. of basic chemicals), and they did not see the expansion of the home market as the *sine qua non* of their growth. The state-based bloc saw the self-employed petty bourgeoisie, state employees, and a large part of small and medium industry as its natural political allies in implementing neo-authoritarian political design.

The labour unrest of the 'Hot Autumn' (1969–70), however, forced the Fordist industries of the auto cycle to take more vigorous action. Their relatively conservative response to the formation of the centre-left coalition had led to a reduction of their political influence.[44] The divisions within capital that emerged during the 1960s further limited their power. Therefore, state policy displayed ever greater autonomy from the demands of private capital: among other instances, the Statute of Workers' Rights (1970) and the reform of the pension system which gave the unions a majority on the boards of directors of the state funds (1969) are symptomatic of this trend. Large private industry believed it needed to seize the initiative again.

Starting in 1972, Gianni Agnelli, chairman of Fiat, began to speak of the possibility of a coalition with the workers' movement, an 'alliance of producers'. This would be a 'Manchesterian' bloc (analogous to the English Anti-Corn Law League of the 1840s) that would aim at eliminating the 'parasitic' elements in the Italian economy, such as the petty bourgeoisie and large parts of the state bureaucracy.[45] For industries like Fiat, these inefficiencies were seen as pushing up labour costs. If health, transportation, and housing, for instance, could be reformed so that they provided better services more cheaply to the workers, pressures for wage increases would be alleviated. This, rather than the desire to increase the market for Fiat products, was the reasoning that led Fiat and others to support a reformed welfare state that would provide a higher level of service. This reflected in turn their strong export orientation. These reforms also happened to be a major goal of the unions, as they sought to convert the new wave of militancy into gains more permanent than wage increases that were vulnerable to inflation.

The large private firms, then, with Fiat in the lead, were prepared to contemplate a form of neo-corporatist arrangement with the unions; the revision of the *scala mobile* wage-indexation mechanism in 1975, which Agnelli signed as President of Confindustria, was an earnest of their willingness to deal with their union counterparts. A series of factors, including above all the political divisions between and within the three union confederations, made a corporatist-type accommodation impossible, but the employers' side had shown its interest in numerous ways. Fiat and its allies, too, developed relations with a variety of political forces, not simply the DC, for they envisaged political stability as the result of a social contract with the working-class organizations rather than the clientelistic purchasing of consent. The small Republican Party, which represented business views but was open to an agreement with the Communists, was particularly favoured by Fiat.

During this period, Italy finally began to conform to the Fordist mode of regulation, as the corresponding regime of accumulation strengthened itself further. However, this progress towards Fordism was still limited by several factors, in particular the weight of the petty bourgeoisie. The extension of workers' pension benefits in 1969, for instance, which played a large role in introducing a full-fledged welfare state in Italy, was accompanied by an even more generous reform of pensions for the self-employed – more generous because a large share of the benefits were financed by workers' contributions and taxes! And the quality of services provided by the public sector – as opposed to simple monetary transfers – remained poor overall. Wage levels, however, did rise in the wake of the Hot Autumn and the system of national industry-wide bargaining, supplemented by plant-level accords, was strongly institutionalized. The failure of large private capital and the workers' movement to conclude a Manchesterian alliance meant that Italian Fordism would always be somewhat imperfect. The opposition of the state-centred fraction of capital to such an alliance also weakened the impulse towards Fordism.

Italy did not develop a truly corporatist form of wage bargaining in this period, but at most a kind of 'imperfect neo-corporatism'. Moreover, its final adoption of the Fordist mode of regulation was delayed until the period when Fordism was already entering into crisis on a world scale – the late 1960s and early 1970s. The quantitative growth of the welfare state and the strengthening of the unions' position coincided with the monetary upheavals and the oil crisis which revealed fully the seriousness of the world crisis. Indeed, one aspect of the 'Hot Autumn', other than wage militancy, was the challenge to the Taylorist organization of work by the assembly-line workers, many of them recent recruits to the factory who were seeking not only to win concrete gains but to form a new collective identity. Thus Italian Fordism was delayed and entered precociously into crisis. By 1976, there were already clear signs that the industrial structure was evolving in a direction different from the Fordist model, even as the political and institutional superstructure continued to adjust itself to the Fordist mode of regulation.

# 3 Wealth and power in contemporary Italian business

As we have noted, industrial capital clearly predominates in Italy; the banking sector remained largely state-owned until the 1990s, and generally played a subordinate role. The one long-term investment bank, Mediobanca, under the direction of Enrico Cuccia, generally supported the large private firms. Without exercising the sort of control or supervision typical in Germany, Mediobanca did help create an Italian sub-species of the 'Rhenish' model of capitalism.[1] Nor are the retail or property sectors of major importance among the largest firms, given the proliferation of small operators in these fields. Three of the major corporations – Fiat, Pirelli, and Riva – are, while diversified, principally involved in the traditional Fordist cycle or in the production of inputs for these industries. Three others – Fininvest, Olivetti/Telecom, and IBM – are centred on the 'new economy', including telecommunications, computers, advertising and the media. The dynamic traditional industries, such as clothing, foods, and footwear, have also gained a significant place among the larger groups in recent years, with five to six of the twelve largest private conglomerates. Nevertheless these sectors and a large part of the capital-goods industry are dominated by small and medium firms.

The main division within Italian capital is between the large groups and these smaller entrepreneurs, who are much more critical of the 'Rhenish' model and strongly in favour of a diminished role for unions and the state. Politically, the smaller capitalists are typically allied to other, petty bourgeois groups that in fact depend on the state for support: the traditional basis of governing parties in Italy. The rest of this chapter will explore in more detail these salient features of Italy's 'production profile'.

## The economy in overview

The industrial structure of Italy today is rather unique among the advanced capitalist countries. In contrast to the situation during the economic miracle, her areas of greatest economic strength are no longer the classically Fordist industries: consumer durables producers and their suppliers, usually highly concentrated and labour-intensive. Her trade balance in these sectors is now, overall, often negative, while her strengths are in first, the 'traditional' high-quality consumer products, such as clothing, shoes, and leather goods, and second, machinery and other capital goods, including machinery for these traditional industries.

A useful approach to categorizing different industrial sectors is the taxonomy proposed by Keith Pavitt,[2] based on the inputs or factors that are most crucial to the success of each type of industry. It divides industries into five main categories:

1 'science-based' or technology-intensive industries, which are essentially driven by research and development (e.g. computing, aerospace, fine chemicals, pharmaceuticals, telecommunications equipment);
2 'specialized suppliers', which both use and generate technological changes, and rely upon adaptability, innovation, and their ability to produce unique products (e.g. capital equipment and machinery);
3 'scale-intensive' industries, which use technology generated elsewhere, but also engage in process innovation themselves, and require a large scale of production to be profitable (e.g. steel, chemicals, automobiles, plastics, rubber, domestic appliances, construction materials);
4 'traditional' industries, where scale is less important though process innovation may be – these are usually, but not always, relatively labour-intensive (e.g. clothing, leather and shoes, furniture);
5 'resource-intensive' industries, in which the crucial factor is the availability of a natural resource that may be difficult or costly to transport for processing (e.g. aluminum smelting, food processing).

The scale-intensive industries are the classically Fordist ones, usually characterized by a high degree of concentration; many resource-intensive industries may replicate their organization. On the other hand, specialized suppliers and traditional industries often include a majority of small and medium firms, whose small size and flexibility may be an asset. Science-based industries tend to be composed of both small, innovative companies and large firms with expensive research programmes. To complete Pavitt's classification, we must add the non-goods-producing sectors of the economy, most considered 'unproductive' by Marx: finance (principally banking and insurance), retail firms, property, utilities, and personal services.

In this framework, Italy's comparative advantages lie clearly in the traditional industries and the specialized supplier sectors (see Table 3.1, groups 7 and 5 respectively: the groupings in the table approximately parallel Pavitt's). In the science-based industries, the heart of the 'new economy', her trade ratio is negative (cf. group 6), as it is in the resource-intensive sector (groups 1, 2, and 3), while in the scale-intensive industries

*Table 3.1* The structure of Italian foreign trade, 1998 (billions of $US)

| Products | a Exports | b Imports | c Balance | d Trade ratio (a/b) |
|---|---|---|---|---|
| 1 Agricultural products | 17.08 | 32.06 | −14.98 | 0.53 |
| 2 Fuels | 2.66 | 12.03 | −9.37 | 0.22 |
| 3 Ores, non-ferrous metals | 3.11 | 9.33 | −6.22 | 0.33 |
| 4 Iron, steel, chemicals, transport equipment, semi-manufactures | 84.94 | 82.44 | +2.50 | 1.03 |
| 5 Machinery | 56.43 | 24.32 | +32.11 | 2.32 |
| 6 Office and telecom equipment | 9.56 | 17.60 | −8.04 | 0.54 |
| 7 Textiles, clothing, other consumer goods | 66.10 | 28.57 | +37.53 | 2.31 |

Source: Computed from World Trade Organization, *Annual Report 1999: International Trade Statistics* (Geneva, 1999), p. 173. Cf. Table 5.4, p. 84 below.

it has fluctuated between a small positive and a small negative balance (group 4). This is a rather singular pattern among the leading industrial countries. The two longest-established capitalist countries, the United States and Great Britain, have comparative advantages in the science-based and specialized supplier groups; the countries with the largest trade surpluses, Germany and Japan, have advantages in the scale-intensive and specialized supplier groups; while France has an advantage in the science-based industries and a roughly balanced position in both scale-intensive and specialized supplier industries. An examination of the structure of output, as opposed to trade, reveals equally clearly Italy's unique position, with a large traditional sector relative to the other leading industrial countries.

This large traditional sector is the most noteworthy feature of Italy's industrial structure. Design, craftsmanship, and tradition have helped to keep it in the forefront of many industries such as clothing, footwear, and leather goods. While not as innovative as many others and characterized by many small firms, as well as a few large ones, this sector is export-intensive, and has a large positive trade balance. Foreign ownership is minimal, and the firms have relatively few manufacturing subsidiaries abroad. These are the sectors which have attracted so much recent scholarly attention because of their use of 'flexible specialization' to take advantage of their skilled labour force and respond to changing market trends.[3]

Many scale-intensive industries producing consumer durables (e.g. automobiles, tyres, appliances) are traditional areas of strength for the Italian economy. All exhibit a high degree of concentration; state owner-ship is not very significant, but foreign-owned firms are important in con-sumer electronics and appliances. Some of these industries are relatively labour-intensive. All of them are export-intensive, and some (rubber and automobiles) have major foreign subsidiaries and other types of overseas involvement (joint ventures, turnkey projects, etc.). On the other hand, only the rubber and domestic appliance industries have a strongly positive trade balance. In the 1980s Italy's automobile trade, in spite of Fiat's position as Europe's largest producer, was in deficit in all years but one (as Fiat is the only significant domestic auto manufacturer, all other cars sold in Italy are imports), and though it returned to a slight surplus in the early 1990s, the deficit reappeared later in the decade. Business machinery and consumer electronics are also deficitary sectors overall, in spite of their export-intensity.

The two major input-producing scale-intensive sectors, the iron and steel and basic chemical industries, both heavily favoured by governments in the past, have experienced considerable difficulty in recent years. The government's privatization programme reduced the state's role in the 1990s. The chemical industry, the object of so many manoeuvres and the basis of so many grandiose schemes, has been considerably reduced in size: the country's trade balance in basic chemicals is negative. The state holding company IRI was able to sell much of its steel capacity to the Riva group. Neither sector is very export-intensive or engages in major ventures abroad; these are among the most 'autarchic' of Italy's industries.

The specialized suppliers, producing machinery and equipment, are Italy's second sector with an overall positive trade performance. They are quite heterogeneous in their make-up. The machine-tool and machinery industry includes both very large and very small companies. State ownership is still significant, especially in heavy engineering, though privatization is imminent, and there is some foreign ownership in electrical and instrumental engineering. The whole sector is both labour-intensive and export-intensive, and much of it (electrical machinery being the main exception) shows a positive trade ratio. Machinery for the traditional industries (woodworking, clothing and textiles, leather, food and agriculture) is a particular strong point. In this sector, too, small firms have been able to use techniques of flexible specialization to produce short runs or unique machines for client firms. It is the larger, heavy-engineering firms that have been less successful in finding markets. None of these firms has engaged in significant expansion abroad.

In comparative perspective, the science-based sector is a weak point of Italy's industrial profile (though it is not a particular strength of Germany or Japan either). These industries, which include the 'new economy' firms involved in the internet and telecommunications, are relatively small and do not show a positive trade ratio. On the other hand, these are some of the fastest-growing and most profitable industries in the country, along with other science-based sectors like pharmaceuticals and fine chemicals. It remains to be seen whether Italy will be able to make up the considerable ground that separates it from the leaders in this field. All the science-based sectors have a high degree of foreign ownership, and the computer industry is furthermore highly concentrated (IBM is the largest foreign subsidiary in Italy). This is the most internationalized group of industries of all: besides a high degree of foreign ownership, they also exhibit a propensity to establish subsidiaries abroad – several Italian pharmaceutical and fine chemical firms have major foreign interests.

Finally, only two resource-based industries are significant in Italy: food processing and energy. Both sectors represent a major net drain on Italy's balance of payments. The state is heavily involved in the energy sector, through ENI, as are several foreign oil companies; it has divested itself of its former presence in food processing. Both sectors are highly concentrated. In both of them, furthermore, state intervention is an extremely important factor: petroleum and other sources of energy are heavily taxed, and their prices are directly set by the government; food prices are governed by the EU's agricultural policy.

As the above summary shows, Italy's productive structure, never as fully Fordist as that of some other countries, moved away from an emphasis on the classic consumer durables sectors between 1975 and 1990. These remain, however, important and dynamic sectors of the economy, especially since they, unlike the traditional industries and many of the specialized suppliers, are highly concentrated and therefore have an economic and political weight that is greater than their place in the economy would warrant. Small and medium industry has not had a strong autonomous voice in the political system, although recently both the Northern League and Forza Italia have bid to perform this function,[1] while in 2000 Confindustria, the employers' association, for the first time elected a declared representative of this tendency within Italian capital as its president.

## The major groups: the private sector

The above description of the productive structure of the Italian economy remains abstract: it is only the foundation on which the edifice of capital's economic and political power is built. The largest concentrations of economic power, both private and public, traditionally have their centre in the Fordist scale-intensive industries, but in the 1990s both the traditional industries and firms representing the 'new economy' became more important. At the same time, as their size and available liquidity grew, the major groups began to venture into the financial sector. However, the relationship between finance and manufacturing remained closer to the 'Rhenish' model in which banks support and sometimes control industry, rather than evolving towards a fusion under the aegis of the large manufacturing conglomerates.

## Fiat

By far the largest and most powerful of the private groups is Fiat, controlled by the Agnelli family. Its central business is still producing automobiles, but it has expanded into a conglomerate with holdings in many diverse sectors. In 1998 the Fiat company and its subsidiaries alone had sales of over 94 trillion lire, and this figure did not include the other firms controlled by the Agnellis.[5] Slightly more than half of the Fiat group's sales were automobiles; this was approximately 40 per cent of the business of all the Agnelli holdings. Besides automobiles proper, the Agnelli group produces industrial vehicles (through Iveco), tractors and construction vehicles (through New Holland), aircraft (through Fiat Avio) and several products both upstream and downstream from auto production: steel (Teksid), machinery and robots (Comau and Magneti Marelli), consumer credit and financial services (FIDIS), and insurance (Toro). The Agnellis also own *La Stampa*, the Turin daily, as well as Turin's beloved soccer team, Juventus. They also own three minor publishing houses, as well as the Rinascente department-store chain. Fiat's major foreign subsidiaries are currently in Brazil, Poland, and Argentina; they produce Fiat cars for sale in those countries and elsewhere.[6]

The vast Fiat empire, like almost all major Italian firms, is family- rather than management-controlled. The typical technique used in Italy to maintain family control is a series of holding companies arranged like 'Chinese boxes'. The Agnellis' control is relatively secure: the family members (led by Gianni Agnelli until his death in January 2003) own virtually all the shares of Giovanni Agnelli & Co.. Giovanni Agnelli & Co. in turn owns 75 per cent of the holding company IFI (Istituto Finanziario Industriale); the rest is owned by the individual family members. IFI and IFIL (another holding company owned by the Agnellis) together hold 38 per cent of the shares of Fiat S.p.A., which in turn controls Teksid, Comau, La Stampa, Iveco, etc., and has approximately 23 per cent of the shares of the holding company Gemina and 42 per cent of SNIA-BPD (armaments). IFIL and IFI independently control Toro (40.5 per cent), La Rinascente, Unicem (cement), and the three small publishers. As the rest of the shares are fairly widely held, the Agnellis have a controlling interest in Fiat (though there have been occasional rumours of takeover bids, for example in 1976, when it was suggested Carlo De Benedetti was buying up Fiat shares), and similarly their significant minority interests in the other companies are sufficient to give them *de facto* control.[7]

Fiat is today the acknowledged leader of Italian business. After the demise of Cefis and his faction, it finally occupied this position; this occurred while Gianni Agnelli was serving as President of Confindustria, and from the mid-1970s until the election of Antonio D'Amato in 2000 all its presidents have had to at least have the approval of Fiat, and several have been close allies of the Agnellis, who promoted them for the post. While the auto industry is of course the quintessentially Fordist industrial branch, Fiat, like other firms, has introduced neo-Fordist methods of 'lean' production, which seek to improve on the traditional assembly line. Furthermore, economic success made it cash-rich, and it has been diversifying into many other areas, in particular finance. The resignation of Vittorio Ghidella, President of Fiat Auto, in November 1988 marked the culmination of a struggle over the future of the conglomerate between Ghidella and Cesare Romiti, President of Fiat S.p.A. Siding with Romiti, Gianni Agnelli accused Ghidella of having too 'autocentric' a vision of the group's future; Romiti, on the other hand, was strongly in favour of diversification. It was rumoured that Ghidella had been pressing for massive investments to upgrade Fiat's automobile production and design capabilities, including the acquisition of the German firm BMW.

The position of Fiat is clearly crucial for the stance of industry on a number of key economic issues facing the country. It is at the centre of the 'old guard' or 'good salon' of Italian industry, and hence is the natural target and natural opponent of projects to open up financial markets and introduce Anglo-Saxon style shareholders' sovereignty, dear both to foreign commentators and the editorial board of the influential daily *La Repubblica*.[8] In its industrial relations, it has pursued a policy of neo-Fordism, with the aim of reducing the workers' margins of autonomy through the introduction of new technology. As a precondition for this, the firm's victory over the unions in the 1980 strike opened the way for a practice of lip-service to the unions' representative role in the factory. Even its attempt to introduce Japanese-style quality control and worker participation in the 1990s has been contradictory and has not been accompanied by an attempt to gain the genuine consent of the work force.[9] At the same time, Fiat has continued to view the unions as necessary at the national level, as part of a strategy for a consensual solution to the major problems of the economy such as the deficit and Italy's entry into the European Monetary System. Agnelli indeed expressed the hope that the centre-left government elected in 1996 would be able to carry out the necessary reforms which the right had failed to accomplish.[10]

At the same time as it supported a policy of rigour and financial orthodoxy, however, Fiat also was suffering from the effects of the rise in value of the lira, and in particular its pegging at 990 to the mark in December 1996, when Italy re-entered the European Monetary System. The combination of devaluation of the lira and austerity at home practised by the successive governments since 1992 had led to a stagnation of the Italian automobile market and a strong surge of export sales. As a major exporter and a direct competitor of foreign imports in the Italian market (Fiat, virtually the sole Italian producer, held 46.2 per cent of the home market in 1994[11]), Fiat wanted the continuation of this currency policy: it claimed the rise in the lira's value in 1996 had cost it a trillion lire in profits, reducing its operating margin from 3.2 per cent to 1 per cent.[12] The very confidence that the new government, through its austerity measures, had generated was in part responsible for the rise in the exchange rate. Nervousness over this prospect led Cesare Romiti, newly appointed chairman of Fiat, to publicly state that the government should consider the objective of reducing unemployment as well as entry into the Monetary Union, and that a delay in Italy's entry would not be a disaster if it allowed the government to increase employment.[13] He was, however, promptly criticized by other major business spokespersons, including the president of Confindustria, Giorgio Fossa.

The best explanation of Romiti's surprising intervention is that it was directed at gaining a temporary respite for Fiat, and pressing the government to negotiate for a low exchange value for the lira's entry into the EMS. In the longer run, Fiat had decided that it had to expand in the growing markets of the developing world, as the European market, like the Japanese and the American, was nearing saturation. It had decided to become truly multinational (in 1994, 67 per cent of its vehicle production was in Italy[14]). As a true multinational, it could better withstand the vagaries of the exchange rate; in any case, the stability of the EMS and later the Euro would be an advantage for Fiat as an exporter, regardless of the rate of exchange, as it would reduce the uncertainties of its business.[15] Furthermore, as a representative of the 'good salon' closely linked to the investment bank Mediobanca, Fiat was concerned about the stability of exchange rates in order to guarantee the returns on international activities, both its own and those of its allies.

Since 1998, Fiat has seen a series of changes that have first strengthened, then weakened, its position in the Italian economy. In the last year's of Cuccia's control over Mediobanca, the historic link between the Milanese bank and Fiat was severed: in 1998, the controlling syndicate put together by Mediobanca was ended, and Cesare Romiti, who had originally been proposed to the Agnellis by Cuccia as a manager, left the chairmanship of the company. The next year, Mediobanca supported a group led by Roberto Colannino in his bid to take over the newly privatized Telecom Italia from a syndicate including Fiat (see below, p. 57). After Cuccia's death, the rift widened: in July 2001, Fiat, in company with the French electric utility EDF, led a hostile takeover bid on Compact/Montedison, which was under the control of Mediobanca (see below, pp. 38–39). These developments marked both the freeing of Fiat from Cuccia's tutelage, and the extension of its control to an important part of the energy and chemical sectors. At the same time, however, Fiat's core business, auto production, was suffering a long-term decline: the company's share of the Italian market fell from 52 per cent in 1990 to 31 per cent in 2002.[16] Then in January 2003 Gianni Agnelli died, to be succeeded at the head of the business by his brother Umberto. Umberto inherited a company in serious difficulty, which needed both peace with the unions to allow for a smooth reduction in manpower, and government assistance to facilitate its recovery plans.

## Pirelli

Pirelli, like Fiat, is an old-established giant of the Italian economy; Leopoldo Pirelli is, like the Agnellis, a charter member of the 'good salon' of Italian business. The Pirelli firm is somewhat anomalous among the largest conglomerates because it is considerably less diversified, concentrating on tyres and cables, which comprise 98.3 per cent of its production. On the other hand, it is the most internationalized of all – 78 per cent of the group's employees are outside Italy, with the principal subsidiaries in Brazil, France, Germany, and the UK; the foreign subsidiaries account for 80 per cent of its sales.[17] It is one of the five major competitors in an international market for tyres, and devotes all its resources to keeping up with or gaining the advantage over its Japanese and American rivals. Its net sales of 10.6 trillion lire (1998) make it a major force in Italian business, but it is still only a medium-sized firm by international standards.

The firm is controlled by the Pirelli family; however, this control is more precarious than that of any of the other large groups' dominant families. The main Pirelli company, Pirelli S.p.A. ('la Pirellona', or 'the big Pirelli', in stock-market slang), is, in classic 'Chinese box' fashion, controlled by Société Internationale Pirelli of Basle, Switzerland, which holds 39 per cent of its stock. This company is in turn controlled by Pirelli & C. ('la Pirellina', or 'the little Pirelli'), which holds 39 per cent of its stock.[18] (Carlo De Benedetti's CIR owns 4.5 per cent of Pirelli S.p.A. and Fiat, through Fidis, 5.24 per cent). The Pirelli family, in turn, own only 5.3 per cent of the stock of Pirelli & C., but exercise effective control thanks to a 'controlling syndicate' (a device at least as common as the Chinese box technique, but with a dubious legal foundation). A controlling syndicate is an association of shareholders who together hold a controlling interest in a company and who agree to vote their shares as a bloc; legally, these pacts probably have the status of simple gentlemen's agreements. The controlling syndicate of Pirelli & C. includes the Pirelli family, Mediobanca (7.9 per cent), Gemina (5.55 per cent), the Orlando family, the SAI insurance company, and Camillo De Benedetti, cousin of Carlo. Pirelli & C. in turn has small holdings in SAI, Mediobanca, CIR, Fiat, and the Orlando companies. Leopoldo Pirelli, in other words, controls his companies with share value that represent less than 1 per cent of the total shares of Pirelli S.p.A., thanks to the support of his friends of the 'good salon' of Italian capitalism.

While Pirelli is closely linked to Fiat, both through the complementarity of their products and the personal and financial connections of the 'good salon', its production profile is significantly different; as a true multinational, it is far less concerned with maintaining a low exchange

rate for the lira. If Frieden's hypothesis concerning the interests of businesses in exchange rate policy[19] is correct, it should be interested in a
stable exchange rate in the first place, and in the second place in a high
value for the currency in order to facilitate investment abroad; Pirelli has
recently been engaged in some bruising takeover battles in an attempt to
gain control of other firms in the sector. These considerations influence
decisions beyond the Pirelli firm, as its president, Marco Tronchetti
Provera, has been the only representative of the major conglomerates to
take an active part in the work of Confindustria since the election of the
centre-left government under Romano Prodi. With the election of Silvio
Berlusconi in April 2001, he continued to be involved, endorsing loyally
the Confindustria's policy of strong support for the new government.

In July 2001, Pirelli made a quantum leap in dimensions when it
acquired a controlling interest in the newly privatized Telecom Italia, in
conjunction with Benetton's Edizioni Holding (Pirelli held 60 per cent of
the shares, Benetton the other 40 per cent, in a company which secured a
controlling 27 per cent interest in Olivetti, which in turn owned 54 per
cent of Telecom[20]). This acquisition gave it a position in a growing branch
of the new economy, albeit a largely domestic-centred one, and marked
yet another step in the shift of the old firms of the 'good salon' from traditional Fordist industries to newer sectors.

## Berlusconi

Silvio Berlusconi has risen from relative obscurity to the front rank of
Italian capitalism. Son of a bank manager, he began his career in construction, then, in the late 1970s, turned his attention to the newly opened
field of private television. He currently owns the three largest private networks in Italy (Canale 5, Retequattro, and Italia Uno). His holding
company, Fininvest, has annual sales of 10.3 trillion lire (1998). Other Fininvest holdings are in advertising, publishing, financial services, and other
media activities (cinemas, film-making, video rental outlets). In particular,
they include the Mondadori publishing house and the control of the daily
*Il Giornale.*[21]

Berlusconi's economic empire, then, is concentrated in the tertiary
sector and the cultural industries. This gives it a 'post-modern' character (in
fact, he was bitingly satirized by Federico Fellini in the film *Ginger and Fred*)
which goes beyond 'post-Fordist' models such as flexible specialization. It is
not surprising given this concentration in the tertiary sector that Berlusconi
is even more directly dependent on good relations with the state than the
heads of the other major groups, even though they too are in constant need
of orders, subsidies, tax concessions, and other forms of state aid. Since they
make use of a public good – the air waves – Berlusconi's television networks
are subject to direct legal regulation. For example, the 1975 decision of the
Constitutional Court which permitted private radio and television stations

forbade the formation of national networks; Berlusconi circumvented this restriction in part by simultaneously broadcasting the same videotaped programme on all the local stations of each network, but it precluded him from offering a national news programme or live sports events. Furthermore, parliament turned its attention to limiting concentrations of ownership in the media and regulating the interruption of televised films and artistic events by commercials. In 1985, Berlusconi was able to secure passage of a decree-law (the so-called 'Berlusconi decree') sanctioning his networks until a comprehensive law governing radio and television was passed, and in 1990 he saw the 'duopoly' RAI-Fininvest in the television sector sanctioned by the Mammì law.[22] Berlusconi's friendship with Bettino Craxi, Socialist leader from 1976 to 1993, was clearly a major factor in these political favours his networks received.

In the early 1990s, Berlusconi attempted to expand into the French and Spanish television markets, but in the end the French venture led to large losses while he failed to gain control of the Spanish network Telecinco, and he was forced to fall back on Italy, where since 1991 profit margins had been reduced to a minimum. In late 1993, when local elections showed that the left was on the rise and could well win a general election expected for the following year, Berlusconi was determined to enter politics. All observers agree that at least one of his motives was to defend his business empire from unfavourable government regulation. Much of the subsequent story of Berlusconi and Fininvest is tied up with his political party, Forza Italia, and his roles as Prime Minister and opposition leader. It is worth noting, though, that, besides their dependence on government regulation, the Fininvest businesses are not export-oriented or import-competing. They are naturally protected, and therefore have no interest in exchange-rate stability or in a low value for the lira; indeed, a high-valued lira would reduce the cost of their inputs, such as imported television programmes. Nor do they have a large blue-collar work force, and labour costs are relatively low; Fininvest does not have to deal with the metalworkers' or chemical workers' unions that have organized Fiat, Olivetti, or Pirelli. Berlusconi, naturally, in his activity as a politician takes account of more than the business concerns of Fininvest, but there is much evidence that, even as Prime Minister, he continues to take a close interest in his companies.

Berlusconi is and always has been kept an outsider by the establishment centred on Mediobanca. Cuccia, its long-time president, hated and despised him, even though Mediobanca assisted Fininvest in a restructuring that involved the conversion of Mondadori into a public company (though still under the control of Berlusconi) and the placing of its shares on the stock market in 1993.[23] Significantly, Berlusconi (like De Benedetti) was not invited to take part in any of the major financial operations orchestrated by Mediobanca. Berlusconi, in turn, has different political sympathies from those of the old oligarchy: as a politician, he was motivated by an extreme anti-communism, in spite of the transformation of the old PCI into the PDS, and did not hesitate to ally with the neo-fascists of the National Alliance, one of the actions which repelled Cuccia. His first election campaign, indeed, was characterized by attacks on the 'poteri forti' ('powers that be') of the economy, and he was critical of Confindustria for its support for many of the measures of the Ciampi government (1993–94), a 'technical' ministry that enjoyed parliamentary support from the left. Against this background, we can explain why the first Berlusconi government fell foul of the old guard of Italian capitalism. What needs explanation, however, is why Berlusconi was the only new political force produced by the Italian centre-right at this time. We shall address this question in Chapter 6.

### Compart/Montedison

The chemical industry has never been a particular strong point of the Italian economy; it has often been criticized for concentrating too heavily on the production of basic chemical inputs – i.e. semi-finished products – and of neglecting the 'fine' chemical lines with higher value added. The predominance of foreign-owned firms in the Italian pharmaceutical industry is taken as a proof of the domestic industry's backwardness, but even in basic chemicals Italy runs a trade deficit. Nevertheless, since the mid-1960s, the chemical industry has been the centre of a series of power struggles and major financial operations, most of them involving Enrico Cuccia and Mediobanca: first, as we have seen, the Montecatini giant passed into the hands of Edison, which in turn passed into the hands of the state, in the guise of ENI. The state by 1981 succeeded in divesting itself of its dominant interest in Montedison, first through an agreement to set up a controlling syndicate in which it would place only an amount of shares equal to those placed by the private parties, principally Fiat and Mediobanca acting through the Gemina holding company, then by supporting the idea of making it a widely held 'public company' under the presidency of Mario Schimberni.

The Ferruzzi group, led by Raul Gardini, the son-in-law of a Ferruzzi, grew to prominence in the field of agricultural commodities, in particular sugar, starch, and soy beans. Its holding company was Ferruzzi Finanziaria (Ferfin). In 1987, it took control of Montedison, after a campaign of stock purchases which was strenuously opposed by Mediobanca. Gardini and Schimberni parted ways at the end of 1987, and Gardini soon developed the idea of a fusion of Montedison with ENI's chemical subsidiary, Enichem, thus creating a single giant Italian company in the chemical sector. A new company, Enimont, was formed in July 1989 to manage the Enichem assets, with ENI and Montedison each holding 40 per cent of the shares, but in 1990 Gardini, through the votes of the private holders of the remaining 20 per cent, attempted to take effective control. At this point the government vetoed the takeover, negotiating with Gardini for his Enimont shares, for which the state paid an inflated price. Some of this money in return found its way into the coffers of the parties that had engineered the deal, and this transaction led to Gardini's subsequent arrest and suicide in 1993, when the Ferruzzi group was in dire financial straits in any case.[24]

At this point Mediobanca intervened to organize a salvage operation and prevent the break-up of the company to satisfy its creditors. Cuccia persuaded the banks that had advanced money to the company to accept shares in exchange for their loans. Without Cuccia and Mediobanca, the banks would undoubtedly have demanded that Montedison go into bankruptcy and liquidated its assets. By the summer of 1995, Cuccia decided that the best permanent solution for Ferfin/Montedison would be to merge it into a new, vast conglomerate nicknamed 'SuperGemina'.[25] The Gemina holding company, controlled by Fiat and Mediobanca (see Table 3.2), would receive Ferfin/Montedison shares from the banks, and shares in Fiat's chemical, fibres, and arms company, SNIA-BPD, from Fiat. In return the banks would receive not cash, but Gemina shares, while Fiat and Mediobanca would retain the controlling interest in Gemina and Fiat would receive both cash and Gemina shares for SNIA-BPD. This plan, announced on 1 September 1995, was roundly criticized in the financial press as a typical old-style Cuccia operation, in which the 'usual suspects' of the 'good salon' – Fiat plus its allies, such as Lucchini and Pesenti – combined to carry out an operation outside the market in which the interests of both the banks and the minority shareholders were ignored – exactly the opposite of the open, transparent, capitalism based on free markets (the 'Anglo-Saxon' model) that so many observers thought Italy needed to adopt. Furthermore, SuperGemina would be a conglomerate second only to Fiat, with annual sales of some 40 trillion lire, and, given the role of Fiat in Gemina, a subsequent fusion with Fiat could not be ruled out. In other words, the SuperGemina operation would give rise to an unprecedented (even for Italy) concentration of economic, and hence political, power.

The SuperGemina operation failed, because of the discovery that Gemina had sustained huge losses, due to its Rizzoli-Corriere della Sera subsidiary, losses that had not been reported previously, though they must have been known at some level in the company; these irregularities led to a charge of falsifying company statements for several managers of the company. Now Gemina was an unsuitable vehicle for the Ferfin/Monedison shares, and Cuccia was forced to abandon his original plan. However, on 23 October he had the Ferfin board vote an increase in share capital of 1100 billion lire, and by early 1996 Mediobanca and its allies, after various temporary difficulties, were able to secure a controlling interest in the company. Mediobanca held *c.*20 per cent of the shares, and its allies such as the Banca Commerciale and the Credito Italiano held enough to give it

*Table 3.2* The controlling syndicate of HPI (ex-Gemina): percentage shoes, 1994

|  | *Share of syndicate* | *Share of all shares* |
|---|---|---|
| Fiat | 41.7 | 18.8 |
| Mediobanca | 26.8 | 12.1 |
| Assicurazioni Generali* | 5.3 | 2.4 |
| Italmobiliare (Pesenti) | 10.0 | 4.5 |
| SMI (Orlando) | 4.2 | 1.9 |
| Pirelli | 4.0 | 1.8 |
| Sinpar (Lucchini) | 3.9 | 1.7 |
| Compart/Montedison | 2.1 | 1.0 |
| Total syndicate | 100.0 | 45.1 |

Source: *La Repubblica*, 6 Mar. 1997, p. 26.

Note
*Controlled by Mediobanca.

control. At this point the inauspicious name Ferruzzi Finanziaria was changed to Compart. Then, as described above, in 2001 Fiat in company with the French EDF took over Montedison in a hostile takeover bid, ending the historic role of Mediobanca in this sector.

The group's principal activity is in agricultural products, notably sugar, starch, and animal feed. It is also involved in chemicals and pharmaceuticals, and in construction and construction materials, such as cement, and it controls an insurance company (La Fondiaria). More recently, it has expanded into the electricity and energy sectors, with an eye to the eventual privatization of ENEL, the state electricity company, which ironically absorbed the electrical business of Edison, the ancestor of Montedison, in the mid-1960s. Its annual sales (exclusive of La Fondiaria) are 25.6 trillion lire (1998).[26] The group as a whole is not strongly involved in the classic Fordist sectors; it has been able to use neo-Fordist methods of industrial organization, but it is very capital-intensive. Therefore, it has had greater margins for collaborative relations with the unions in its own plants. It also has a very strong international presence (60 per cent of production was outside Italy in 1993).

### De Benedetti

While he is no longer the major figure in the Italian business world that he was in the late 1980s, Carlo De Benedetti still merits mention in this context because of his unique role. Even today he remains an active member of the economic elite of the country, even though his holding company, Cofide, today controls firms with sales of only 3.6 trillion lire (1998).

Carlo De Benedetti did not inherit a position in the firmament of major Italian capitalists. His father owned a small industrial firm, and

*Table 3.3* The largest firms and groups, 1998

| Name | Sector | Controlling interest | 1998 sales (billion lire) | Italian sales (%) | Employees (1998) | Employees in Italy (%) |
|---|---|---|---|---|---|---|
| a  The 12 largest private industrial groups | | | | | | |
| Fiat* | Vehicles, agricultural machinery | Agnelli family | 88,621 | 37.1 | 220,549 | 60.2 |
| Olivetti/Telecom | Telecommunications, information tech., business machines | Group of investors (Gnutti family and others) | 51,404 | 86.8 | 140,708 | a |
| Compart | Agricultural products, chemicals, energy | Mediobanca, other banks | 25,574 | 21.7 | 33,076 | n.a. |
| Pirelli* | Tyres, cables | Pirelli family | 10,624 | 15.0 | 38,209 | 21.9 |
| Fininvest | TV, advertising, retail, publishing | Berlusconi family | 10,278 | a | 13,537 | a |
| Parmalat | Foods | Tanzi family | 9,833 | 23.0 | 39,349 | 8.6 |
| Riva | Steel products | Riva family | 9,456 | 76.3 | 23,092 | a |
| IBM Italia | Computer products and services | IBM (USA) | 9,188 | 46.6 | 18,384 | 73.1 |
| Edizione Holding | Clothing, retail, restaurants | Benetton family | 9,148 | 66.5 | 30,478 | a |
| HdP | Clothing, publishing, paper | Fiat, Mediobanca, others | 9,008 | 47.9 | 18,532 | a |
| Ferrero | Foods | Ferrero family | 7,402 | 27.0 | 15,839 | 37.3 |
| Italcementi* | Cement, building materials | Pesenti family | 5,844 | 29.5 | 14,478 | 36.7 |
| b  The 3 major state-owned groups† | | | | | | |
| ENI | Oil, gas, chemicals | State | 54,875 | 63.7 | 78,906 | a |
| ENEL | Electricity | State | 38,951 | 100.0 | 84,938 | a |
| IRI | TV, transportation, engineering, shipbuilding | State | 30,875 | 64.4 | 112,651 | a |

Source: Calculated from data in *R&S*, 1999 (data for end of 1998).

Notes

*Fiat, Pirelli, and Italcementi are themselves owned by holding companies, respectively IFI (total sales 94,420 billion lire), Pirelli & C. (total sales 11,159 billion lire), and Italmobiliare (total sales 6,209 billion lire), each controlled by the family listed in the table.

†In process of privatization: IRI was dissolved in June 2000, and ENEI shares had been offered to the public; plans for ENI were less advanced.

a Figure not available, but close to 100 per cent.

Carlo rose to prominence as a financier and reorganizer of companies.[27] So successful was he that the Agnellis hired him in 1976 to reorganize Fiat, then in considerable difficulty; but his suggestions proved too radical at the time, and the relationship soon ended. In 1978, however, he gained control of Olivetti, the office machinery firm, and succeeded in restructuring it and restoring it to profitability. In the late 1990s, after a series of losses, he reduced his share of ownership in the firm, and in 1996 withdrew from operative management.[28] The new management planned to sell the personal computer division and concentrate on telecommunications, in particular cellular telephones: Olivetti controls Omnitel, the second cellular network in Italy.[29] Later, control of Olivetti was acquired by Bell, a Luxembourg company representing a syndicate of investors led by Emilio Gnutti.[30] As we shall see below, it then launched a successful takeover bid for the recently privatized telephone giant, Telecom Italia. De Benedetti has also divested himself of the French auto parts firm Valeo, so that his principal holdings remain in auto parts, machinery and equipment, advertising, and the publishing company that prints the weekly *L'Espresso* and the daily *La Repubblica*.

De Benedetti has in the past been regarded as the *enfant terrible* of Italian capitalism. He is an opponent of the old economic 'oligarchy', and a champion of 'modern', 'Anglo-Saxon' business methods. For instance, he has often, and successfully, turned to the capital markets to finance his various operations, and as a result his control over the firms in his conglomerate has been more tenuous than that of the other major capitalists. He has stated his preference for public market dealings rather than private, secret compacts, and championed the rights of minority shareholders. His political actions and pronouncements have also been more open to the left than those of other major capitalists. He has engaged in more purchases and sales of companies than they have, so much so that he has been dubbed a 'raider' by some, particularly during his failed attempt to gain control of the Société Générale de Belgique (SGB) in 1988. Though he is an expert at restructuring firms in difficulty, he is more a financier than an industrialist at heart.

It is possible to link De Benedetti's distinctive political and economic position to the nature of his principal business interests, present and past. Olivetti, his former flagship company, was chiefly engaged in the 'post-Fordist' business of computer manufacturing, an activity with a large research and development component. White-collar workers outnumber blue-collar at Olivetti – the latter are only 15 per cent of the work force of the parent company – and De Benedetti was above all interested in labour peace and fostering a collaborative culture in his work force. This means he avoided the confrontational positions adopted by Fiat *vis-à-vis* the unions in its efforts to control costs and tame union and worker power. His conglomerate is also highly internationalized: roughly half of Olivetti's work force was outside Italy, as are many of his remaining holdings. The fact that the entrepreneur with the most clearly 'post-Fordist' holdings also appeared as the recognized leader of the 'progressive' wing of Italian capitalism is not accidental. At the same time, his stands in favour of a free and open market, while attracting the applause of the left because they were attacks on the 'powers that be' of Italian business, Fiat and Mediobanca, foreshadow an 'Anglo-Saxon' style of capitalism. The fact that the left has not perceived him in this light is a product of its own particular attitude to the free market and capitalism. (Berlusconi's hold-ings also have a somewhat 'post-Fordist', or, as we have said, even 'post-modern' character, but he has assumed the leadership of the more backward wing of capital, and he does not favour a genuine free market, but rather depends on state support.)

In fact, De Benedetti had aimed at constructing a second pole of Italian capitalism, in competition with Fiat; he had taken over the Credito Romagnolo bank, and bid for the Mondadori publishing house and for companies in the food sector. However, his failed attempt to take over the SGB not only weakened him financially, but was the beginning of a decline, accelerated by the losses of the Olivetti personal computer divi-sion, which he felt that he could not sell in the Italian market, even though he saw it was necessary.[31] Finally, in the fall of 1995 he had to seek Mediobanca's support for an increase in capitalization of 2,257 billion lire for Olivetti. As he himself put it, 'I had no alternative, because no one in Italy can put together so large a sum of money, over 2000 billion, no one except Mediobanca'.[32] This episode demonstrated, in De Benedetti's words, that 'I am *establishment* and at the same time *antiestablishment*'.[33] While a critic of the Mediobanca-Fiat nexus and its practices, De Benedetti remained in an ambiguous position. This was particularly so under the centre-left government of Romano Prodi, towards which the 'good salon' also demonstrated considerable sympathy.

## The state sector

The Italian state sector, while currently in the midst of a process of privati-zation, has long been one of the largest in the capitalist world, but its peculiar character has often made its role difficult to assess. Are these enterprises to be considered a part of capital, and, if so, of what sort? Or are they simply appendages of the state itself? As we shall see, the archipel-ago of state industry is so variegated and fragmented that no single answer, valid for the whole group of companies, is possible.

Until the recent privatization programme, which began in earnest only in 1992, the Italian state sector was extremely large and omnipresent in the economy. The three largest institutes (*enti*), IRI, ENI, and EFIM, had 578,000 employees in 1987, and total sales (excluding banking) of nearly 80 trillion lire. Even more significant, of the 1640 largest companies, state-owned firms accounted for 34.6 per cent of net sales.[34] By 1994,

EFIM had been dissolved, but IRI was still the country's largest conglomerate, slightly larger than Fiat, and ENI was the third-largest with 63 trillion lire in sales. To these three could be added the national electric firm, ENEL, with 35 trillion lire total sales, and a few smaller state-owned companies.

Perhaps even more striking is the variety of the activities in which the state sector was involved. IRI controlled three major banks, holdings in the food industry, steel plants, the public television and radio corporation (RAI), the national telephone company (Telecom Italia), telephone and telecommunications equipment producers, most shipbuilding companies, several engineering companies, an aircraft producer, several motorways and the restaurants on them, construction companies, and several other banks, not to mention numerous minor holdings. Besides oil, gas, and chemicals, ENI has been involved in construction, engineering, and newspaper publishing.

There are several possible ways in which state-owned firms could be characterized. If they behave in the same way as private firms, they could be classified unproblematically as part of capital, in no essential way different from the private sector. Of course, private-sector behaviour does not necessarily mean a single-minded pursuit of the maximum profit. Especially in the era of large-scale oligopolies, private firms often aim at expansion or stability ahead of profit-maximization; in any case, there are often legitimate doubts about the most profitable course of action, which can lead private firms to adopt very different strategies for achieving the same ultimate goal. While the state, as the major shareholder, may not press its firms to maximize profits as private shareholders would, we have seen that the large monopolies are also controlled *de facto* by one person or family, and therefore relatively free from market pressures as well. This is indeed what is held to distinguish the Rhenish and Japanese forms of capitalism from the Anglo-Saxon, where the demands of the financial markets for short-term profitability predominate.

State industry may also, as it has done in many countries, pursue not its own interests, however defined, but those of the private sector, offering services and infrastructure at moderate cost, particularly in the case of 'natural monopolies'. It may also undertake infrastructural investments which are too large and risky for private capital, carry out research and development for the benefit of the private sector, etc.; the derivationist school has stressed the importance of these state functions for the accumulation of capital. In performing this role, state industry may in fact favour one fraction of private capital over others, by offering infrastructure and services to it in particular, and thereby promote its own strategy for the country's economic development: this was the role of ENI under Mattei. ENI did not offer its gas at cost price to consumers, as public utilities often do; instead, it charged a monopoly rent and used the proceeds to further its own vision of Italy's economic future.

Third, state industry may promote general, national economic goals that do not so directly serve the interests of private capital. These may include Keynesian stabilization policies, the pursuit of a particular type of economic development (industrial policy), or the defence of the country's balance of payments position. The latter sort of policy clearly strengthens the state's hand, even if this may not be in the interests of capital or any significant fraction of it. Not all of these goals can be 'derived' from the needs of capital; often they are manifestations of state autonomy and indeed in many cases also further that autonomy.

Finally, state industry may pursue non-economic goals, primarily related to legitimation: e.g. the maintenance of employment, the salvaging of unprofitable firms, regional policy, and the provision of rewards for the government's supporters.

How should we characterize Italian state industry? Which of the above roles has it played, and which have been predominant? The answer is not simple, for two related reasons: in the first place, there has been no agreement either among the managers of the industries or among their political 'masters' on the role and objectives of state industry. All of the above-listed goals find some support among both groups, with different emphases.[35] For instance, a survey of 360 public-sector managers revealed that 5 per cent believed they should pursue the maximum profit, 14 per cent that they should 'follow the indications of the market', 46 per cent that they should operate as efficiently as private firms, and 35 per cent that they should achieve the objectives of economic planning at the least cost.[36]

Secondly, there is no clear division of powers and responsibilities within the state sector; this situation engenders considerable confusion and frequent conflict, so that it is very difficult to identify the real decision-making body in many cases. Grassini has very aptly compared this situation to a decaying empire, where there is no coherent system of rules and many overlapping jurisdictions contend for power.[37]

Within the state sector, there were three (sometimes four) levels of command. Until 1993 there was a further level, the Ministry of State Holdings (Partecipazioni Statali). It was supposed, in theory, to lay down policy and exercise control over all the state holdings; since its abolition by referendum, the government as a whole could be considered the senior level of management and control over state holdings. At the highest formal level were the major institutes (*enti*), charged with overall supervision of their variegated empires. (Currently, only ENI remains of the three original *enti* – IRI was broken up in 2000.) Below them were the sectoral holding companies (*finanziarie*) in IRI, or sectoral leading companies (*società caposettore*) in ENI. These generally controlled all the group's operations in a particular industry – e.g. Stet was the IRI holding company in the telephone and telecommunications sector; Snam is ENI's leading company in charge of its pipeline and distribution operations.

Finally, the operating companies actually carried out the work and ran the plants. Sometimes there was an intermediate firm between the holding company and the operating company – e.g. Stet controlled Italtel, the manufacturer of telecommunications equipment, which had subsidiaries of its own.

The powers of these levels were ill defined, so that conflicts often emerged. One of the most notable was that between the Ministry and the Intersind, the association formed by the IRI companies after they left Confindustria, over Intersind's support of Confindustria's decision not to renew the wage-indexation mechanism in 1982. Similarly, different public companies often entered into conflict with each other: an accord between Aeritalia (IRI) and Boeing to produce a vertical-take-off aircraft was opposed by Agusta (EFIM), which had already agreed to enter a European consortium to produce a similar plane.[38] One reason for the conflicts is that virtually all managers owed their jobs to political nomination, even if they were chosen for non-political qualities, and therefore could not be effectively disciplined or controlled by those above them in the hierarchy.[39] This means that, in effect, the largest share of power was wielded by the managers of the operating companies or of the holding and leading companies. This conclusion is supported by the results of the above-cited survey.[40]

Therefore, the state sector cannot be viewed as a single whole with a single set of goals, as the managers of the different companies exercised a large amount of discretion in choosing between different objectives. It seems at first glance that this is the only sector of the Italian economy where 'managerial capitalism', as theorized by Berle and Means, Burnham, Galbraith, and others, flourished (we have already seen that it is very rare in the private sector). However, unlike the managers of this classic line of theory, state managers in Italy are not a self-perpetuating group who co-opt their own successors; instead, they are chosen by the politicians in what was until recently at least a fierce struggle between the different governing parties and their factions, and is still a highly politicized process. While the majority of those chosen have the technical knowledge and background for the job as well as the support of a party, this frequent injection of exogenous elements or considerations has prevented them from developing a completely 'managerial' set of goals.

Enrico Mattei pursued a strategy that was above all political in inspiration, and far from the cautious, stability-oriented policies held typical of managerial firms. His successor, Cefis, abandoned many of Mattei's causes (in part because some of his battles had been won by 1963), but continued to pursue an independent line, conditioning rather than being conditioned by the political parties. After Cefis' departure from ENI for Montedison in 1971, the parties, partly as a result of the Socialists' growing appetite, partly because Cefis had accommodated them more than Mattei had done, began to assert fuller control over appointments in the state sector. Throughout the 1960s and especially the 1970s, the state sector became increasingly 'politicized' by party appointments, while at the same time losing efficiency and dynamism. Cefis, as we have seen, did not follow Mattei's line of seconding the rise of the Fordist firms such as Fiat, but instead began to evolve a different strategy, based on the highly capitalized input-producing sectors and on financial speculation.[41]

The increasing politicization of appointments in the state sector did not, however, lead to a shift in the locus of power from the managers to the politicians. The politicians were able to nominate most of the senior managers, but unable to then issue them directives. There was no unified political will in the government, no agreement even on the role of state industry, so no such directives could be formulated. The political parties sought in general to control appointments for their own sake, to reward followers and extend their power to provide further rewards, rather than to influence the industrial policies of the public-sector companies. Furthermore, each manager, while often the 'candidate' of a particular party or faction, owed his (very rarely her) nomination to a complex bargaining process rather than a single individual or group. As a result, the politicization of appointments could condition, but not eliminate, the considerable independent power of the state managers.

These political appointees may well have used their own powers to make appointments on political criteria, but such clientelistic practices are always incidental to the major policy directions of the firm. Where larger-scale political objectives are concerned, state managers all tend to reject the salvaging of industries with no future, in spite of the undoubted political benefits that might ensue; they will take on such firms only when required to do so by the political authorities.[42]

The principal motivation of state managers, as it emerges from surveys and their day-to-day behaviour, is in fact very similar to that of private-sector managers: to ensure in the first place the stability and continued existence of the firm, and in the second place, if possible, its growth (this is not far different from the behaviour of the non-managerially controlled private oligopolies, where immediate profitability is not uppermost in the owners' minds). In addition to these primary goals, they may secondarily pursue some collective economic goals, such as improving the balance of payments or promoting the development of the South, in much the same way as private-sector managers may pursue profit maximization as a secondary objective after growth. Often the very existence of the firm is viewed as an important national goal – e.g. a firm like Italtel, whose managers thought it was important that there should be an Italian presence in the world-wide telecommunications industry.

In the case of some utilities, like ENEL, or, in part, Telecom, these objectives were of course present, but were strongly constrained by the requirement to serve the accumulation of private capital through an accommodating pricing policy. These firms need to be considered as a group apart from the rest of state industry: as stated above, the fragmentation of the system makes it impossible to generalize about all public-sector firms.

The relative independence of the management of state industry from the politicians is well illustrated by the terms of the 'two professors' as presidents of the largest institutes: Romano Prodi during his first term at IRI (1982–89) and Franco Reviglio at ENI (1983–89). Both were appointed to reorganize the two institutes and bring them back to financial health, and they succeeded in large degree. While Prodi was a Christian Democrat and Reviglio a Socialist and former Minister of Revenue, both had spent their careers as professors of economics, and both were determined to resist political pressures. They brought the two institutes back to profitability after years of losses (ENI in 1985, IRI in 1988), shedding personnel and restructuring where necessary. Realizing the large degree of autonomy enjoyed by their managers, they sought to recruit the best, often from the private sector. They carried out several significant privatizations as well, not for ideological reasons, but to sell off holdings in non-strategic sectors or, more important, to improve their overall balance-sheets.[43]

IRI, for example, sold Alfa Romeo to Fiat in 1986, and ENI sold the Lanerossi textile firm to Marzotto. Both institutes also offered more shares in their companies to the public: by 1988, IRI and ENI companies accounted for 20 per cent of the value of shares traded on the Milan stock exchange.[44] It is true that Prodi was blocked by the politicians in his attempt to sell SME (food processing) to De Benedetti,[45] but his other thirty privatizations went ahead. The two professors also attempted to conclude significant accords for co-operation and joint ventures with the private sector: Prodi between Italtel and AT&T, after the failure of an attempt to combine with Fiat's Telettra, and Reviglio between Enichem and Montedison. The second was to lead to considerable bad blood between public and private partners after Reviglio's departure, but was a logical move for the Italian chemical industry.

The two professors received high marks from informed observers and the public for their performance, but were criticized by numerous politicians, who objected to their opposition to political appointments and also to their privatizations, which reduced the number of political appointments available at a time when conflict within the majority over the division of these positions was reaching new levels of intensity. Ironically, ideological predispositions had very little to do with the politicians' positions on privatization. The most critical were the Socialists and some of the Christian Democrats from the centre and right, who stood to lose most by this diminution of their patronage powers. The professors' successors were Franco Nobili (DC) at IRI, and Gabriele Cagliari (PSI) at ENI (since 1979, the Socialists had claimed the presidency of ENI as theirs, while that of IRI belonged to the DC; that of EFIM was assigned to one of the minor coalition partners). They displayed more sensitivity to the politicians' wishes – Nobili, for instance, declared an end to privatizations, and showed himself more accommodating in the nomination of bank directors and managers.[46]

The consequence of this situation is that state industry's position *vis-à-vis* the government and the state has been essentially similar to that of private industry – i.e. it has sought to influence the state for much the same reasons and in much the same ways. There are, of course, important differences: we have seen that the politicians attempt to influence appointments and certain strategic decisions in the state sector, such as the sale or acquisition of a company, and that their nominees may have secondary economic policy goals which they pursue as well as their primary objectives of stability and growth. On the other hand, as we shall see, state managers have important advantages in lobbying politicians, advantages usually not available to private industry: their close political contacts, and their ability, as public-sector enterprises, to offer politicians a wide range of benefits that fall short of outright corruption. There is, in sum, a greater interpenetration of state and public enterprises, but the latter, represented by their managers, nevertheless remain independent subjects with their own interests and objectives. These considerations apply down to the mid-1990s: since 1993, when governments have embarked on the privatization programme that has led to the demise of IRI and envisages the eventual privatization of ENI, the state managers have been engaged in a significant rearguard action, aimed at retaining as large a degree of control as possible.

## Banks and financial capital

Until the early 1990s the majority of Italian banks, with over 75 per cent of total deposits, were in the public sector. This pattern of ownership was chiefly a result of the collapse of 1931, which led IRI to take over the three 'banks of national interest', the Banca Commerciale, Credito Italiano, and the Banco di Roma. There were also the six large 'public-law banks', the Banca Nazionale del Lavoro, the Istituto San Paolo di Torino, the Monte dei Paschi di Siena, and the banks of Naples, Sicily, and Sardinia. Several of the latter were not corporations with share capital, but 'foundations' with boards of directors nominated by different governmental or other bodies. There were also the publicly owned special credit institutions (for long- and medium-term credit) and many local savings banks (*casse di risparmio*, etc.) controlled by local authorities; furthermore, some of the ordinary banks were also controlled by IRI or other public institutions. As a result, five of the seven largest banks by size of deposits were still in the public sector as late as 1997, and nine of the fourteen largest, with 76 per cent of the total deposits, were public.[47]

*Table 3.4* The seven largest banking groups, 1998

| Name | Controlling interest | Assets (billion lire) | Revenues (billion lire) |
|---|---|---|---|
| San Paolo-IMI | Charitable foundation and banks, Fiat | 300,528 | 9,544 |
| Banca Intesa* | Crédit Agricole, Cariplo and other local savings banks | 289,341 | 10,838 |
| Unicredito | 3 local savings banks and Allianz insurance (Germany) | 277,372 | 12,177 |
| Banca Commerciale* | Banca Intesa | 213,291 | 7,788 |
| Banca di Roma | Cassa di Risparmio di Roma (savings bank) | 195,821 | 7,145 |
| Banca Nazionale del Lavoro | Banca Bilbao Vizcaya, INA insurance, Banca Popolare Vicentina | 163,144 | 6,385 |
| Monte dei Paschi di Siena | Local governments | 154,213 | 6,413 |

Source: *R&S*, 1999 (data for end of 1998).

Note
*Banca Intesa obtained a controlling interest in the Banca Commerciale Italiana in 1999, reducing the number of large banking groups to six.

The process of privatization began in 1993. Although the government intended to promote widely diffused shareholding by limiting the number of shares any individual or firm could hold, the privatizations of the Banca Commerciale and the Credito Italiano in 1993 and 1994 resulted in the control of the two ex-IRI banks falling into the hands of informal syndicates organized by Mediobanca. In fact, the limits on single blocks of shares made it most likely that groups who already operated together in other sectors would be able to co-ordinate their share acquisitions in order to form a controlling block. In the Banca Commerciale, 21.3 per cent of the shares were taken up by large shareholders; of this 21.3 per cent, 10.8 per cent was held by foreign banks, many of them allies of Mediobanca.[48] Another 4.37 per cent was held by companies controlled by or traditionally allied with Fiat and Mediobanca (Gemina, Cartiere Burgo, Lucchini, Ligresti, and Pirelli). A further 4 per cent was held by newer participants, the Benetton and Cerutti families and Diego della Valle. Subsequently, the Assicurazioni Generali, controlled by Mediobanca, became the largest shareholder, raising its holdings to 3.07 per cent, enough to ensure it *de facto* control.[49] As for Credito Italiano, 22.18 per cent of the shares were taken up in large packets, of which 9.39 per cent by foreign institutions, 4 per cent by Fiat and traditional allies, and 7.8 per cent by a group of eight other Italian family businesses, including Benetton and della Valle again.[50]

A 'nocciolo duro' (hard core) of controlling interests had formed in spite of the government's plans. When Benetton, one of the new entrants, realized that 'privatization had resulted in the transfer of ownership from the state to the usual well-known group of private businesses',[51] it sold its interest in Credito Italiano at once, keeping its Banca Commerciale shares only because their price had fallen too far. Later Gemina, the holding company controlled by Mediobanca and Fiat, acquired an 8.99 per cent interest in Credito Italiano.[52] Subsequently, however, and in spite of its tremendous efforts, Mediobanca lost control of these two major privatized banks. Credito Italiano was gradually taken out of its orbit by the German Allianz Insurance, one of the four large financial institutions that stood at the centre of German finance capitalism. A fusion was engineered with three local savings banks, to produce the new, larger Unicredito, controlled by these banks and Allianz.[53] As for the Banca Commerciale, Mediobanca attempted to secure its control through a fusion with the Banca di Roma, but this was repulsed by the Banca Commerciale management, who felt they had been slighted under Cuccia's tutelage. In the end, the Bank of Italy denied approval for the fusion, and subsequently the Banca Intesa, a fusion of local savings banks in association with the French Crédit Agricole, made a successful bid to take over the Banca Commerciale, creating the largest banking group in the country.[54]

The most significant other privatization involved the Istituto Bancario San Paolo di Torino, the largest single Italian bank. It was originally controlled by a charitable foundation of the same name. In the course of privatization, it first fused with the Istituto Mobiliare Italiano (IMI), a state-controlled medium-term investment bank, and then came under the control of a syndicate including a group of other banks and Fiat, represented through its holding company, IFI. This is one case of a major industrial conglomerate acquiring a significant stake in the control of a privatized bank. Significantly, it occurred when relations between Fiat and Mediobanca were beginning to cool, before the conflict between them came into the open in the struggle for control of Telecom Italia. The other large state-controlled banks, Banca di Roma and the Banca Nazionale del Lavoro, went to a local savings bank and to a syndicate headed by the Spanish Banca Bilbao Vizcaya, respectively. While large, these were not particularly well managed institutions, and were destined to be the targets of merger attempts.

In Zysman's typology,[55] then, the pre-1993 Italian credit system would appear at first glance to have been a 'state-led' one, but in fact the different banks and credit institutions did not have the same unified direction and sense of purpose as is provided by the Trésor in France or the Ministry of Finance in Japan. The banks were mostly in the public sector, but, as we have seen above, public-sector managers exercised a large degree of autonomy. The banks were limited in their activities by the banking law of 1936, which was intended to prevent crashes such as had occurred in 1931. It forbade the creation of 'mixed' banks, and instead outlined a system of specialized institutions, some dealing with short-term credit, some with long-term industrial finance, etc. The large banks listed above were all ordinary banks – i.e. they were forbidden to undertake long-term commitments to firms, and in particular could not buy their shares or bonds. This situation created the need for 'special credit institutions' that could engage in such long-term financing, and the state created many of these, though not enough to satisfy the demands of industry. The most famous of them is Mediobanca, founded in 1946; the largest are IMI (Istituto Mobiliare Italiano) and Crediop, founded to finance public works.

The ordinary banks, like the rest of the state sector, gave priority to stability; in this they were encouraged by the legal limits on their activities, and the reliance of governments and the Bank of Italy on monetary policy to regulate the economy. They followed a very conservative line, preferring to invest in treasury bonds or other guaranteed financial instruments rather than in loans to industry. This propensity also reflected the interests and inclinations of their depositors, the mass of the saving petty bourgeoisie. This led to frequent cases of 'double intermediation', in which the banks purchased the bonds of the special credit institutions, which in turn advanced funds to industry. On the other hand, firms have been traditionally highly dependent on credit for finance, as the public's propensity to buy stocks and private-sector bonds was very low in the 1960s and 1970s. In the 1980s, those firms willing to issue shares (mostly the larger ones) were able to once again seek funding from the stock market, and the largest companies' balance sheets had improved so much that self-financing accounted for a much larger proportion of their investment. Small and medium firms, on the other hand, remained much more dependent on credit.

The issuing of credit has not been governed by any clear economic criteria. The special credit institutions often applied political rather than economic standards (e.g. priority to public-sector companies, priority to investments in the South), while they and the ordinary banks showed a marked propensity to favour large over small borrowers. Many of the banks lacked the professional capacity to properly assess risks in any case, and for this reason also stuck to their safe, established clients. (In a few cases, especially some of the local savings banks, political affiliations may also influence credit decisions).

The banks, then, have not constituted a powerful fraction of capital to rival industrial capital for political power; this is an important difference between Italy and Britain. Nor, with the important exception of Mediobanca, have they taken the lead in financing and controlling industry, as in Germany. Nor is the credit market the powerful instrument of government policy that it is in France or Japan, though the Italian state, particularly through the special credit institutions, has often attempted to use it to favour certain projects and firms, particularly in the South. Rather, the banks have to a fair degree passively conformed to the given economic power structure, favouring the already established firms and particularly the state sector. They have not, in the process, been particularly efficient in channelling the very large savings of the Italian people into productive investment; in recent years, they have been diverted from this task by the need to finance the growing government deficit.

In the 1980s the large private conglomerates, with their large reserves of cash, were able to reap profits from financial as well as industrial operations; in fact, the prevailing high-interest policies made such operations especially lucrative. They also sought to expand into the banking sector themselves: Fiat, through Gemina, acquired the Nuovo Banco Ambrosiano, and De Benedetti purchased the Credito Romagnolo. This trend to the diversification of industrial groups into banking (the formation of 'finance capital' through a process inverse to that described by Hilferding) was, however, opposed by the Bank of Italy and numerous political groups, who sought to forbid such combinations by law.

In the 1990s, the privatization of most of the banking sector did not in fact see the continuation of this trend, with the single and important exception of the significant Fiat stake in San Paolo-IMI. The new banks appear to be most interested in expanding into as many areas of financial services as possible, following an Anglo-Saxon rather than a Rhenish model.

## Medium and small industry

Beside the major groups discussed above, there are few medium-large firms in Italy; there is a significant gap between the few very large and the myriad of small firms. Several of the intermediate-sized companies are foreign-owned or have their principal business activity abroad. One exception is the Riva group, which grew suddenly when it became the principal shareholder of the privatized Ilva steelworks in 1995. Another is Benetton, the clothing manufacturer which grew exponentially by using modern methods of marketing, sophisticated, rapid communications between the sales points and the manufacturing operation, and sub-contracting in the 'industrial district' of Treviso and neighbouring zones. Benetton is one of a series of 'pocket multinationals' which have developed in recent years, often in traditional industries, and expanded worldwide in spite of their initially modest dimensions; others include Mr Tod's shoes (Diego della Valle), Luxottica eyewear (Del Vecchio), Carraro tractors, the Marzotto textile group, and Merloni appliances.[56] Benetton is the exception in that it has, through Edizione Holding, diversified into other areas of activity, including supermarkets. The Marzotto textile group is another of these 'pocket multinationals'. It attempted to achieve diversification through its fusion with Gemina, the stronghold of the 'good salon'. These capitalists who have experienced recent growth often continue to reflect the mentality of the small entrepreneurs of the industrial districts from which they emerged, though the recent attempted Marzotto-Gemina fusion suggests that with growth and success may come co-option by the existing economic 'powers that be'.

While the small and medium firms of the 'Third Italy' have been economically crucial, they traditionally had very little weight in national politics. In the North-East, for instance, the DC was solidly implanted for many years, receiving support because of its subcultural roots, a network of clientelistic ties, and pork-barrel projects. Similarly, the strong Communist subculture in the 'Red' regions allowed the party to consider their support a given. While at the local level, political leaders facilitated the economic growth of these regions, national policy continued to channel subsidies primarily towards the major firms (in the case of industrial policy) or the South.

In general, the firms of the 'Third Italy', which are heavily involved in exporting, should favour a low, stable exchange rate, though certain quality lines are insulated from fluctuations in the currency. They favour easier credit and lower interest rates, as they tend to depend on loans rather than self-financing. At the same time, their major interest with respect to the budget of the state is the high level of taxation; many perceive that they receive little from the state in return for the taxes they pay, and there is widespread sympathy for tax evasion. While many of this group, especially in the North-East, have adopted extreme *laissez-faire* positions and supported the Northern League and Forza Italia, they are not always in support of the 'hard line' in labour relations advocated by Fiat and some of the larger groups: for example, during the 1996–97 negotiations for the metalworkers' national contract, many of the North-Eastern firms concluded plant-level deals with their workers even before the national contract was signed.[57]

Meanwhile, the larger industrialists in these regions, the 'pocket multinationals', often showed themselves ready to extend at least the benefit of the doubt to the centre-left government of Romano Prodi, even when the leadership of Confindustria was taking a much tougher stance. Mario Carraro, the president of the federation of industrialists of Veneto, the regional federation of Confindustria, was forced to resign for criticizing the attacks on the government by Confindustria president Giorgio Fossa, while Diego della Valle spoke as an invited guest at the February 1997 Congress of the PDS (Democratic Party of the Left, ex-Communist), expressing hope that the government could solve the long-standing problems of the Italian economy; indeed, he believed that the Prodi government was a unique opportunity to carry out reforms without provoking insurmountable opposition in society, adding that many other industrialists thought the same.[58] And Gilberto Benetton stated that the Prodi government 'is doing things, after decades of disorganization and thieving', and called tax evasion 'the real cancer'.[59]

Obviously, these larger, more 'enlightened' business leaders from the 'Third Italy' do not represent completely the views of the mass of smaller entrepreneurs: it was pressure from the base that had forced Carraro's resignation. For instance, large, well-known firms find it harder to evade taxation or social security contributions or pay less than the national labour contracts stipulate; hence Benetton's views on tax evasion. But their fundamental objectives – cutting social security contributions, reducing taxes and labour costs, reforming the inefficient state – are common to large and small, in spite of their different views on the parties and on governments.

## The ruling class: unity and division

The above survey has concentrated on the different components of the capitalist class, without discussing in any detail the crucial question of their unity and cohesion. In part, this will be answered by the treatment of their political organization and action in Chapter 6, since social interests are in part shaped by politics and the state; as has often been pointed out, they cannot be considered a given which is constituted in the economy or civil society and then simply acts on the political system.[60] Nevertheless, the social and economic make-up of the capitalist class is clearly relevant here as well.

Many sociological studies informed by the elitist problematic devote considerable attention to the common social background and personal ties linking members of the ruling circles.[61] From a Marxist point of view, which lays emphasis on common material interests, this factor is much less important, but still significant. In this respect, the Italian capitalist class differs somewhat from those of most other major industrial states, in that it does not share a robust common cultural or social background that sets it apart from the rest of society. It does not have a small, exclusive group of elite educational or social institutions in which its members develop close personal ties:[62] there is no Italian equivalent of the Oxbridge-public school nexus (with its panoply of associated clubs, regiments, and other institutions), the Ivy League, the French *grandes écoles*, or Tokyo University. As Martinelli and Chiesi have pointed out,[63] there is relatively little differentiation between Italian institutions of higher education, though Milan's Bocconi and Catholic universities (both private) and the Milan and Turin polytechnics have turned out more than their share of industrial managers and promoted an *esprit de corps* among their graduates, and the LUISS, a private university in Rome run by Confindustria, may do the same in future. Furthermore, the persistence of family control of the largest corporations has meant that expertise and professional qualifications are less important than in other countries in any case. Nor do other institutions (clubs, churches, etc.) fulfil the social-ization and certification roles usually played by education. More recently we can note a tendency for foreign qualifications, particularly from the top-ranking English-speaking institutions, to identify and promote their holders as members of the business elite; however, these institutions cannot further ruling-class cohesion in the same way that domestic Italian universities could.

This absence of unifying institutions reflects the rather fragmented character of the Italian ruling class. This is in part a result of its persisting regional character.[64] The aristocracy did not provide a unifying element, or model, for the rising capitalist class in the same way as in England: the Italian aristocracy, by and large, entered a period of economic decline with the onset of industrialization, and participated little in the develop-ment of industry. The bourgeoisie concluded very fruitful alliances with the landowners (many of whom were aristocrats), as in 1887, but never truly fused with them. In any case, such a fusion would have contributed less to their cohesion as a class, as the Italian aristocracy was itself region-ally based. The lack of a clearly dominant ideology, even among the ruling classes, in the post-Risorgimento period also militated against the founda-tion of important cohesive institutions; the liberalism of the governing elite was contested by the Church and by both conservative and radical intellectual movements.

While there are no truly exclusive institutions to prepare the ruling class, the total number of persons with higher education was in the past (and still is, by comparison with the rest of Europe) quite small, and this larger group forms a broader elite which is demarcated from the rest of the population and has a certain minimum cultural background in common. What mobility there is into the higher ranks of the capitalist class is from within this group, and almost never from the lower reaches of society (blue-collar workers, artisans, farmers, small business), as is relat-ively frequent in the US or Japan. For instance, the two major oligopolists who did not acquire their positions by inheritance or marriage came from this wider cultural and professional elite: De Benedetti, the son of a small industrialist who came in turn from a family of financiers, and Berlusconi, the son of a bank manager.

Nor does ideology provide a truly unifying cement for the Italian capitalist class. As Abercrombie and Turner have pointed out, there is seldom agreement within the dominant class on a common ideology any-where in the era of advanced capitalism.[65] This is even more true in Italy, where managerialism and the modern welfare state have never been accepted by large fractions of the bourgeoisie. Martinelli and Chiesi suggest that the capitalist class is currently divided between adherents of a free-enterprise ideology and those with a Christian-Socialist vision derived from the two major ideological currents in the country.[66] Some of the most evident lines of cleavage do not precisely follow this divide, however, but are between those who promote a more market-oriented, Anglo-Saxon brand of capitalism, with greater reliance on the stock market, strong anti-trust legislation, and more competition, and, on the other hand, defenders of the more concentrated, state-protected, oligopolistic *status quo*. While there may be broad agreement between capitalists on some policy goals, there are few common ideological or cultural points of reference.

In this situation, the unity and cohesion of the capitalist class, to the extent that they exist, have been created by the activities of the class itself, through relations between families, interlocking directorships, informal meetings, and formal associations. These mechanisms are not lacking. Confindustria, the employers' association, has at times been an instrument for achieving the unity of the class behind the major firms, though in the last few years it has also reflected major divisions as the first president elected 'against' Fiat, Antonio D'Amato, has steered a course closer to the wishes of small and medium industry (see Chapter 6). We have already mentioned (p. 32 above) the 'good salon' which contains the 'old guard' of Italian capitalism, a closely interconnected group of dynasties who attempt to retain control of all the commanding heights of the economy. Its charter members are the Agnellis and Pirellis, along with other families of the second rank with which they have long had close relations – Orlando (metals), Pesenti (cement), Lucchini (steel products), Ferrero (chocolates), Bonomi, and a few others. They meet not only informally, but on the boards of directors of major companies such as Gemina (see Table 3.2, above) and the privatized banks.

The institution which, more than any other, has acted as the support, forum, and agent of the 'good salon' is Mediobanca. The majority of its shares were until 1993 owned by the three IRI 'banks of national interest', but they took a passive role in its management, so that a theoretically public institution paradoxically became the bulwark of the old guard of private capitalism, who are now, after its privatization, its major private shareholders. The *éminence grise* of Mediobanca for fifty years was Enrico Cuccia, who organized and facilitated most of the major financial operations in Italy in the post-war period: the rescue of Ferfin, the SuperGemina scheme, and the privatization of the Banca Commerciale and Credito Italiano, described earlier in this chapter, are some of the most recent. Many of the 'Chinese-box' structures of ownership and the controlling syndicates were devised and implemented by Cuccia, who devoted most of his career to protecting the power and position of the major capitalist dynasties. As a special credit institution, Mediobanca controls large amounts deposited with it by other banks, and often uses these funds to buy minority holdings in important companies. It typically uses these holdings to shore up the position of the owning family. It also controlled, along with its ally Lazard Frères of Paris, the largest widely-held company in Italy, and the largest insurer, Assicurazioni Generali, with its abundant financial resources (42.1 trillion lire in investments in 1996[67]).

Towards the end of the 1990s, however, differences between Cuccia and the Agnellis, long hidden beneath the surface, began to appear. In 1998, the agreement constituting the controlling group of Fiat shareholders, which gave Mediobanca a key role, expired; in the same year, Cesare Romiti, who was very close to Cuccia, retired as Fiat chairman. In early 1999, Mediobanca supported the bid for the newly privatized Telecom Italia launched by Olivetti, headed by Roberto Colannino; Fiat was a leading member of the group of private shareholders who had just assumed control of it.[68] In the meantime, Fiat had taken a major interest in the fused IMI-San Paolo bank. Later in 1999, Meidobanca, through the Assicurazioni Generali which it controlled, countered IMI-San Paolo's bid for the INA (National Insurance Institute), in a move described by Umberto Agnelli as 'arrogant'.[69] In April 2000, Enrico Cuccia died. However, the events of the previous few years had shown that his Mediobanca no longer held the same central position in Italian capitalism, and in the subsequent period, under Vincenzo Maranghi, it lost further ground as the newly privatized banks fused and challenged it, while it was defeated in the battles for Montedison and Telecom.

Both De Benedetti and Berlusconi, though not members of the 'club', had, as we have seen, to seek Cuccia's assistance in their efforts to raise capital. De Benedetti continues to polemically attack the 'old guard', even while acknowledging his debt to Cuccia, while Berlusconi, though an outsider, has no strong motive to destroy the current power structure in favour of Anglo-Saxon market capitalism; his own television networks depend on the frequencies assigned by the state. Also largely outside this network of influence is the state sector, though state managers are not fundamentally different from private-sector managers in their background (except that more come from the Centre and South) and many have had careers in both the public and private sectors. Finally, the 'good salon' perforce excludes the thousands of small and medium capitalists, whose operations are largely local. This is the prime limit of a mechanism of cohesion which relies on present-day personal contacts and relationships rather than a shared background or widely held common values.

In fact, some authors have identified the primary fault line within Italian capitalism as that dividing the large from the small and medium firms. For Augusto Graziani,[70] the larger firms and Mediobanca in the mid-1990s favoured a stabilization of the currency, autonomy for the Bank of Italy, lower social security spending, and privatization with the formation of controlling syndicates of major shareholders (*noccioli duri*). On the other hand, the small and medium industrialists favoured devaluation and less autonomy for the central bank, while having nothing to gain from the passage of state industry to private hands. They did not suffer as much as the large from the blockage of government spending on public works and industrial subsidies, in which they had taken less part. They could agree with the aim of lower social security spending, while at the same time suffering less from high labour costs than the major groups. In Graziani's view, the parties of Berlusconi's Pole of Freedom (Polo) were able in 1994 to unite the pressure from the 'Third Italy' for a lower exchange rate with the desire of the South for more public spending and the retention of a large bloc of state industries. While the enterprises of the North-East were anti-statist, the reduction of public spending was urgent after 1992 because of the need to meet the Maastricht criteria for entry into the Single European Currency, and if this latter objective was less important to them, then so was budgetary rigour.

While sharing *grosso modo* Graziani's characterization of the objectives of the 'good salon', which he calls the 'technocratic' right, Marco Revelli[71] contrasts it not with the small firms of the 'Third Italy', but with the middle strata, the social base of the 'populist' right. The latter he sees as divided between a Northern fraction which resents paying taxes and a Southern one which, on the other hand, depends on government expenditure.[72] The 'technocratic' right, including many managers of state industry, pursues a hard line in the factory with its own workers, while seeking compromises with the working class at the national level; the populist right does the reverse, opposing national 'concertation' with the unions while supporting redistributive spending policies. Revelli does not explicitly refer to two fractions of *capital*, as Graziani does: the industries of the 'Third Italy' are in fact not explicitly mentioned in his analysis. On the other hand, he does point to an objective difference of interests between the Southern small business and middle strata, who want to maintain state expenditure, and their Northern counterparts.

For Alan Friedman, on the other hand, the crucial issue is the creation of open, free markets, especially in the financial sector, so that he tends to see any opponents of Mediobanca and the 'good salon' as part of the 'new' wing of Italian capitalism. This analysis is founded on a contrast between 'ins' and 'outs' rather than on an investigation of the production profiles of the actors. It has in this some objective foundation, but captures only a part of the fault lines within the capitalist class.

Our investigation in this chapter has shown that, while the insights of Graziani and Revelli are valuable, they do, like all such brief sketches, simplify in order to illuminate. To make sense of the divisions within the capitalist class, we should first distinguish between:

1   the 'good salon' and its allies;
2   the industrialists of the 'Third Italy', including two sub-groups, the larger 'pocket multinationals' and the myriad of other small and medium firms;
3   the 'parasitic' strata, both entrepreneurs and middle classes, that depend on state expenditure.

This final group is concentrated in the South, and is, strictly speaking, mostly outside the capitalist class proper, though it has links with one part of it.

The 'good salon' favours a strong anti-inflationary stance and a stable currency, in spite of the hesitations expressed by some of its members, like Romiti, over stabilizing the lira at too high a level. While centred on exporting and import-competing industries, it includes multinationals like Pirelli and has financial interests as well. Therefore, it saw participation in the European Monetary Union as an important objective. Hence it also supported an autonomous role for the Bank of Italy, and limits on the overall level of public expenditure. On this point too, though, it displays some ambiguity, as it favours measures of industrial policy that will benefit it directly, such as the reactivation of public works after the Tangentopoli investigations, or the January 1997 programme of subsidies to consumers who wished to replace cars over ten years old with new ones. For the 'good salon' it is evident that cuts must come in social spending and the public sector. It supports privatization, if it leads to the formation of syndicates which it controls. And as we have seen, it takes a tough line on labour costs within its own factories, while attempting to negotiate with the unions on national wage guidelines and budgetary and macroeconomic policy. In a newer and more restrictive situation, the 'Manchesterian' option of the mid-1970s has been revived in part: the unions are invited to participate in the 'reform' of the welfare state, a reform whose main objective is to cut costs, but in which the excluded, 'parasitic' strata of society (the petty bourgeoisie and public employees) may lose the most.

Small and medium industry, as we have seen, favoured a lower value for the lira, perhaps counting on its ability to export regardless of Italy's position in Europe; it is less internationalized and less involved in finance than the 'good salon'. The 'Third Italy' is also strongly in favour of lower interest rates, given its heavy dependence on loans, and therefore opposed to an autonomous central bank such as the European Central Bank which manages the euro. It is less ambiguous than the large groups on public spending, favouring cuts across the board, though it did not have the same interest in meeting the Maastricht criteria as quickly as possible. While maintaining more consensual labour relations on the shop floor, it is suspicious of, or at best indifferent towards, national tripartite arrangements, where its voice is very weak compared to the large groups': it believes it can maintain labour peace in its own back yard without having to reach accords with the national union leaderships, whereas the negotiations at the large groups are subject to national scrutiny.

Much of Southern industry, and the Southern middle strata, like the small and medium firms of the North and Centre, favour devaluation and lower interest rates, and they are especially opposed to national wage bargaining, which they believe imposes Northern wage levels on the South.

However, they also support continued high public spending and an inflationary solution to the problem of public debt, and this differentiates them strongly from the 'Third Italy'. European integration is especially threatening to this group, who realize, if only dimly, that it means the eventual end to many of the corrupt and illegal practices which have allowed it to survive, such as 'black' labour – i.e. workers who are not paid the wages specified by the national labour contracts, and for whom the employers do not pay social security contributions or taxes. Already the drive to reduce the government deficit has cut the flow of funds to the South and concentrated public attention on abuses such as the widespread false disability pensions. These comments do not apply, of course, to all industry in the South: recently, students have noted the appearance of embryonic 'industrial districts' there too, capable of eventually surviving without evading the law, while the Abruzzo region has seen so many firms of the 'Third Italy' set up shop that its unemployment rate has fallen below the national average.[73]

As a largely non-exporting conglomerate, Silvio Berlusconi's Fininvest stands apart from the other large groups in that it did not share their concerns about the value of the currency or Italy's participation in the European Monetary Union. Hence the drive to meet the Maastricht criteria was also of less concern to the company. Nor are industrial relations as crucial in a firm where labour costs are smaller relative to sales and the unions present are not major industrial federations like the metalworkers or chemical workers. Berlusconi's exclusion from the 'good salon' is not simply a matter of personal relations; it also reflects a difference in the nature of his business and his interests from those of the rest of this group. For this reason, he was able the more easily to form alliances with the second and especially the third groups of businesses identified above. His main interest, of course, remains to protect his television frequencies from governmental regulation.

The pronounced division of Italian capital that we have just described has become even more accentuated over the past decade, as Confindustria has moved outside of the Fiat orbit and offered its wholehearted support to Berlusconi and his coalition. While the 'good salon' tried to make the best of the situation, and offered support to many of Berlusconi's policies, the underlying conflicts remain: in many respects, the centre-left government was more in tune with the needs of the dominant fraction, which is now even more in need of the assistance of an active state and co-operative unions. As Poulantzas wrote, the division of the capitalist class into fractions is one of the principal reasons for the relative autonomy of the state – in Italy, it helps explain the overall political weakness of capital. While the Fiat empire may be weakened by recent developments, this does not signal a shift in underlying economic power to the more backward fractions represented by Berlusconi – the fractionalization of Italian capital will persist.

This chapter has traced the production profiles of the major components of Italian capital. In the following chapter, we shall place Italian capitalism in a comparative perspective, and in Chapter 5 we shall discuss the second major influence on Italy's economic policy, the international environment.

# 4    Italian capitalism in comparative perspective

The previous chapter has outlined the 'production profile' of Italian capitalism, and described its principal fractions. However, any description would be incomplete without any reference to the large literature in political economy on the various 'models' of capitalism that different authors have identified.[1] Much has been written about the differences between Anglo-Saxon, market-dominated, deregulated capitalism and the 'Rhenish model' or 'social market' economy of Germany and similar continental states, characterized by corporatist industrial relations and bank involvement in industry. Some typologies add a separate Asian model, while others include a state-led form of capitalism embracing the East Asian economies (and France before 1981).[2] These models differ significantly in the political relationships between capital, the working class, and the state which accompany them. The Regulation School has given rise to another, only partially overlapping, family of models, centred around the distinction between Fordism and different varieties of post-Fordism.[3] There have been, however, few discussions of Italy in this debate,[4] in spite of its significance as a country in which the class struggle has known moments of great tension, and the working class has developed sophisticated programmes and methods of struggle against capitalist hegemony. The analysis of the last two chapters suggests that Italian capitalism does indeed possess significant peculiarities, and that a single, one-size-fits-all theory of the capitalist state is insufficient to account for the Italian case, where capital is politically weak and has relied to a significant degree on state support. Hence in this chapter we shall discuss the value of the literature on models of capitalism and then critique the manner in which it has been applied until now to the Italian case, in order to arrive at a characterization of the form of capitalism in Italy.

Any discussion of forms and models of capitalism must begin with (and return to) the work of Marx. In *Capital*, in which England is taken as the pattern and prototype of a capitalist economy, Marx presents a theory of capitalism with few suggestions of national differences. Later, looking back on his major work, he tried to dispel the impression that this was a 'general theory' which necessarily applied to all capitalist economies.[5] And in his political writings, such as *The Eighteenth Brumaire of Louis Bonaparte*, Marx was very much aware of the different forms which capital could take on. *Capital* appears to trace an outline of the development of capitalism which allows principally for differences between more and less advanced countries, depending on how far they have travelled along that path. In certain sections, however, such as the chapter on counter-tendencies to crises in Volume III,[6] the possibility of national differences (e.g. in the development of foreign markets) is clearly left open, though not developed by Marx. At the end of Volume III, he lays the groundwork for his unfinished treatment of social classes with the threefold division of surplus value into profit, interest, and rent,[7] and in the *Eighteenth Brumaire*, Marx refers to the fractions of the French capitalist class, and to the pre-dominant role of the financial bourgeoisie among them.[8] Here there is little question that he is discussing a particular national form of capitalism, with its own economic make-up, apart from its political tendencies and divisions.

After Marx, of course, many in the Marxist tradition have identified distinctive forms of capitalism. The most noteworthy earlier contribution remains that of Hilferding, whose *Finance Capital* (1910)[9] attempted to sum up the changes that were already beginning when Volume I of *Capital* was published. Hilferding noted the need of late-follower capitalist countries to provide large pools of capital to their companies, in order to undertake the expensive fixed investments that were now necessary to enter the leading industries such as steel or chemicals. (In England, on the other hand, a slower and more gradual development based on self-financing and loans from local banks had been possible). In these late-follower countries, banks had provided these large stocks of capital, and in turn had taken an interest in the management of the companies concerned, exercising their influence either as lenders or (more typically) as shareholders with a direct stake in the companies' success. The state often played a role in fostering industrial growth as well, especially in the case of industries such as steel and shipbuilding which supplied the military. The banks, with the encouragement of the state, in turn were able to facilitate the formation of cartels among the industries they controlled; hence the free-market model, on which *Capital* is premised, was replaced with a monopolistic or oligopolistic form of capitalism. Hilferding identified the cartels as the prime movers of imperialism: having secured the home market, they then sought further outlets for their production, both in the colonial world and in the orders that would come from the state in its pursuit of an aggressive foreign and colonial policy.

Hilferding's account had the virtue of theorizing and accounting for major trends of his day, including the rush towards world war. Capitalist competition no longer simply took the form of the peaceful exploitation of labour and vicious competition in the market place, but had transmuted itself into inter-imperialist conflict and, eventually, warfare. And he explicitly recognized national differences, though he believed that England, the major exception among the great powers to his theory of finance capital, was destined to go the same way as Germany (his prototype country) and the others.[10] Furthermore, *Finance Capital* does not ignore the relationship between politics and economics, giving politics a more explicit treatment than Marx does in *Capital.* While Hilferding's work appears very much a product of its own time, the age of growing imperialist rivalry before World War I, the basic insight that the mobilization of large pools of financial capital will become more and more necessary for capitalist development applies today with even more force. The German model of the universal bank is one of the methods by which this can be done, but others have been developed. (In England in the first Industrial Revolution, this had been accomplished in large part by means of 'primitive accumulation': in this case, the profits of colonial trade and plunder, merchants' profits, landlords' rental income, etc., as described by Marx in Volume I, Part VIII of *Capital*).

Hilferding's insights were adopted by Lenin to develop his theory of imperialism;[11] as is evident, Hilferding linked the emergence of finance capital to the concentration of capital and the formation of monopolies. 'Monopoly capital' itself became a much-used category of analysis, particularly in the period of the Third International, and was identified as the social basis of fascism. While these different forms of capital were typically conceived of in a teleological manner, as stages of development necessarily following each other, nevertheless they also allowed a differentiation between national varieties of capitalism as well, even if only between more and less 'advanced' forms. In this vein, Poulantzas wrote of different stages of capitalist development, ending with 'state monopoly capitalism', the label used by the French Communist Party for the current phase.[12] These analyses attempted to link the dominance of monopoly capital with the tendency of capitalism to economic 'stagnation', which was held to be the forerunner of economic crisis. Thus, they were unable to account for the unprecedented economic growth of the post-war period, now dubbed by some authors the 'Golden Age of Capitalism'. This task was taken up in the 1970s by a new trend in political economy, the French 'regulation school'.

While inspired by Marxism, the regulation school developed a typology of capitalisms that reflected more closely the actual course of economic growth. They postulated a key distinction between 'extensive' and 'intensive' development, and the associated 'regimes of accumulation' and 'modes of regulation'.[13] The Fordist regime of accumulation, based on the mass production of consumer durables as its driving sector, is by far the most fully developed in the work of the school. It requires a Taylorist organization of work within the factory, and a system of wage regulation that ensures the working class will have sufficient purchasing power to buy the durable goods (automobiles, etc.) produced by the dominant sectors.

The regulation school contrast it to the previous regime, based on heavy capital goods on the one hand (railways, ships, etc.) and on light consumer goods (textiles, clothing) such as characterized the first Industrial Revolution on the other. To underpin a policy of relatively high wages, Fordism typically finds most compatible a Keynesian fiscal and monetary policy, a nationally co-ordinated system of wage bargaining, and a developed welfare state; and on the side of capital, oligopolistic regulation of the market is held to be a necessary complement of Fordism: above all, firms must not attempt to compete by lowering wages, and at the limit competition is restricted to styling, etc. Other elements functional to the Fordist regime of accumulation could also be added (e.g. popular culture or city planning); it is already evident, however, that no capitalist state ever completely fitted the model, and that some approached it more closely than others (one could argue that Sweden and Germany had a more highly developed version of Fordism than its country of origin, the United States, although the latter remained more autocentric, rather than export-oriented, in keeping with the original Fordist model).

The regulation school agrees that Fordism entered into crisis in the early 1970s, but there is less agreement on what has succeeded it. The models proposed tend to be characterized by new work relations in the factory and by new types of product lines, but leave in the background the link between production and consumption that was the starting point and key insight of the 'Fordist' model. Various authors have proposed 'flexible specialization', 'diversified quality production', 'flexible mass production', and 'neo-Fordism' as successor regimes of accumulation,[14] but seldom has any of them been seen as hegemonic or has a full-fledged regime of accumulation similar to Fordism been sketched for any of them. While the wave of neo-liberalism that has washed over the capitalist world since the late 1970s has *de facto* restored the competitive (i.e. market-based) mode of regulation in many sectors of the economy, after the defeat of the left and the trade unions in many of their strongholds, this has not led the regulation school to present a new model which fully reflects this reality, in spite of some suggestive attempts by authors such as Davis and Lipietz.[15]

In relation to the theory of state monopoly capitalism, the model of Fordism differs in several ways. Most importantly, it places industry, rather than finance, at the centre of the analysis, and indeed the Fordist period is described as one favourable to industrial capital and generally unfavourable to rentiers and financial capital. And it sees the stimulation of the home market, rather than cartelization and imperialism, as the primary factor counteracting the tendency of the rate of profit to fall. Like the theory of state monopoly capitalism, it postulates an oligopolistic form of regulation of the market, though it does not reserve a special role for banks in this process, and it sees the involvement of the state in an active role in support of capitalist accumulation, though in different forms (maintenance of purchasing power above all). For the post-Fordist era, it

has attempted a characterization of recent trends, while the more traditional Marxist theory has not been able so far to incorporate them fully
into its analysis.[16]

Another author inspired in many respects by Marxism, Robert Cox, has
attempted to synthesize some of the most important recent developments
in the world capitalist economy, distinguishing between two types of state:
the hyperliberal state, which attempts to re-establish the market as the
determinant of wages, on the one hand (e.g. Thatcherite Britain and the
USA under Reagan); and, on the other, the neomercantilist state, which
attempts to maintain working-class purchasing power and the welfare state
and to aid its core industries.[17] Cox's analysis focuses on the forms of regulation of the labour market, which he identifies as 'modes of social relations of production': for him, the hyperliberal state represents a
regression to modes of regulating the labour market that were predominant earlier in capitalism, such as the 'enterprise labour market' mode,
where wages are determined simply by supply and demand. Cox's major
innovation is the attempt to link domestic forms of regulation with the
world economy and international political developments: he postulates
that certain world orders are more conducive to certain forms of state and
production,[18] whereas more traditionally Marxist authors saw international relations as a function of the domestic economic and political
make-up of the individual states. Cox also attributes to the state a strong
role in shaping the forms of regulation of the labour market. His framework is therefore considerably more state-centred and oriented to the
international economic regime than previous Marxist approaches.

With the regulation school and Cox, the Marxist-derived theories
approach the characterizations of different models of capitalism
developed by non-Marxist writers. The most popular typology has been
that proposed by Michel Albert in *Capitalism against Capitalism*: he contrasts the 'Rhenish' model with the 'Anglo-Saxon'. In the former, industry
is controlled by banks, somewhat in the fashion described by Hilferding.
The banks provide it with 'patient money' which is prepared to wait for
long-term projects to mature; this long-term perspective has allowed the
firms to provide guarantees to their workers and to enter into multi-year
agreements with their unions. The Rhenish model is typically accompanied by a degree of corporatism – peak-level bargaining between unions
and employers' associations – and by a highly developed welfare state. The
Rhenish model, indeed, seems to offer the most appropriate mode of
regulation for a Fordist regime of accumulation, sustaining the purchasing power of the workers while guaranteeing orderly labour relations to
industry.

By contrast, the Anglo-Saxon model of capitalism is characterized by
the much greater influence of markets, both for capital and for labour.
Firms typically derive a much larger share of their capital from the stock
market than from the banks, which are legally prevented from holding

controlling interests in firms. The market investors study the companies' quarterly financial reports, and are prepared to sell out their interests if they are not satisfied. Hence the so often lamented 'short-termism' of British and American companies, and their inability to undertake costly, multi-year projects that detract from short-term profitability. The same pressure of the financial markets for immediate results leads Anglo-Saxon firms to take a tougher line with labour, seeking to reduce costs in any way, including breaking the unions if necessary, and to demonstrate intolerance of regulations and costs imposed by the state.

From a regulation school perspective, we could say that the Anglo-Saxon countries never achieved the most complete form of Fordism even during the 'Golden Age': in the US, significant areas of the country (e.g. the South) were outside the Fordist circuit, and the welfare state remained underdeveloped, while in Britain financial capital in the form of the City of London remained dominant, and industry itself was slow to introduce Taylorist methods. And the very autocentric character of the American economy, combined with the privileged position of the dollar in the Bretton Woods system, allowed for a 'looser' form of wage regulation (pattern bargaining in the major consumer goods, capital goods, and defence industries, with large parts of the work force non-unionized or with much weaker unions) than in continental states such as Germany or Sweden, where the balance of payments was a constant reminder that wage-push inflation had to be controlled. Britain, on the other hand, was exposed to payments crises and paid for its failure to develop a tighter form of incomes policy. Against this background, it is not surprising that Britain and the US were the first to break with Fordist modes of regulation entirely.

Albert's typology recalls in part that of Alfred Chandler, who contrasts personal capitalism, competitive managerial capitalism, and co-operative managerial capitalism.[19] The first is found typically in Britain, the second in the USA, and the third in continental Europe and Japan. Chandler's perspective is based principally on the internal organization of the firm, and there is some question as to whether the differences between personally controlled and managerially controlled firms are as significant as he has postulated (though the distinction has been much discussed in Italy, where it is suggested that family control has limited the growth of many firms[20]). Nevertheless, he too notes the difference between American competitive capitalism, which he considers more highly developed, and the continental and Japanese types.

In a similar vein, Lester Thurow, in *Head to Head*,[21] develops at length the contrast between individualistic capitalism of the Anglo-Saxon type and communitarian capitalism, best typified by Japan but also found in continental Europe. While the former places shareholders first, then customers, and finally workers, communitarian capitalism gives pride of place to its workers, followed by its customers and finally its shareholders. For Thurow, the competitive advantages of the communitarian form of capitalism are evident: long-term planning and co-operative relationships between management and labour. Furthermore, partly for historical reasons, but also because of the interrelationship between industry and the state, the state in these countries has played a more active role in supporting capitalist enterprise: in the first place by providing excellent primary and secondary schools as well as technical and vocational training.

Will Hutton is in certain respects a British Thurow, calling attention to the weaknesses of British capitalism, even in relation to its American cousin.[22] He suggests that the problems of individualistic capitalism are tempered in part in the US by the role of banks operating in individual states and by government intervention in favour of housing construction, defence contracting, and industries vulnerable to foreign competition. Britain, he argues, has neither these advantages nor those of European 'social market' capitalism or of the East Asian model, which Hutton sees as having even more closely managed financial markets. Hutton's principal focus is on financial markets, which he knows well; he points out how the Japanese banks' close knowledge of their customers' business permits them to lend them far more than British banks and at more favourable rates.[23] Similarly, this intimate knowledge permits German banks to lend to small and medium enterprises as well as large. In Britain, on the other hand, the market alone links saving and investment, with results that are far less favourable for growth.

Finally, John Zysman, among others, distinguishes between the market-oriented Anglo-Saxon economies, those with corporatist structures and strong universal banks (e.g. Germany), and those where the state itself plays the leading role in directing the economy (Japan and France, among the G7 countries).[24]

The classical Marxist analyses, starting from Hilferding, put the emphasis on relationships between sectors of capital, rather than on the capital-labour relationship. They tend to view finance capital as less dynamic than industrial capital and, in the long run, likely to lead to stagnation and crisis in the capitalist economy. On the one hand, cartelization and monopolies restrict growth, as they lack the competitive stimulus and tend rather to restrict production in the interest of profit-maximization. On the other, financiers tend to be cautious in their lending, to risk less than industrialists, with a more intimate knowledge of production, would, and to seek political guarantees where possible. In part this reflects the greater risk-aversion of the small savers whose money they manage. Keynes was later to note the inefficiency of financial markets in allocating capital to productive uses. Moreover, on the political level financial capital favours sound-money policies over growth-oriented, expansionist ones, though even where financial capital is dominant, this effect has to be mediated through the political system. (Nevertheless, in the late nineteenth century, more and more countries adopted the gold standard[25]).

In many contemporary treatments, however, such as Hutton's and Thurow's, this relationship appears reversed: where financial institutions are directly linked with industrial companies (whether it be via the German universal banking system, the Japanese *keiretsu*, or other forms of conglomerate), growth appears to be stimulated, while the dominance of financial markets seems to limit it. First, true cartels have not emerged in these countries, where in any case competition in export markets has become central for many firms. Second, the dominance of financial institutions, and the restricted financial market, have insulated firms from the potential short-termism of small savers; whereas, the American and British stock markets and institutional investors are much more effective transmission belts of their demands. Third, the close intertwining of finance and industry has prevented the financial institutions from adopting a strong sound-money stance that sacrificed domestic growth.[26]

While these approaches focus on the relationship between financial and industrial capital, Cox and the regulation school centre their typologies on the capital-labour nexus. While Hilferding, like the regulation school, saw overproduction as the primary crisis tendency of capitalism, for him the limitation of production by cartel agreements and the aggressive search for foreign and colonial markets were the chief responses of capital. Meanwhile, the regulation school views the various modes of regulation as attempts to match demand and supply, in the case of Fordism principally by the creation of a mass market for consumer durables. While for Hutton and Thurow, corporatism and the acceptance of a role for unions are seen primarily from the supply side, as factors that enable a co-operative relationship between management and labour, the regulation school sees them from the demand side, as a way to ensure a mass working-class market, while Cox is principally interested in the form of the political and power relationship between capital and labour, rather than its strictly economic effect.

Categorizations such as Zysman's, which highlight the role of the state, are also interested in political relationships and the locus of power, in addition to the concrete shape of the economy. At the opposite end of the spectrum, Chandler considers the individual firm and is principally interested in its economic capabilities.

The literature we have just surveyed, then, is inspired by two different problematics. The prevalent one is that of economic growth, and involves the attempt to identify the types of systems that are conducive to growth or, on the other hand, stagnation and crisis.[27] Marx and Hilferding were concerned with the tendency of capitalism to generate economic crises; Thurow, Hutton, Albert and Chandler compare contemporary versions of capitalism and seek the roots of their performance in institutional and political factors. For the regulation school also, starting from a Marxian problematic, economic performance is still central. And Zysman, while he introduces the state's role as an important distinguishing feature of certain types of capitalism, is nonetheless concerned primarily to explain economic performance. On the other hand, the problematic of political power and how it is distributed is also present in many of these approaches: Hilferding is concerned about the political support behind European imperialism, and foresees a political crisis (an inter-imperialist war) arising out of the economic contradictions of capitalism. The advocates of co-operative capitalism also note, and generally approve of, a more egalitarian distribution of income and of political power where it is established, by contrast with the United States and Britain. Nevertheless, it is only an account like Cox's that, while stressing the close interrelationship between politics and economics, makes power rather than growth the primary *explanandum*.

In this study, our primary concern is the distribution of political power: specifically, the power of Italian capital. Therefore, a framework such as Cox's would seem the most appropriate for our purposes. However, the question cannot be solved so quickly, and not only because Cox's is not the only possible typology of capital-labour relations. As the scholarly debate on political power has demonstrated, power is itself a highly contested concept.[28] A defensible concept of power seems to require some sort of identification of the 'true' interests of the actors before their ability to realize them can be assessed. This is a task which is nearly impossible even apart from its normative implications. Thus, as has often been pointed out, the true, long-term interests of capitalists, as distinct from their subjective preferences, are difficult to identify, as they depend on a series of assumptions about the future which are necessarily speculative.[29]

The best solution to this dilemma has been offered by Göran Therborn, who has pointed out that it arises from the subjective conception of power as held by persons.[30] As a Marxist, Therborn conceives of the prime actors in history not as individuals or groups of people, but as impersonal forces and tendencies, such as, for example, capital itself. While the interests of capitalists cannot be identified with certainty, the tendencies of capital, the social relationship, can. Therefore particular policies can, at least in principle, be considered to favour the expansion of capital and others to obstruct it. And certain policies favour the political domination of capital while others do not (these are in the 'second-order' interest of capital). We do not need to enter into the debate on the transformation or disappearance of the working class in modern capitalism, or assume that the proletariat as a class for itself is a necessary complement of capitalism (it plainly is not) to conclude that the working class may, when it constitutes itself as a class for itself, with a consciousness of its own identity and power, represent a tendency that resists capital's drive to self-expansion, on the factory floor and in the state.[31]

A perspective such as Therborn's allows us to resolve the problem of power. Even though our account of the tendencies of capital will naturally be itself contestable, it will at least permit us to avoid some of the philosophical objections to a subjective account of power. One might be tempted to argue that since the self-expanding tendency of capital is the mainspring of economic growth, the two problematics mentioned above are conceptually linked. In other words, economic growth (the self-expansion of capital) may be taken as a prime index of the power of capital. However, this ignores the fact that periods of crisis and stagnation are physiological in capitalism, in fact necessary phases of its self-expansion, and that the growth of profits and economic surplus is not always accompanied by the growth of national income. In addition, the political dominance of capitalism may be furthered by policies that restrict economic growth, keeping it below its potential path.[32]

Hence the problematic of political power is different from that of economic growth, although the two are in fact closely linked. And, from our point of view, the former must be the central feature of any typology of forms of capitalism. Cox distinguishes between forms of state and modes of social relations of production, allowing for different modes within the same state – tripartism, enterprise corporatism, management-labour bipartism, and the enterprise labour market (free labour market) are the most common modes found in modern capitalism. For Italy, he suggests that in much of the post-war period there was a 'cartel state', a more relaxed and benign form of fascism, which 'appears to effect a transformation of state corporatism into tripartism'.[33] Cox's framework allows for distinct national mixes of modes within the broad categories of the hyperliberal state and the neomercantilist variety, both reflecting important trends in the world economy which in the long run are tending to reduce the differences between states. It also has the virtue of focussing on the labour market, a central aspect of the balance of power in advanced capitalist societies. On the other hand, while, for example, the 'enterprise labour market' plainly gives capital the upper hand in that labour is disorganized, these institutional forms are not always a sure guide to the relative power of capital and labour; tripartism, for instance, is compatible with situations in which capital is able to secure major concessions from labour and government, as well as with arrangements which effectively constrain capital.

Cox, while providing a clear and useful framework, devotes only brief sections to the Italian case, where he fails to provide a complete account, though he suggests that tripartism broke down in the late 1970s under the impact of the economic crisis (in truth, it never really came into being in Italy at that time, thanks to the divisions within the trade-union front and the weakness of governments). Thus, while the 'cartel state' concept reflects a significant insight into one aspect of Italian politics, the alternation of authoritarianism with the incorporation of the opposition in the governing party or coalition ('transformism'),[34] it does not have a clear counterpart at the level of modes of social relations of production.

Of those who have taken the Italian case as a distinct object of study, Mario Regini has concluded that it constitutes a model *sui generis*, or at least did so in the 1980s.[35] Much influenced by the regulation school, Regini points out that while the state's redistributive policies favoured large firms (e.g. with subsidies), its other, less explicit policies (such as the failure to pursue tax evasion) did not, but rather allowed smaller firms, practising flexible specialization rather than diversified quality production or flexible mass production, to flourish. Meanwhile, the industrial relations system was characterized by antagonistic relations at the national level and in some large firms like Fiat, and by 'micro-concertation' in many other firms practising flexible specialization or diversified quality production. Regini, then, gives pride of place to the small and medium-sized firms of the 'Third Italy' (the North-East and the Centre), which he sees as at the distinguishing feature of a separate model of capitalism.

In spite of the significant differences between types of enterprises, Regini sees Italy as a single capitalist system. Richard Locke, on the other hand, takes the differences which both Cox and Regini see between firms of diverse types even further, and postulates that there is no single national model of capitalism in Italy, but rather a mixture of sub-national patterns, of which he identifies three: policentric, polarized, and hierarchical.[36] Where policentric local networks prevail, he argues, labour relations can be co-operative and consensual, as opposed to the conflictual relations that are found in the other two types. Once again, the *explanandum* (even more than for Regini) is the pattern of industrial relations. But for Locke the focus is on industrial relations at the local level. He arrives at his conclusions by overplaying the differences between local situations (e.g. Turin and Milan), while at the same time conflating fundamentally different realities (e.g. Alfa Romeo in Milan and the Biellese woollen district) that he believes have the same type of local network. And, while local differences are indeed noteworthy, as we shall see below it is wrong to underestimate the importance of the national balance of class power within which the local situations are inserted.

In a more traditionally Marxian vein, one of the most acute writers on the Italian economy, Napoleone Colajanni, sees it as an example of finance capital, in which production is socialized through the nexus savers-banks-state-firms. The form of this nexus – a holding company, a conglomerate, or bank control of industry – is less important than the substance, the rule of finance capital, which tends to generate stagnation. In this analysis, Colajanni is following the path laid out by Pietro Grifone in his classic study of the birth of IRI out of the collapse of the classic form of 'finance capital' (universal banks with industrial shareholdings) in the early 1930s.[37] For Colajanni, the Italian state has never pursued an industrial policy, as distinct from a monetary policy, in the post-war period, and attempts by Enrico Cuccia of Mediobanca to fill the gap have been insufficient. Hence Italy has few really large enterprises, and they have not been able to secure a balanced or lasting form of economic growth for the country. While basing himself theoretically much more on Chandler's typology of the firm, Giulio Sapelli, another careful student of the Italian economy, has also pointed to the relatively small number of large firms as a peculiarity of the Italian economy, and linked it to the pattern of family ownership, which makes companies reluctant to grow if this involves a dilution of family control.[38] Sapelli also relates the failure of the bourgeoisie to become directly involved in politics to this relative weakness – a cultural, as much as an economic insufficiency.[39] Hence the absence of a true industrial policy in Italy, where at most conjunctural policies are exploited by firms to serve their own ends.

Against the background of these diverse opinions, how can we characterize the Italian model of capitalism? We must first concede its relative temporal 'backwardness' compared to the other advanced capitalist economies. This means simply that certain changes that took place elsewhere at various times in the past have been delayed in Italy, not that these changes constitute a desirable norm (as implied by much of the journalistic and political debate in Italy) or an inevitable stage of capitalist development (as some traditional Marxist analyses would have it). A prime example of this relative backwardness is the persistence of a large petty bourgeoisie, even after the decline of agricultural employment. The self-employed constitute 29 per cent of the Italian work force, the highest fraction of any of the G7 countries, approached only by Japan (see Table 6.1). From a political point of view, this group has had a crucial impact on the state, constituting as it does a prime reservoir of votes for governing parties, such as the Christian Democrats, but requiring in turn subsidies and regulatory favours. The petty bourgeoisie shade off into the vast number of small businesses, which share their relationship with the state. A significant group of these constitute the basis of the 'Third Italy', which has proved a dynamic element of the economy from the mid-1970s, but which is unlikely to be able to perform this role indefinitely.

A second, but not unrelated, form of Italian backwardness is the delayed establishment of a full-fledged Fordist mode of regulation, noted in Chapter 2, in spite of the early introduction of Taylorist methods of mass production in the factories. It was only with the 'Hot Autumn' of 1969 that wage levels began to catch up with the productivity gains made possible by Taylorism, and at the same time the welfare state was expanded to quantitative levels approaching those of Northern Europe, in spite of its selective and clientelistic elements and the persisting low quality of many public services. And, very significantly, no truly corporatist or tripartite system of wage determination was established until 1993.[40] Not only did Fordism triumph late and incompletely; while the small enterprises of the Third Italy have been seen as prime examples of a post-Fordist regime of accumulation, the large firms, Fiat in the lead, have been slow and reluctant to abandon the traditional Fordist model, preferring to reform and streamline it with technological changes until they finally attempted to incorporate some features of the Japanese industrial model ('Toyotism').[41]

As far as the composition of its national product is concerned, as well, Italy has never developed a significant presence in the technologically most advanced industries. As we have seen in the previous chapter, its areas of strength remain the traditional consumer goods sectors (clothing, leather goods, ceramic tile, etc.) and the engineering and metal-working sectors producing capital goods ('specialized suppliers'). In both of these types of industry, the small and medium firms of the 'Third Italy' have developed into formidable competitors on the world stage. However, the failure to expand into new sectors will eventually cost the economy dearly. As far as the state and the political system are concerned, it would perhaps be mistaken to speak of 'backwardness' given the unique character of the Italian experience, a trajectory quite different from the other advanced capitalist countries. Only if we took the British (or the American) political system as a necessary *terminus ad quem* could we refer to the Italian system as 'backward'.

While marked by these elements of backwardness, Italy is without doubt one of the major advanced capitalist economies. Its major features can be summed up as follows:

### Industrial relations

This feature is crucial, as the balance of power between capital and labour is central to any discussion of models of capitalism. After several abortive or only partly successful attempts, Italy had, by the mid-1990s, established an industrial relations system of a broadly 'tripartite' form. After over a decade of uncertainty, during which the employers attacked the old system of inflation indexation of wages (*scala mobile*) while the unions were broadly on the defensive, a series of negotiations eventually resulted in the framework agreement of 3 July 1993.[42] This agreement preserved two levels of bargaining, the industry level and the plant level, in spite of the employers' unhappiness with this situation. The wage provisions of the national industry-wide contracts were to be negotiated every two years, taking account of the planned level of inflation agreed among the parties as a result of semi-annual tripartite meetings with the government. This provision introduced *de facto* an incomes policy which the parties at the bargaining table were bound to respect. Subsequently, if inflation (net of imported inflation) proved to exceed or fell below the planned level, the next contract would reflect that difference. Plant-level bargaining was to proceed within the framework of the national contracts, and provide for productivity increases, profit-sharing, etc. Other provisions regulated the election of the factory councils that would conduct the plant-level bargaining. The government, for its part, gave the employers the right to hire new workers under 'apprenticeship' (*formazione lavoro*) contracts at rates below the industry minimum, and reformed the unemployment benefit system to provide better benefits for workers outside the largest plants.

While allowing a fair amount of room for plant-level bargaining, this accord did seal a tripartite pact between workers, employers, and government to jointly manage wage levels and related issues. This became evident in the subsequent years, when successive governments engaged in tripartite discussions on topics such as the reform of the pension system and fiscal and taxation policy. These negotiations were not without moments of conflict, such as the general strike and demonstrations organized by the unions after their talks with the first Berlusconi government broke down in the fall of 1994. But in the end, even then the government reached an agreement with the unions. The following year, the employers' organization (Confindustria) refused to sign the agreement on pension reform sponsored by the Dini government, having taken part in the negotiations, as a gesture of protest against the limited savings that would result. However, this did not mean the end of the practice of 'concertation'. In fact, the following year the Prodi government negotiated significant aspects of its budget with the unions and employers' associations, in particular the special surtax aimed at meeting the criteria of the Maastricht treaty (the 'Euro-tax'). While the employers were the least enthusiastic participants, the practice of consultation with the 'social partners' (*parti sociali*) was, by the mid-1990s, becoming well established.

This evolution occurred, as Salvati points out, as a result of the changes in the political system in the early 1990s. First of all, the revolution in the party system removed the major reason for rivalry between the three union confederations and their components – their erstwhile political points of reference (DC, PSI, and PCI) disappeared or at a minimum transformed themselves. Hence the unions could present a united front. Similarly, the government of 'technicians' headed by Carlo Azeglio Ciampi could, for the first time, give the unions some guarantees of political support for the agreements, including the fufilment of the measures to be implemented by the government itself. Thus the two major reasons for the failure of previous 'neo-corporatist' bargains, such as the January 1983 Scotti agreement, had been removed. At the same time, all three partners had been weakened – the unions by unemployment and the employers' offensive since 1980, the employers by the recession and the charges of corruption many of them were facing, and the government by the discredit the corruption investigations had thrown on the political system. Hence the agreement was a useful means for all three to reinforce their legitimacy.

At the same time, the financial crisis of 1992, culminating in the forced exit of the lira from the European Monetary System, had impressed on all the parties the need for a national effort to contain inflation and industrial costs while ensuring social peace. Italy, in other words, saw itself more clearly as an exposed, open economy similar to those discussed by Peter Katzenstein in *Small States in World Markets*.[43] Financial deregulation and the internationalization of business had not proceeded to such an extent that Italian firms could do without corporatist-style accords, as some writers such as Kurzer suggest is now possible in the globalized economy.[44] (This may be seen as another aspect of the 'backwardness' of the Italian economy; however, the role of plant-level bargaining in the July 1993 accord demonstrates the desire of firms for flexibility in contemporary world market conditions, as well as the desire of the unions to maintain the two levels of negotiation[45]).

The election of the second Berlusconi government in 2001, coupled with the presidency of Antoni D'Amato at Confindustria, has put severe strain on the method of concertation instituted in the previous eight years. Even Berlusconi, however, considered it important to attempt agreements with the union confederations, or at least the two more moderate ones, CISL and UIL. The fundamental parameters of the Italian industrial relations system have not yet been changed.

### Relations between financial and industrial capital

The relationship between industry and finance in Italy is unique in its institutional forms, but, as Colajanni points out, the substance of the relationship is what counts; and, in substance, the relationship in Italy is closer to the 'Rhenish' model of integration between finance and industry than to the 'Anglo-Saxon' system. In Britain and the US, shareholders' expectations and financial markets have overwhelming influence over industrial decisions; in Italy, the controlling groups of most large firms are almost completely insulated from the stock market and virtually unassailable. Since they are typically family groupings, not managers as in the German or Japanese cases, their decisions may nevertheless reflect the short-term interests of the family members who are also the controlling shareholders, but Italian firms have not been prey to the compulsive 'short-termism' which has been one of the principal weaknesses of Anglo-Saxon business. Indeed, some of the major industrial conglomerates have not only been capable of self-financing, but have invested parts of their surplus and expanded into the financial sector,[46] so that a fusion of industry and finance has sometimes occurred through a process opposite to that taken in Germany.

On the other hand, the banking sector has not played the active role that it has in Germany or, in different ways, in Japan. The 1936 banking law, in reaction to the crash of 1931, forbade commercial banks to take up shareholdings in industrial firms or engage in long-term credit (see pp. 50–51 above). At the same time, over 80 per cent of the banking system was brought within the state sector. This effectively neutralized the banks politically, so that they never constituted a lobby, similar to the City of London, in favour of freer financial markets or sound money. Subject to controls on the amount of credit they could offer, the banks however pursued conservative, safe lending policies, preferring to loan to larger, established firms, or, even more, to invest in state-backed securities. In the 1960s, the bonds of the special credit agencies set up by the government to aid industry in the South or otherwise in need of assistance proved popular; in the 1970s and 1980s, with the growth of public debt, the government's own bonds became a prime outlet for the banks' cash. In fact, the banks, by rolling over short-term credits, did also develop long-term relationships with some large companies. In this they were simply conforming to the contours of the existing distribution of economic power; they did not develop real expertise in the industrial operations of their clients, and could not therefore play the dynamic role of backing new firms or ideas. As a result, Italy has a high savings rate but a relatively low rate of accumulation, in part because of the nature of the banking system.

A partial exception to this picture are the long- and medium-term credit banks, established to fulfil the functions denied to the commercial banks. The most noteworthy of these is Mediobanca, controlled from its foundation in 1946 until his death in 2000 by the now legendary Enrico Cuccia (see above, pp. 56–57). While its resources are far less than those of the German universal banks, for example, Mediobanca has been able to use them strategically to exercise great influence on the Italian economy. And Cuccia's policy was typically to support the established great families of Italian capitalism, such as Agnelli, Pirelli, Falck, Lucchini, Orlando, and Bonomi – the so-called 'good salon' or 'noble wing'; informed observers believe his long-run goal may have been to unite this group, through alliances and cross-holdings, with the centres of German and French capitalism.[47] He was able to intervene to save them in moments of crisis, and above all was the author of prodigious feats of financial engineering, aimed at keeping the control of the major conglomerates in family hands. While Mediobanca also tried to engage in industrial policy by these means, and Cuccia achieved some major *coups*, such as the creation of the Montedison chemical giant, in the long run its activity contributed chiefly to maintaining and strengthening the structure of industrial capital rather than shaping it.[48] While it does not conform to the German or Japanese pattern, Mediobanca is the prime example of the close relationship between financial and industrial capital in Italy.

Overall, and with these qualifications, the bank-industry relationship in Italy has been considerably closer to the German or Japanese pattern of close integration than to the Anglo-Saxon model of separation, though the result in terms of industrial policy and economic growth is less positive. Established large firms have had the dominant role in their relations with the banks, and the latter do not constitute a separate fraction of capital, as they do in Britain, pressing for policies inimical to the interests of industry. The formation of large private banks over the past decade has yet to change these essential features of the bank-industry nexus.

### Large vs. small industry

Much has been made of the importance of small and medium industry, especially in the 'Third Italy'; while those who take it as the defining feature of a separate Italian model of capitalism have exaggerated its role, the clear distinction between large and small firms is notable and significant. In industrial relations, for example, small firms tend to have more informal, less antagonistic relations with their unions, and wage rates are 20–25 per cent lower than in large companies. The small firms enjoy some advantages with respect to public policies as well – the regulatory hand of the state *de facto* lies more lightly on them.[49] Small and medium industry is more dependent on bank capital; it is constrained by its family ownership from expanding or issuing shares on the market. For these reasons it tends to be less able to invest on a large scale, for instance in research and development. However, these firms make a major contribution to Italy's balance of payments; they are present in the dynamic, export-oriented traditional sectors of clothing, textiles, footwear, leather goods, ceramics, furniture, etc., but also in the machine tool and metal products industries and in a host of other consumer-goods and specialized supplier industries.

Over and against the proliferation of dynamic small industry, we must put the domination of the Italian business scene by a small number of large conglomerates. Of these, Fiat is in a class by itself, but the industrial and financial empires of Berlusconi, Pirelli, and in the recent past De Benedetti, as well as the troubled chemical and food giant Montedison/Compart, also have turnovers in the ten billion dollar range or above, and are principal centres of political and economic power (see Chapter 3). As has often been observed, what Italy lacks is a large, well-established group of middle-sized firms, although some such groups have begun to appear in the 1990s.

At any rate, the 'model' of industrial relations and the balance of class power is not fundamentally different in the smaller firms than in the large. They generally adhere to the national labour contracts ('black' and 'grey' labour is more prevalent in the South), although their practices with respect to bonuses and plant-level bargaining tend to be less generous.[50] As Hutton has pointed out, Germany too has dynamic small and medium firms, which enjoy close relations with the banks that support them:[51] Baden-Württemburg is often cited as a *Land* where industry has a structure similar to that of the Italian 'industrial districts'. Exponents of the regulation school have laid stress on the organization of production and work in these firms, which is characterized by flexible specialization or diversified quality production, unlike that in the largest companies, where 'neo-Fordism' tends to prevail. While tripartism is indeed the form of regulation most suitable to Fordism, it can be adapted to the requirement for flexibility of the industrial districts; there is if anything a greater need for co-operative relations between labour and management in the specialized plants and workshops of the 'Third Italy'.

The contrast Locke notes between the generally consensual climate in certain districts (e.g. Biella) and plants (e.g. Alfa Romeo) and the antagonistic situation in others (e.g. Fiat) may be valid, but does not cancel the fact that at the national level Fiat and its workforce take part in bargaining a contract for the sector. Overall, while the small and medium firms represent a source of serious division within the capitalist class and do constitute a peculiar feature of Italian capitalism, they are not sufficiently distinctive to differentiate Italy fundamentally from the other tripartite forms of capitalism.

### The role of the state

In Italy, the state has not performed the directing or co-ordinating role that it has had in the economies of France or Japan, for example. This reflects the acute divisions within the capitalist class and its political weakness, both of which we have described in previous chapters. Nor has it furnished the cadres for business in the way it has in these countries; the state has notoriously lacked the expertise, as well as the authority, to play a leading role in the economy, and its recruitment policy has favoured graduates of Southern law and related faculties, who lacked the skills necessary to play such a role. The only partial exception to this was the function of state industry in preparing managers for the private as well as the public sector. In general, the business and the political elites have been quite separate, the former largely Northern and the latter with little business background and a large Southern presence. Nor has the banking system (largely state-owned) filled the role of training managers, as it has in Germany. Only the Bank of Italy has played a significant, but limited, role in the management of the economy.

Albeit belatedly, the Italian state has set up a system of welfare which, while not as broad in coverage as those of Northern Europe, provides fairly generous pension, unemployment, and sickness-disability benefits for the core of guaranteed workers, while leaving the others to the operation of particularistic and clientelistic mechanisms such as false disability pensions, or indeed without any protection except the support of their families. The only exception to this is a universal, though relatively low-quality, public health service.[52] This welfare system complements the tripartite system of wage bargaining by providing a series of social shock-absorbers in cases of industrial restructuring and cyclical downturn.

At the same time, the state has maintained consensus by satisfying a large petty bourgeois clientele; the welfare state itself and the expansion of public employment have been among the vehicles for this policy (e.g. social security contributions are lower for the self-employed). In addition it has provided a series of general background policies of considerable utility to business, from the construction of essential infrastructure to opportune tax reductions and export credits.[53] As Regini pointed out, many of the explicit redistributive policies favour large firms, but others which are not explicit, such as the failure to repress tax evasion, operate in the interest of the smaller enterprises. But the state has not been able to pursue any genuine industrial policy. In the words of one writer, conjunctural policy has played the role of structural policy – the high-interest policies of the early 1980s, for instance, forced an industrial shakeout and recourse to massive new investment.[54] Similarly, as we have noted, Mediobanca's efforts to pursue an industrial policy have been frustrated.[55]

In sum, the state's role has often been facilitating, but not directing, and other aspects of its activity, such as support for the petty bourgeoisie and similar exercises in consensus-creation, have produced results that have been unfavourable to capital, while state-provided infrastructure has often lagged behind what is available elsewhere in Europe. The direction of industrial growth has been determined largely by industry itself, interpreting in its own fashion and according to its own experience and goals the signals of the market, at times in consultation with Enrico Cuccia, but seldom with any genuine contribution from the state.

The Italian model of capitalism, then, is not, at least in the recent period, *sui generis*, but is a particular variant of the continental, or 'Rhenish', corporatist form. Its particularities consist in the weak role of the banks and the state relative to industry itself, in the importance of the small and medium enterprises of the Third Italy, and in its relative backwardness in some fields. In spite of the recent assertiveness of small and medium businesses, represented by Antonio D'Amato as president of Confindustria, and the difficulties of concertation under Silvio Berlusconi, if we consider the relative power of the major social classes, and the institutional forms of this power, these peculiarities do not differentiate Italy fundamentally from the other countries where the Rhenish form of capitalism is present. As we saw in the previous chapter, the capitalist class is seriously divided, but the coalition of small industry and the petty bourgeoisie led by Berlusconi has not achieved hegemony. Unlike Japan, the other non-market-driven model of capitalism, Italy lacks a strong state, while its industrial relations system accords much greater weight to the unions. As Italy attempted to meet the Maastricht criteria for European monetary union, it is not accidental that its political economy converged with those of the other principal European capitalist states it hoped to join. And as we have seen, the pressure to meet the criteria forced employers, the unions, and the state to enter into a collaborative relationship that had been attempted without lasting success on previous occasions.

# 5 Italian capital in the global economy

The literature in political economy has increasingly focussed on the process of 'globalization' and its impact on the politics of the developed capitalist countries. The dominant view is that it has augmented the power of capital by increasing its mobility, and thereby its bargaining power *vis-à-vis* both labour and the state. At the same time, it has blunted many of the state's policy instruments: in particular Keynesian demand management is ineffective if an increase in purchasing power leads to an inflow of imports and a payments crisis. The failure of the reflationary policy of the Mitterand government's first year is taken as proof of this point. International agreements and trade blocs such as the European Union also limit the ability of governments to intervene on the supply side. All of this has led to the breakdown or weakening of tripartite arrangements, as capital loses the incentive to bargain with domestic labour when it can transfer production elsewhere.[1] While in the popular view the competition of cheap labour in less developed countries appears as the most significant root cause for this weakening of labour, the literature places the greatest emphasis on the liberalization of financial flows, which has put governments in a position of weakness *vis-à-vis* the money markets more rapidly than the hypothesized longer-term relocation of production capacity could undermine their power.

At the same time, many scholars have cautioned against a one-sided stress on the globalization of the economy, which could lead to a neglect of the national aspect. Hirst and Thompson pointed out, for instance, that there were no truly transnational firms, in that all had a home country to which they were linked and from which they drew the overwhelming majority of their management. Moreover, the world's largest firms still made two-thirds of their investments, on average, in their home countries, and capital flows were chiefly between the developed countries.[2] Panitch notes that globalization is far from being an ineluctable, impersonal process – it was rather the result of the choices of national states, influenced by domestic actors whose interests were served by those choices.[3] Milward makes a similar point with respect to the formation of the European Community.[4] Nor is the political result of greater internationalization of the economy self-evident: Garrett found that, empirically, internationalization combined with a strong left led to more, not less, government spending and higher deficits, as the state acted to compensate for the disruption caused by globalization, even at the price of higher interest rates.[5] And it is worth noting that Katzenstein's classic study of corporatism, *Small States in World Markets*,[6] attributed the tripartite bargaining systems of the smaller European states to their open economies and the consequent need to adjust smoothly to an international environment they could not control.

While Katzenstein was writing about an era in which the flow of trade to and from these states was relatively open, but capital was less mobile, the same sort of argument could apply *mutatis mutandis* in the new and even more open economies of today. While some of the forms and institutions created in the pre-globalization era may be outdated, the possibility of a corporatist-style bargain with new contents has not been ruled out by the new economic conditions.

Chapter 3 described the production profile of Italian capital as a factor that influences economic policy-making; this chapter will consider the weight of the international context, and particularly the growing internationalization of the Italian economy. This will involve first of all an investigation of the effective degree of internationalization it has reached, including its impact through the production profile of Italian business. We shall then discuss the impact of the European Union, and especially the Maastricht Treaty and the criteria for monetary union, on Italy's domestic economic policy.

## Globalization and the production profile of business

### Trade

For many years, Italy has been a major trading nation with a high ratio of exports to GDP. In 1999, exports of goods amounted to 25.5 per cent of GDP, while imports were 23.5 per cent.[7] This ratio has been increasing over time since World War II, and places Italy at an intermediate level among the more internationalized major economies (see Tables 5.1 and

*Table 5.1* Italy: exports as a percentage of GDP, 1913–99

| | |
|---|---|
| 1913 | 12.0 |
| 1950 | 7.0 |
| 1973 | 13.4 |
| 1987 | 15.4 |
| 1995 | 21.3 |
| 1999 | 25.5 |

Source: Angus Maddison, quoted in R.O. Keohane and H.V. Milner, eds, *Internationalization and Domestic Politics* (Cambridge: Cambridge University Press, 1996), p. 12, and OECD (see Table 5.2).

5.2), considerably ahead of the US or Japan, but behind Germany and the small export-dependent European economies. Over half of Italy's foreign trade is with the other countries of the EU, though this proportion has declined in recent years as markets in Eastern Europe and the developing world have grown (see Table 5.3). In terms of sectoral composition, the latter show a greater propensity to buy the products of Italian scale-intensive industries and specialized suppliers, while the traditional industries find better markets in the highly developed world.

Italy's significant payments surplus is the product of the very different performances of the different sectors of the economy. As Table 3.1 (above) demonstrates, agricultural products, fuels, and metals – i.e. foods and raw materials – are deficitary sectors, while manufacturing as whole provides Italy's export earnings. Table 5.4 below gives a more detailed breakdown of manufacturing trade: it lists the trade balance for each sector as a percentage of domestic production. Italy's export earnings are generated by a group of traditional industries – textiles, clothing, leather goods, furniture, etc. – machine tools, and some of the scale-intensive industries such as

*Table 5.2* Exports as a percentage of GDP, leading industrial countries, 1999

| | |
|---|---|
| Japan | 10.4 |
| USA | 10.7 |
| Germany | 29.4 |
| France | 26.1 |
| UK | 25.9 |
| Italy | 25.5 |
| Belgium | 76.5 |
| Netherlands | 60.6 |
| Sweden | 43.7 |
| Switzerland | 42.1 |
| Norway | 39.0 |
| Denmark | 37.4 |
| Canada | 43.7 |
| Austria | 45.1 |

Source: OECD (http://www.oecd.org/std/bss, consulted 27 July 2001).

*Table 5.3* Destination of Italian exports, 1999 (percentages)

| | |
|---|---|
| European Union | 57.4 |
| Germany | 16.5 |
| France | 13.0 |
| UK | 7.1 |
| Eastern Europe | 6.0 |
| North America | 10.4 |
| Asia | 10.4 |
| Latin America | 4.0 |
| Africa | 3.5 |

Source: Centro Studi Confindustria, *Rapporto sull'industria italiana*, May 2000, p. 63.

*Table 5.4* Italian trade balances, manufacturing sectors, 1999 (percentages of domestic output)

| Sector | |
|---|---|
| *Traditional industries* | |
| Food and beverages | −5.1 |
| Textiles and yard goods | 39.5 |
| Clothing | 38.3 |
| Shoes and leather goods | 41.7 |
| Furniture, wood products, home furnishings | 39.6 |
| Glass and ceramics | 56.9 |
| Paper, publishing | −6.6 |
| *Scale-intensive industries* | |
| Energy products (refined) | −4.1* |
| Chemical products | −21.4 |
| Construction materials | 47.3 |
| Rubber and plastic products | 30.6 |
| Automobiles | −18.3 |
| Other transportation equipment | 19.1 |
| Metals | −37.7 |
| Metal products | 52.5 |
| Mechanical and electrical equipment | 43.8 |
| *Specialized suppliers* | |
| Machine tools | 45.7 |
| Electronic machinery | 14.0 |
| *Science-based industries* | |
| Precision instruments | −14.8 |
| Electronic equipment | −18.1 |

Source: Centro Studi Confindustria, *Rapporto sull'industria italiana*, May 2000, p. 62.

Note
*1997–98.

metal products and construction materials. The industries producing basic inputs for other processes – chemicals, metals, and energy – as well as the high-technology science-based sectors, are in deficit, as well as, interestingly, the automobile sector. The invisibles account is traditionally in deficit, as the positive tourism balance is outweighed by an outflow of investment income and by transportation and other services.

### Direct investment

While the Italian economy is highly internationalized as far as trade is concerned, Italian capital has been slow to invest abroad, relative to the other advanced capitalist economies. In part, this is the result of the previously mentioned financial weakness of Italian capitalism, and the dependence of some sectors on state protection. In part, it reflects the large number of small and medium firms for whom international expansion is more difficult. The traditional sector, in which Italy specializes, typically has smaller firms and often depends on special labour skills and networks of suppliers and clients found only in Italy (e.g. the case of the 'industrial districts'). The same is true to some extent of the specialized suppliers. As a result, only 11 of the 450 largest multinationals (1994) were Italian (vs. 60 British, 32 German, and 26 French firms on the list).[8] Moreover, until the later 1980s the largest firms were responsible for the lion's share of foreign direct investment, but from 1988 the base of investing firms has broadened considerably. Nevertheless, in 1994 6 firms still accounted for 60.4 per cent of overseas investment (by number of employees), and 48 firms with over 2000 employees in Italy accounted for 81 per cent; only 11 per cent of direct investment was by firms with under 500 employees in Italy.[9] As we saw in Chapter 3, Pirelli has only one fifth of its work force in Italy, while Olivetti has 61 per cent of its production abroad, and Fiat, which already makes one third of its cars outside Italy, has increased its overseas presence, particularly in Poland and Argentina.

The principal motive for direct investment abroad until the 1990s appears to have been the desire to capture market share: 58.9 per cent of investments by number of workers (1994) were in OECD countries.[10] However, in the 1990s the lower labour costs in some countries, particularly in Eastern Europe, also came to play a role: 37.6 per cent of all new overseas investment in 1992–94 went to Eastern Europe.[11]

In spite of the roughly equal inward and outward flows of direct investment in the 1990s, the stock of foreign direct investment in Italy remains larger than Italian investment abroad if measured in terms of sales (141.4 trillion lire versus 98.7 trillion lire[12]), though not in terms of employees (see Table 5.5) or book value: by 1999, Italian direct investment abroad exceeded inward direct investment in value by 57 per cent.[13] Italy has an average quota of inward foreign direct investment, compared to the other major European economies, while its outward investment still lags somewhat behind (see Table 5.5).

What is noteworthy about inward direct investment, however, is its concentration in the high-technology, science-based sector of the economy: 31.5 per cent of total foreign investment is in this sector, with 46.7 per cent of all workers in these industries employed in firms with foreign participation, while the foreign presence in the traditional sector is very low (5.4 per cent of the total foreign investment, with only 3 per cent of all workers in the sector). Nearly 60 per cent of workers in the electronics and telecommunications industry, and over 45 per cent of those in the chemical and pharmaceutical industries, work in firms with some foreign participation.[14] These data highlight the weakness of Italian capital in the technological and science-based industries.

Direct investment abroad, however, has insulated many Italian firms in part from the vicissitudes of the currency and the local political system. This applies not only to the largest groups, but also to some of the medium-sized

*Table 5.5* Outward and inward foreign direct investment, major industrial countries (employees as a percentage of domestic manufacturing employment)

| Country | Outward | Year | Inward | Year |
|---|---|---|---|---|
| Italy | 18.5 | 1993 | 16.0 | 1993 |
| Germany | 24.0 | 1992 | 17.0 | 1992 |
| France | 30.1 | 1992 | 16.4 | 1990 |
| Great Britain | 22.9 | 1981 | 14.9 | 1990 |
| USA | 20.8 | 1991 | 10.8 | 1991 |
| Japan | 8.1 | 1991 | 1.0 | 1990 |
| Sweden | 47.0 | 1990 | 11.5 | 1990 |
| Netherlands | 60.5 | 1987 | 14.0 | 1987 |
| Norway | 2.5 | 1981 | 6.4 | 1989 |
| Austria | 34.1 | 1982 | 36.5 | 1985 |

Source: Centro Studi Confindustria, *Previsioni dell'economia italiana*, IX, 1 (June 1995), p. 169.

Note
Outward investment is measured as the ratio of the employees in foreign subsidiaries to domestic manufacturing employment; inward investment is the ratio of employees of foreign-owned subsidiaries to total domestic manufacturing employment.

firms – the so-called 'pocket multinationals' – which include some of the most dynamic and successful of the firms of the 'Third Italy', such as Luxottica, Merloni, Benetton, and Della Valle. This has, as we shall see, had an impact on their positions on many economic issues.

### Portfolio investment

Much of the literature on globalization places a great deal of emphasis on the role of portfolio investment – the mobility of financial capital, which can have a massive impact on markets for currencies and securities, and in turn place nearly irresistible pressure upon governments. The September 1992 speculative attack on the lira is the most noteworthy demonstration of the power of mobile capital in recent Italian history – and here the capital which provoked the crisis was not Italian, but 'offshore', though the danger of an outflow of domestic capital was of course present. This illustrates how a government may be affected by the humours and speculative flows of international financial capital, regardless of its own regulations, if there is sufficient off-shore trading of its currency and securities. And unlike direct investment, movements of financial capital can occur very rapidly, and thus exercise a more concentrated influence on policy.

As a result of European Community regulations, exchange controls were finally eliminated entirely in Italy in May 1990. This did not lead to an immediate exodus of funds, but to a greater internationalization of Italy's financial position (see Table 5.6).

*Table 5.6* Italy's financial position with the rest of the world (trillions of lire; August 1996)

|  | Assets | Liabilities |
|---|---|---|
| Direct investments | 168 | 109 |
| Portfolio investments | 308 | 425 |
| Commercial credits | 150 | 174 |
| Bank credits | 268 | 363 |
| Bank of Italy reserves | 110 | – |
| Balance | – | 66 |

Source: Banca d'Italia, *Bollettino economico*, n. 27 (Oct. 1996), p. 34.

Of particular interest is the fact that 321,110 billion lire of the portfolio liabilities were in government securities, approximately 15 per cent of the total government debt. This represented a significant increase in foreign investment in the 1990s: previously only 5–10 per cent of the government debt was foreign-held. In 1993 alone, there was a net inflow of 103 trillion lire in all types of foreign portfolio investment, the majority of which were government securities.[15] But this capital was volatile, and foreign holdings of government bonds can vary significantly from day to day – at one point, they reached 23 per cent. In fact, 2 per cent of the entire stock of Italian government debt (2.2 thousand trillion lire at the end of 1996) is traded every day on the secondary market.[16] The 1990s also saw the appearance of a futures market for government bonds, which allowed speculative investments without the actual purchase of securities. The 'BTP future' (the BTP is a longer-term government bond) became a significant benchmark for market reaction to government policy; the principal futures market for the 10-year BTP is the London LIFFE market.

These changes in Italy's international financial position on the one hand have increased the power of international markets and those who trade on them; on the other, internal political decisions were also a necessary precondition for this increase in the markets' power. The issuance of government debt to foreigners is clearly a consequence of the high level of debt accumulated in the 1980s; similarly, the speculative attacks on the lira were motivated by the observation that it was overvalued with respect to the 'fundamentals' of the economy (relative price levels and inflation rates). This in turn was a result of the 'strong lira' policy pursued by the government and the Bank of Italy since 1981. The international markets are not impersonal mechanisms – they reflect the judgements and prejudices of those who trade on them, so that for instance the success of a privatization programme may come to represent in traders' minds a test of the seriousness of a government in implementing its whole economic programme. Nevertheless, their movements are not dictated by directly political motives, and on numerous occasions the international financial markets have judged Italian government policy quite differently from business spokespersons and the political right in Italy. For example, the markets' view of the budgetary policy adopted by the Prodi government in late 1996 was substantially favourable, in spite of the sharp criticisms coming from the Confindustria and major industrial leaders.[17] In this case, the markets were focussed once again on the economic 'fundamentals', in particular the significant fall in inflation and the healthy balance of payments, and not only on the government's plans to reduce the deficit.

### Immigration and emigration

Discussions of 'globalization' often ignore patterns of immigration, as labour is the one 'factor of production' which has proved far less mobile than the others, both because of the preferences of the workers and because of a series of legal and *de facto* barriers (language, etc.). In fact, many theories trace the shift in power towards capital to its superior mobility relative to labour. Nevertheless, in the case of Italy the past twenty years have seen a startling and unprecedented change in the pattern of labour migration. Until the 1970s, Italy sent emigrants abroad to a wide variety of destinations (permanent emigrants to the Americas and Australia, more often temporary emigrants to Germany and other Northern European countries), and immigrant labour in Italy was restricted largely to domestic service. In that decade, the outward flow of migration diminished considerably, while towards its end immigrant labour began to become important in Italy itself, first in agriculture in some parts of the South, then in industry as well.

In theory, the pressure of immigrant workers could weaken the power of the Italian unions *vis-à-vis* the employers, even more than the possibility of capital exports and plant relocations. In practice, this has been the case only in small measure. The flow of immigrants has not been planned or co-ordinated with the labour market or the needs of employers, but has been the largely haphazard result of weak frontier controls, grants of asylum, and pressure from inhabitants of Third World and East European countries, especially those that are nearby and suffer from labour surpluses. The immigrant work force tended to gravitate to the informal or 'black' economy; lack of skills prevented many immigrants from competing for regular industrial employment. This fact makes estimates of the size of the immigrant labour force particularly unreliable and an accurate statistical account of its growth very difficult. The National Statistical Institute estimated that in 1989 there were 85,000 regular and 580,000 irregular workers from outside the EU, plus 181,000 residents of all types from EU countries, of whom over half can be assumed to be workers.[18] By 1996, their numbers had probably increased by at least one-third,[19] meaning that they were equal to some 5 per cent of the number of workers in the official employed work force, but probably only 4–4.5 per cent of the total work force, including 'black' labour.

## The European Union and Italian policy

It is difficult to argue that considerations of 'high policy' in the inter-national field have had a large direct weight in Italy's economic policy-making: foreign and defence policy have a relatively low profile with the voters, and foreign policy is generally treated in relation to its impact on domestic politics rather than in its own right.[20] The major, if partial, exception to this generalization is the impact of the Cold War on the domestic alignment of political forces; the exclusion of the Communists and their successor parties from the government for the forty-nine years from 1947 to 1996 was made possible in part by the international situ-ation, and this in turn had major consequences for the policies of succes-sive Italian governments. The Cold War was important not primarily because of its connection with Italy's national interests, but because of its role as a discriminant between the government parties and their principal opposition. This form of international influence, in other words, was exer-cised through and in combination with the balance of political forces in the country.

International economic developments, however, have had an extremely significant impact on Italy through its membership in the European Union. Its adherence to the European Economic Community in 1957 was a major factor contributing to the economic boom of the following years: domestic wages trailed productivity, and growth was export-led. The EEC sustained this model of development by providing export markets for Italian consumer durables and traditional products.[21] As Milward argues, European integration was supported because it furthered the economic goals of the national governments. On the other hand, each further step toward unification, while sustained by the interests of the national govern-ments collectively, places each one individually in a position in which it must choose not between further integration and the *status quo*, but between participation in the next step and exclusion, where the con-sequences of exclusion are not fully clear but potentially serious.

In Italy, the positive ideological connotations of 'Europe' and the wide-spread fear of being relegated to the rank of a 'Mediterranean' or 'African' country add to the pressure for integration: in early 2000, for example, Italians were more likely to have a 'positive image' of the Euro-pean Union than citizens of any other EU country (67 per cent vs. an average of 43 per cent for the whole EU), and less likely to identify them-selves by their nationality alone, rather than as simply Europeans or as European and citizens of their nation-state (25 per cent vs. an average of 41 per cent for the EU).[22] This strong support for European integration operated in particular at the time of the signing of the Maastricht Treaty in 1992, when the Italian representatives believed that it was impossible for them not to sign, on pain of having to admit to their constituency that Italy would not be fully part of 'Europe'.[23]

## The Maastricht Treaty

While it reinforces the European Union in many other ways, some of the Maastricht Treaty's most important provisions concern the formation of the European Economic and Monetary Union (EMU)(see esp. article 109J, article 101C and the Protocol on Convergence Criteria).[24] The Treaty provided for the establishment of a common European currency (since named the Euro) by 1 January 1999; only those EU countries that met certain criteria of economic stability would be able to participate in this monetary union. (The Treaty provided in fact for the possibility of an earlier decision to launch the common currency, if a majority of member states met the criteria; since a majority did not do so in advance of 1998, the default date of 1 January 1999, when the currency was to be launched by those states that had met the criteria, whether a majority or not, became the operative one). The criteria were intended to ensure that the future Euro would not be undermined by inflation and high government debt, identified by the signatories of the treaty as the principal sources of currency instability. The criteria set out in the treaty, which were destined to occupy the centre of the political stage in Italy as in many other European states, are:

1    Inflation: The inflation rate of the candidate country must be no more than 1.5 per cent above the average of the three countries with the lowest inflation rates.
2    Interest rates: Interest rates (measured as interest on long-term government debt) must be no more than 2 per cent above the average of the three countries with the lowest inflation rates.
3    Government debt:
    a    The current public sector deficit must be no more than 3 per cent of GDP.
    b    Total public sector debt must be no more than 60 per cent of GDP.
4    Exchange rate stability: The value of the candidate country's currency must remain for at least two years (i.e. 1997 and 1998) within the normal margins of fluctuation of the European Exchange Rate Agreements, without any devaluation *vis-à-vis* the currencies of the other member states. (In 1993, the margins of fluctuation of the European Monetary System [EMS] were widened from $+/-2.25$ per cent to $+/-15$ per cent.)

While the Treaty does not specify this, it was subsequently decided that the period in which criteria 1–3 must be met would be the calendar year

1997; in the first half of 1998, the European Commission and the European Monetary Institute (EMI: the future European central bank) were to evaluate the performance of the different countries of the Union with respect to the criteria, and the European Council would ratify their conclusions.

While the criteria are stated in explicit and clear, even somewhat crude, terms (many economists would have preferred, for instance, that the government's 'structural' deficit – i.e. adjusted for the influence of the economic cycle – be used as the criterion, rather than the actual deficit, and/or the relationship of the deficit to the rate of economic growth, since a deficit equal to growth does not increase the debt/GDP ratio;[25] furthermore, the use of gross debt as the indicator is also open to serious criticism), the Treaty also allows the Commission, the EMI, and the Council some room for judgement. Not only were they required to take account of 'the development of the ECU [European Currency Unit], the results of market integration, the evolution of the current account and the balance of payments, the evolution of unit labour costs and other price indices'; they could decide to admit to the EMU a country whose debt/GDP ratio did not meet the criterion, but was falling 'at an adequate rate', or whose deficit/GDP ratio was over 3 per cent, but was falling 'in a substantial and continuous way' and was near to meeting the criterion. These margins for political decision were the only concessions that the Italian representatives who signed the Treaty in January 1992 were able to wrest from the other EU countries: at that time, Italy was far from meeting any of the four criteria.

In fact, of the five different criteria, the one on which political attention was concentrated most closely was 3a, the deficit/GDP ratio. The exchange rate condition could be met by all the currencies in the EMS (Italy rejoined in December 1996). In 1996, ten of the fifteen EU states met the inflation criterion (2.6 per cent), and eleven met the interest rate criterion (8.7 per cent); the European Commission forecast that all but Greece would meet these two criteria in 1997.[26] In 1996, the European Council judged the public deficit/debt of Ireland and Denmark 'not excessive', in view of their progress in reducing their debt/GDP ratios, even though these were still estimated at 75 per cent and 70 per cent respectively for that year.

Italy could not hope to meet the 60 per cent criterion for the debt/GDP ratio, as it had already reached a 104 per cent ratio at the end of 1991, and this was growing at an accelerating rate, but did hope to be able to meet the public finance condition anyway if it made progress on the deficit. Furthermore, Belgium's debt/GDP ratio, at 133 per cent in 1996, was even higher than Italy's (121 per cent),[27] yet it would have been difficult to exclude Belgium from the EMU for this reason alone. The inflation and interest rate conditions were reachable, although they would require constant attention by the authorities. Adhesion to the EMU was voluntary for member states (in fact, Britain and Denmark requested and obtained special status: they would not be obliged to enter the monetary union until their own constitutional procedures had been satisfied).

For Italy, joining the EMU soon became a central objective. This posture was rooted in domestic economic and political factors more than in developments at the EU level. For internationalized businesses and financial institutions, membership in the currency union was important, as it was for exporters – at this stage, the level at which the lira would enter the EMU had not been specified. For all business, membership in the EMU would, it was hoped, bring lower interest rates and lower inflation, on the pattern of Germany, as foreign investors would no longer demand a risk premium for their lira holdings, while the convergence criteria would force the Italian government to deal with the issue of public debt and deficits as well. As early as the late 1980s business representatives looked forward to a common European currency as the solution to many of the ills of the Italian economy.[28] At the same time, governments saw the common currency as a way of ending the exchange crises that periodically afflicted the lira, and reducing the deficit significantly by lowering the interest rate they had to pay on the public debt. Moreover, the consequences of exclusion from the currency area might be unpleasant; to protect themselves from the danger of 'unfair competition' resulting from a devaluation of the lira, the countries participating in the EMU might adopt 'countervailing' measures against Italian exports, perhaps in the form of exchange regulations. This would obviously be extremely serious for large segments of business. At a minimum, exporters would lose some of their competitiveness to firms within the union, because the latter would be able to sell without the costs, risks, or trouble of a currency exchange. In a stable environment, these factors could cancel out the potential advantages of monetary sovereignty, i.e. the power to devalue.

On the other hand, the convergence criteria were not only crudely formulated, but their achievement would, it was widely feared, produce deflationary consequences or at the very least stifle employment growth. This was pointed out by the unions but also, as the deadline for convergence neared, by various employers' spokespersons, including Cesare Romiti, chairman of Fiat.[29] This was the most evident and most often expressed reservation about the Maastricht Treaty. Public sector workers might fear having to bear a larger share of the burden than others, especially if the reduction of the deficit involved rationalization of government services. In addition, most of the large tertiary sector, including most of the self-employed and companies such as Berlusconi's Fininvest, had no particular interest in a stable or competitive exchange rate as they were almost exclusively domestically oriented (the tourist industry is a partial exception). And with a single European currency and the interest rate convergence criterion, Italian bond-holders would receive significantly lower real returns, as they would no longer reap the same 'risk premium'.

But in addition to these particular interests that were indifferent or threatened, many sectors feared the general, if not the specific, consequences of monetary union and further European integration: a tightening up of many regulations and their enforcement, and the end of many 'Italian' (but not specifically Italian) practices involving favouritism, collusion, privilege, and state subsidization or protection of particular groups and firms with political connections. The general aim of the EU is to achieve equality in the market place between domestic and other European actors: this means an end to closed bidding lists for public contracts, as mandated by the Single European Act of 1985 (the '1992' programme), and to special relationships between certain firms and the state. The EU has also ruled out many forms of subsidy to industry; privatization has been promoted to encourage greater competition in the sectors where state-owned firms operated, and anti-trust legislation has been mandated. Moreover, the Maastricht criteria have inevitably led to a greater interest in the problem of tax evasion, which can easily be presented as one of the principal causes of Italy's public sector deficits. Not only tax evaders, but all those groups that are able more easily to survive and take advantage of inflation, such as shopkeepers, felt a certain uneasiness about monetary union. More generally, businesses that compete with imports or that are currently protected and fear foreign competition would be opposed to further integration.[30] In Italy, this includes a large part of the service and retail sectors.

However, there were in addition to these sources of vague uneasiness about EMU other intangible but important benefits that many actors expected from union. Many believed that exclusion from the union would lead to a loss of contacts, knowledge, and overall 'total factor productivity' that would be the result of participation. Full exposure to the competitive environment of Europe, they felt, was necessary for the growth of the economy, apart from any specific gains or losses.[31] In the end, the combination of political and economic factors weighing in favour of joining the monetary union proved exceptionally strong, though as we shall see opposition, often in covert and subterranean form, was not absent (see below, pp. 139–141).

### Other EU policies

As mentioned above, many other EU policies have had a significant impact on Italian domestic politics, from the assignment of quotas to agricultural producers to the ban on industrial subsidies and preferential government purchasing. In some cases, the role of the Italian government in the formulation of the policies has been minimal, and this has brought criticism from domestic interest groups. In these cases, the policies often appear as externally imposed restraints on the national government; however, many of them are simply the logical and predictable consequences of the economic union which Italy entered into along with the other states.

We can end this chapter with a provisional conclusion: while Italy lags behind both Germany and Britain in indicators of trade volume and financial openness, the degree of underlying internationalization of the Italian economy has increased significantly, to a level comparable to France's, as has the role of the European Union as a constraint on domestic policy-making. Most significantly from our point of view, the internationalization of the economy has strengthened the domestic forces that favour further internationalization and the removal of barriers that restrict it – forces such as multinational companies, exporters, and financial institutions with international interests. To a certain extent, it is a process that feeds on itself. The ways in which internationalization has significantly affected the stances of the actors and of the government on major issues of economic policy will be explored in the coming chapters.

# 6 Business and the political system

The political system exercises its own independent influence on policy, which can never be conceived as an automatic result of either the production profile or international pressures.[1] In Italy, this is perhaps even truer than in many other industrial democracies: the state has had a major, autonomous role in economic development, and the party system itself to a considerable degree grew downwards from the state rather than upwards from civil society. During the so-called 'First Republic', the dominant Christian Democratic Party enjoyed a significant degree of autonomy from the capitalist class. Given the serious divisions in Italian business, this allowed it to throw its weight into the balance on one side or the other, often proving decisive. In the 1950s, while different factions had different orientations, the strength of Mattei within the Party meant that much of government policy was oriented towards the more dynamic, emerging industries of the automobile cycle, as opposed to the traditional electrical/chemical bloc that continued to hegemonize Confindustria and business opinion.[2] The traditional bloc remained close to the small Liberal Party, encouraging it to lead the opposition to the 'opening to the left' (the admission of the Socialists to the governing coalition) even after this strategy had been decided on by the majority of the DC.

The state in this instance did not act as the site of compromise between different fractions of capital; its role was biased towards one of them, the one which promised the more rapid development of the country, with all the electoral benefits that entailed. This was the one which was in the best position to exploit the opportunities of the Fordist phase of capitalist development. After the turbulent 1960s, however, the centre of gravity of the Party, like the state industries to which it was increasingly tied, shifted to a position closer to the more conservative, authoritarian strategy of Eugenio Cefis, chairman of the Montedison chemical giant (see Chapter 2 above).

While the DC tried subsequently to build and maintain bridges to the more dynamic elements of capital, led by Fiat and Pirelli with Mediobanca in the background, these never really trusted it, as it was so close to small industry and the petty bourgeoisie. This distance between the major governing party and the dominant fraction of business was a background factor that helped contribute to the downfall of the DC regime: it lacked the ability to forge a compromise between fractions of capital, and at the same time its policies did not reflect either the current logic of capitalist development or the abstract general interests of the country and state. Since the political revolution of the early 1990s, this situation has altered somewhat with the appearance of new parties such as Forza Italia, led by Silvio Berlusconi, and the Northern League.

Since Berlusconi has so far been unable to act as honest broker between different fractions of capital, the left has been in a better position to play this role, as it demonstrated when in power from 1996 to 2001. In this chapter, we shall first discuss the political system of the so-called 'First Republic' as it existed until 1992, outlining the bases of the relative autonomy of the political system. Then we shall consider the changed scenario of the post-1992 period: in this second section, we shall look both at the emerging new political system and at the various governments that have succeeded each other during this rapid transition from the DC regime. Finally, we shall look at the representation of interests as one aspect of the political system, with particular emphasis on the role of business interests.

## The political system of the 'First Republic': the DC regime

The Italian political system from 1945 to 1992 was defined by two characteristics, one strikingly evident and the other slightly less so: it saw the same party, the Christian Democrats, in power continuously as the sole or principal governing party; and, a crucial component of the Christian Democrats' social basis was the petty bourgeoisie.[3] These two characteristics, which the DC shared with the Japanese Liberal Democratic Party (and which the Indian Congress possessed to a slightly lesser degree), allow us to call it a 'regime party'; they are mutually related, as the DC's social base ensured it its dominant role, and its possession of state power permitted it to consolidate its ties to this base.

These two characteristics are sufficient to define, but not to explain the regime party system. Several other factors contributed to its formation. The Christian Democrats inherited the extensive Catholic subculture and the active support of the Church in the first post-war elections, and they also benefitted, as the principal anti-communist force, from the ideological divisions of the Cold War. The DC were complemented by the Italian Communist Party (PCI), which had similarly come to represent the larger part of Italy's Marxist subculture; because of its own policies and above all the ideological hostility it provoked, it was destined to remain for decades in the position of permanent opposition. Hence there was no feasible alternative to a government dominated by the DC. However, the PCI was strong enough for the DC to convince conservative and moderate

opinion that it constituted a threat to the established order, and thus reinforced the DC's role as that order's principal bulwark.

Italy, then, while undoubtedly a capitalist democracy, was governed by a
party which was not the direct, organic representative of the capitalist
class. This situation, far from being paradoxical, was in keeping with
Gramsci's theoretical insight:

> The problem arises of whether the great industrialists have a perman-
> ent political party of their own. It seems to me that the reply must be
> in the negative. The great industrialists utilise all the existing parties
> turn by turn, but they do not have their own party. This does not
> mean that they are in any way 'agnostic' or 'apolitical'. Their interest
> is in a determinate balance of forces, which they obtain precisely by
> using their resources to reinforce one party or another in turn from
> the varied political checkerboard.[4]

Gramsci went on to note that in England the industrial bourgeoisie in
times of crisis turned to the party of the landowners (i.e. the Conserva-
tives), because 'the landowners are "politically" far better organized than
the industrialists, attract more intellectuals than they do, are more
"permanent" in the directives they give, etc'.[5] In the countryside, the
landowners were often able to maintain a 'bloc of all the elements of agricultural production', while in the cities no such bloc existed, partly
because of the 'corporativism or narrow economism' of the urban bourgeois parties.[6] Both England and Germany were cases where the bourgeoisie 'might not enjoy any intellectual or moral prestige, i.e. might be
incapable of establishing its hegemony', and hence 'the leading personnel
of the bourgeois class organized into a State can be constituted by elements of the old feudal classes'.[7]

Writing of Italy, where the aristocracy was relatively weak, Gramsci identified a different type of situation in which the industrial bourgeoisie did
not rule directly through a party of its own: there economic classes were
less clearly structured, and 'The government in fact operated as a
"party"'.[8] Both in the period of liberal transformism, and, implicitly,
under Fascism, Gramsci argued that political parties were weak and the
state in fact shaped them through the use of corruption, fraud, and viol-
ence by the government. While Poulantzas contends that bourgeois rule is
masked and hence in fact stabilized when the 'reigning class' is not the
bourgeoisie itself, Gramsci sees the Italian situation, unlike the English
and German, as fundamentally unsatisfactory for the capitalist class,
because the state, replacing political parties in their vital functions, does
not exercise true intellectual and moral hegemony. Both writers, however,
have noted the difficulties the capitalist class faces in organizing its own
political party: capitalists are reluctant to see organizational solidarity as
the principal strategy for success, preferring competition, and are in any

case unwilling to devote time and energy to politics when they regard the state as a body that should remain peripheral to their activities. They are, as Gramsci noted, less well organized, as well as less constant in their interests and demands, than other classes such as the landowners.

The Christian Democratic regime party continued this Italian tradition. It could trace its origins to Catholic doctrine, and this ideological grounding made it more secure than its liberal and Fascist predecessors, but this was not the principal basis of its strength – it exercised intellectual and moral hegemony only over a minority of the population. It extended its power by using the resources of the state (corruption), and by posing as the paladin of anti-communism.

For a party which owes its strength to its control of the state, the most natural social basis is the petty bourgeoisie. This class, though it often espouses anti-statist ideologies, today depends on the state for its very survival as a class: without subsidies, protective legislation, tax exemptions, and other types of assistance, it would be defenceless against the tendency towards concentration inherent in modern capitalism. And in Italy, the self-employed petty bourgeoisie are particularly numerous – they still represent 29 per cent of the employed population, far more than in any other G7 country (see Table 6.1).

The DC took full advantage of this situation, forging permanent, organic links with different sections of the petty bourgeoisie. The Catholic peasants' organization, the Coltivatori Diretti (Smallholders' Federation), for instance, included some 85 per cent of the peasantry and ran the Federconsorzi, the state agency through which subsidies and other forms of assistance (marketing, etc.) are distributed to the peasants. For a long time, the Coltivatori Diretti were a distinct faction within the DC. Other petty bourgeois categories, such as shopkeepers and independent professionals, were also well served by collective benefits distributed by the DC regime, and organized in similar associations, less openly but no less effectively tied to the ruling party. Chubb has pointed out that these

*Table 6.1* Self-employed workers as a percentage of total civilian employment, 3rd quarter 1996

| | |
|---|---|
| Italy | 29.1 |
| Japan | 18.2 |
| UK* | 14.1 |
| France | 11.7 |
| Canada | 11.3 |
| Germany | 9.7 |
| USA | 5.6 |

Source: OECD, *Quarterly Labour Force Statistics*, no. 4, 1996: civilian employment less employees (seasonally adjusted figures).

Note
*3rd quarter 1995.

collective benefits were supplemented by direct clientelistic ties to individual members of these categories, stemming chiefly from local governments' licensing and regulatory powers.[9]

Furthermore, many public sector employees were also part of the DC's clientele; if they did not owe their jobs or promotions to the party, the majority of them were organized in Catholic CISL unions or corporative 'autonomous' unions which sought nothing but material benefits for their members and could easily be integrated into the politics of the DC regime. Public employees enjoyed many privileges compared to private sector workers, especially in the field of social security. While this group is in many other countries the core of the progressive 'new middle class', in Italy it has retained much of the mentality of the independent petty bourgeoisie, from which most of its members were recruited.[10]

The DC had, of course, many other bases of support. Its control of the state and the resulting patronage resources allowed it to attach to itself many voters besides the petty bourgeoisie and state employees. The chronically underdeveloped South, where many have a crying need for assistance, is a fertile terrain for this sort of clientelistic politics. For instance, DC politicians, especially in the South, could secure disability pensions for workers who were not strictly entitled to them. The party could also do favours for small entrepreneurs (contracts, etc.). Southern entrepreneurs, who are heavily involved in construction and real estate, were in fact subordinate to the DC machine, depending on it for public funds, contracts, and access to credit.[11]

The DC's Catholic base also remained extremely important, giving it a truly 'interclass' character. The Catholic subculture is particularly strong in certain regions, such as the North-East (Veneto, Trentino, eastern Lombardy, and some contiguous provinces); furthermore, the CISL trade-union confederation, though less closely tied to the DC after *c.*1970, still acted as a conduit of influence over the workers, both blue-collar and white-collar, that it organized. It is worth noting, however, that by the end of the 'First Republic' the DC's largest vote share came from the South, where its clientelistic networks were strongest, rather than from the 'white' North-East.

Another source of Christian Democratic strength was the party's role as the only credible bulwark against communism. This drew to it many voters who were neither committed Catholics nor part of its clientelistic structure. Many of the business and professional people who supported it belong in this category. The DC's electoral fortunes typically improved when the Communist 'threat' was strongest, either internationally (1948) or nationally (1976), and ebbed when it receded (1983). The PCI's decision to change its name and re-found itself as a new and different party in 1991 was one of the events precipitating the end of the DC regime.

The DC, then, was a heterogeneous party, whose strongest base of support was among the petty bourgeoisie. As the governing party and the mainstay of anti-communism, it attracted the support of many capitalists, but was not the party of the industrial bourgeoisie. Both its social base and its leadership were predominantly drawn from the petty bourgeoisie. Moreover, their ideological background in Catholic social doctrine did not make them unconditional supporters of *laissez-faire* capitalism; the Church has accepted capitalism, but stresses the social responsibility of capitalists.

The DC's heterogeneity was manifested in its internal structure: since the 1950s, organized factions dominated it. At the XVIII Congress (February 1989), for instance, there were five lists competing for seats on the National Council. Some of them represented more than one distinct grouping, so that in fact there were ten factions or sub-factions present at the Congress (see Table 6.2). As the National Council was elected by the Congress by proportional representation, the table gives an accurate picture of the delegate strength of the different groups.

It is notoriously difficult, however, to specify precisely the policy differences between the factions. Originally, they represented distinct ideological positions or interests within the party: the *dossettiani*, the first major faction, were left-wing but integralist (i.e. they believed in bringing religious principles into politics); New Forces was an emanation of the CISL trade unions; the peasant federation, the Coldiretti, had its own faction. However, with the passage of time and the integration of all the factions into the DC patronage machine, they lost their distinct character and became more and more oriented simply towards the conquest of power.[12] Therefore, it is impossible to establish firm connections between particular factions and specific interests, much less particular sectors of the

*Table 6.2* DC lists and factions, XVIII Congress, February 1989

|  | Seats on National Council | Percentage |
| --- | --- | --- |
| 'Grand Centre' (Gava-Forlani-Scotti)[a] | 67 | 37.2 |
| Left[b] | 63 | 35.0 |
| Andreottiani[c] | 31 | 17.2 |
| New Forces (Donat-Cattin) | 14 | 7.8 |
| Fanfaniani | 5 | 2.8 |
| Total | 180 | 100.0 |

Source: *La Repubblica*, 23 February 1989.

Notes
a Includes the ex-*dorotei* led by Antonio Gava, Arnaldo Forlani's faction, and Enzo Scotti's faction.
b Includes Ciriaco DeMita's group, the broader 'Area Zac' (after former secretary Benigno Zaccagnini), and a group of younger leaders headed by Giovanni Goria.
c Includes 3 councillors belonging to the Popular Movement, representing the integralist religious group Communion and Liberation.

economy or firms; even the especially close association with construction firms established by factions of the Japanese Liberal Democrats did not develop in Italy.

Though the factions did not have distinct social bases or coherent ideologies, they differed subtly in temper and general outlook, and these differences manifested themselves in some policy issues and, in particular, in their preferences for political allies. Indeed, attitudes to other parties as coalition partners became the principal real issue dividing the factions in the 1980s and 1990s.[13] Some factions (e.g. Andreotti's) may have changed sides on this issue, but the differences were more than purely pretexts for struggles over power and influence. In general, the Left, which controlled the party from 1975 to 1989, favoured a *rapprochement* with the Communists and a policy of confrontation with the Socialists, even if the latter were the DC's governmental partners. The Grand Centre, supported in this by New Forces and the *fanfaniani*, was opposed to any form of coalition with the PCI, either as a long-term solution or as a prelude to a more bipolar political system. These factions saw the alliance with the PSI and the other minor coalition partners as a stable formula, and were therefore more accommodating towards the Socialists.

None of the DC factions was the mouthpiece of business or any group within it; conversely, all were open to its influence. On the whole, the influence of the petty bourgeoisie within the DC was an important aspect of the 'relative autonomy' of the state: because the DC had used the state to forge organic links with this stratum, the state was virtually incapable of policy initiatives that would harm the interests of the petty bourgeois groups attached to it. One key example is the health-care system: the 'reform' of 1980 introduced a National Health Service, which was intended to rationalize the public health insurance system and extend coverage to all. However, large amounts were spent on administration, particularly by the notorious Local Health Units (USLs), while the quality of care remained indifferent. The continuing inadequacy of the public system left ample room for private physicians' services and clinics; the medical profession, one of the major petty bourgeois clienteles of the DC, thus preserved its greatest source of income. In fact, in the late 1980s as much money was spent by Italians on private health care as on the public system.

The social composition of the DC's membership confirms the above account of its political complexion (see Table 6.3). More than 58 per cent of its economically active members were either petty bourgeois or public employees. (The data do not distinguish between public and private blue-collar workers, so the actual figure is considerably higher than 58 per cent). Furthermore, many of the private sector employees who belonged to the party worked for artisans, peasants, or other small entrepreneurs.

While the DC was the most important governing party, the governing coalition regularly included other parties – the Socialists (PSI), Social

*Table 6.3* Social composition of Christian Democratic party membership 1982 (economically active members only)

|  | Percentage | |
|---|---|---|
| Entrepreneurs – industrial | 1.5 | |
| Artisans, shopkeepers, etc. | 12.7 | |
| Independent professionals | 5.3 | 31.0 |
| Entrepreneurs – agriculture | 0.5 | |
| Peasants, incl. sharecroppers | 12.5 | |
| White-collar workers – public | 27.1 | |
| White-collar workers – private | 13.7 | |
| Blue-collar workers | 20.2 | 40.3 |
| Employees of artisans | 2.6 | |
| Agricultural labourers | 3.8 | |
| Total | 99.9 | |

Source: Calculated from M. Caciagli, 'Il resistibile declino della Democrazia cristiana', in G. Pasquino, ed., *Il sistema politico italiano* (Bari: Laterza, 1985), Table 6, p. 123.

Democrats, Liberals, and Republicans. The most important of these was the Socialist Party.

The Socialists, who first joined the cabinet in 1963 and were part of it for nineteen of the subsequent twenty-nine years, had their roots in the Marxist working-class movement, but changed markedly in character and outlook since their entry into government and, especially, since the accession of Bettino Craxi to the leadership in 1976. Craxi sought to turn the PSI into a true 'catch-all' party, able to challenge both the DC and the PCI on their own terrain. Less burdened by organic ties to particular social groups, the Socialists were able to act more flexibly than the DC, appealing to 'opinion' voters. These shifts would be expected to make the party more acceptable to business, and indeed the PSI espoused many policies favoured by capital, adopting a 'modern', managerial image: the most spectacular, perhaps, was Craxi's decision as Prime Minister in 1984 to issue an anti-inflation decree that reduced workers' monthly cost-of-living increases by 27,200 lire (*c.* US$20). This programme had not been agreed to by the Communist-led CGIL union confederation, and the Communists requested a referendum to repeal it. The referendum, held in 1985, sustained the decree by a vote of 54 per cent to 46 per cent.

These measures were consistent with the Socialists' aims, which were to broaden their electoral appeal far beyond the working class, to include in particular the 'modern' middle classes. On the other hand, their entry into government also opened up to them the possibility of expanding their electorate through the more traditional methods of clientelism and patronage. Indeed, the Socialists soon proved more adept than the DC at using the resources of the state to solidify their electoral base: their approach to patronage was more systematic and more ruthless. According to one informant, while the DC Minister of Public Works had demanded kickbacks at a fixed rate of 5 per cent, the Socialists increased that rate considerably.[14] Moreover, they demanded increasing representation on the boards and in the management of state-owned industry and other public bodies, threatening to bring down governments over this issue.

This led some commentators to state that with 10 per cent of the votes, the PSI had 30 per cent of the power.[15] Moreover, the PSI's central position in the political spectrum allowed it to form alliances at the local and regional level with either the other centre-left parties (DC and small lay parties) or the Communists. Indeed, its participation was usually necessary for any majority to be formed; often only one type of majority (left or centre-left) was mathematically possible. This frontier situation allowed it to bargain for representation in local government in excess of what its electoral strength would have entitled it to. In 1982, for instance, it was present in the administrations of nearly four fifths of the provinces and provincial capitals, with nearly a quarter of the portfolios in them.

The PSI's eager exploitation of its position in the state can be explained by its lack of the solid subcultural and ideological base the DC possessed. Nor had it the organic links the DC had with the petty bourgeoisie, while its traditional base in the working class had shrunk, in spite of its strong position in the union hierarchy. Its electorate was less stable – only 65–70 per cent of Socialist voters had typically supported the party at the previous election, as opposed to 85–90 per cent for the DC and Communists – and it therefore had to rely more on the state and its resources to attract a following. The 'new' middle classes to which it made a special appeal are in fact often as dependent on the state as the traditional petty bourgeoisie.

While more flexible than the DC because it lacked the latter's organic ties to the petty bourgeoisie, the PSI often found itself opposing business proposals because of its dependence on the state and its resources. It perceived any contraction of the state or the state sector as a threat to its power, and any deregulation it viewed in the same light. The party's leftist heritage was a far less important factor. It did, at times, promote policies not motivated by such short-sighted considerations of party interest, including genuine reforms in the broad public interest. These were generally adopted when they seemed likely to increase the party's appeal as a catch-all party to a broad segment of the electorate (a case in point is the crack-down on tax evasion initiated by the Socialist Finance Minister, Franco Reviglio, in the early 1980s). And the party was open to the influence of particular business people, as the well known friendship between Craxi and Berlusconi, which helps explain the 1985 decree solidifying the position of Berlusconi's networks, testifies.

Among the minor coalition parties, both the Liberals and the Republicans were especially close to business interests. The Liberals were the beneficiaries in the 1950s of massive business backing, and led the campaign against the opening to the left, scoring their greatest electoral success (7 per cent) in 1963 as a result of this stance. For the first thirteen years of centre-left government, they were excluded from the coalition and the cabinet, returning only briefly in 1972–73 in Andreotti's 'centrist' government. After the period of 'national solidarity', however, they once again became potential coalition partners, and since 1980 the typical governmental coalition was a *pentapartito* (five-party alliance), including the four 'centre-left' parties and the Liberals. The Liberals traditionally supported *laissez-faire*, pro-business policies, playing the role of a typical lay conservative party.

The Republicans (PRI), who have continued to exist since 1992 under the same name, though running under the umbrella of other lists (e.g. Rinnovamento Italiano in 1996), have been a much more dynamic representative of business interests in the political system. Many of their post-war leaders came from the Action Party of the Resistance era, the original home of many important figures of the centre and left of the political scene. These, including the party's long-time secretary, Ugo La Malfa, enjoyed great intellectual and moral prestige. Moreover, under La Malfa the PRI distinguished itself for its innovative and progressive position within the coalition, promoting the centre-left and later foreshadowing the possibility of an opening to the Communists as well. At the same time, the PRI has always championed economic 'rigour'; it promoted incomes policies in the 1960s, and in the 1980s was the most outspoken opponent of deficit financing. In this, it continued a long tradition of Italian liberal economic thought, a tradition with which even the Communists displayed a surprising affinity.[16]

The Republicans are not a mass-membership party, although they have a traditional base in the Romagna region (Ravenna and Forlì provinces). They enjoy their greatest success in the large cities of the North, where they appeal to the middle classes as a progressive, honest party that endorses capitalist values and virtues. In 1983 they achieved their greatest success, scoring 5.1 per cent nationally, with 12.3 per cent of the popular vote in Milan and 10.2 per cent in Turin, where they were the third largest party. The Republicans are especially popular among capitalists, with 23 per cent of businessmen questioned by Martinelli and his collaborators about their vote in 1976 supporting the party.[17] It is well known that the Agnelli family's sympathies lie with the party; Gianni Agnelli's sister, Susanna, was a Republican deputy and mayor. Former Fiat chairman Cesare Romiti has also indicated that he inclined towards the party at the time.[18]

The third minor party, the Social Democrats, were closer to the Socialists than the Liberals and Republicans in their social basis: they were in the governmental area since 1947, when they broke with the PSI, and sank deep roots in the state apparatus, which they also used to generate electoral support. While the Liberals and Republicans could rely largely on opinion voters and business contributions, the Social Democrats depended on their political position. Their importance declined in the last years of the old regime, and in 1987 they obtained only 2.9 per cent of the popular vote. With the end of the Cold War, their virulent anti-communism was no longer an electoral drawing card, and they attempted to create a new constituency by posing as the champions of pensioners.

An illustration of the social bases of the political parties of the First Republic is the make-up of the parliamentary parties. As Table 6.4 shows, businesspeople were not strongly represented in the ranks of the deputies and senators, even in the governing parties. (Of course they were over-represented relative to their weight in the population at large, while workers and peasants were vastly under-represented). Only 9 per cent of DC deputies had business backgrounds. On the other hand, a decisive majority of the parliamentarians on the government side came from the public sector or were career politicians: fully three-fifths of the DC's deputies, for instance, were politicians, public sector managers or func-tionaries, or members of state-employed professions. Moreover, the table understates the strength of public employees: some of the subordinate employees (at least half in the case of the DC deputies) were in the public sector; some of those classified as business managers may in fact have been employed in public enterprises, but not have declared their employers; and a certain number of the professionals classed as 'other', that is not state-employed (especially doctors), may have derived all or part of their income from the state and its agencies.

The DC's parliamentary party, then, was principally composed of career politicians and public employees. The party's petty bourgeois constituency was hardly represented in proportion to its electoral significance (small business is included in the business category), and businesspeople were scarcely present. This helps to account for the perception that 'Rome' was a foreign, hostile place for business. But more than a perception is involved. The main concerns of the deputies and senators were shaped by their political backgrounds, and they tended to focus on their political advantage; they had little appreciation of the priorities and concerns of business.

## The emergence of the 'Second Republic'

The DC regime was brought down in the early 1990s by a concatenation of factors, of which the most spectacular were the corruption investigations known as 'Tangentopoli' (Bribesville) (see below, pp. 120–122).[19] Begin-ning in March 1992, these unveiled a network of payoffs and corrupt prac-tices whose extent surprised even cynical observers of the Italian scene. Many other changes contributed to the political 'revolution', however: the end of the Cold War, symbolized by the fall of the Berlin Wall in 1989, had made it less necessary for the right-wing forces to rally around the Christian Democrats, and induced the Communist leadership to trans-form their party into the more moderate Democratic Party of the Left.

*Table 6.4* Social composition of governing parliamentary parties, Tenth Legis-
lature 1987–92 (percentages)

| Occupation | Party | | |
| --- | --- | --- | --- |
| | DC | PSI | Lay parties* |
| a *Chamber of Deputies* | | | |
| Politicians | 16.2 | 22.3 | 14.3 |
| Functionaries and managers, public sector | 23.9 | 18.1 | 18.4 |
| State-employed professions (teachers, judges, military) | 20.1 | 19.1 | 20.4 |
| Other professions | 26.5 | 23.4 | 38.8 |
| Business (owners or managers), except agriculture | 9.0 | 4.3 | 6.1 |
| Agriculture (except workers) | 1.7 | 1.1 | 2.0 |
| All subordinate occupations (workers, clerks, technicians) | 2.6 | 11.7 | – |
| Total | 100.0 | 100.0 | 100.0 |
| N | 234 | 94 | 49 |
| b *Senate* | | | |
| Politicians | 18.3 | 17.8 | 5.9 |
| Functionaries and managers, public sector | 17.5 | 6.7 | 11.8 |
| State-employed professions (teachers, judges, military) | 20.6 | 26.7 | 17.6 |
| Other professions | 30.2 | 37.8 | 52.9 |
| Business (owners and managers), except agriculture | 9.5 | 6.7 | 11.8 |
| Agriculture (except workers) | 2.4 | – | – |
| All subordinate occupations (workers, clerks, technicians) | 1.6 | 4.4 | – |
| Total | 100.1 | 100.1 | 100.0 |
| N | 126 | 45 | 17 |
| Unknown (N) | 1 | 0 | 1 |

Sources: *I deputati e senatori del decimo Parlamento repubblicano* (Rome: La Navicella, 1988) and Camera dei deputati, Servizio prerogative e immunità, *I deputati della X legislatura* (Rome: Camera dei deputati, 1987). Author's classification; in case of conflict, the former source prevails.

Notes
*PRI, PLI, PSDI.
a 'Politicians': The table is intended to record the social origin of the parliamentarians, many of whom had been full-time politicians for a long time. Therefore, a parliamentarian is classified as a 'politician' only if there is no declared occupation plus a long *curriculum* of political office-holding, or if the only declared occupation is 'party functionary' or similar, or if the only declared occupation is 'journalist' or 'publicist' and there is no evidence the parliamentarian has ever worked for any non-party publication. This category therefore includes those who never had any occupation other than politics. Office-holding or work for a collateral organization (union, peasant organization, etc.) is considered equivalent to party work.

The signature of the Maastricht Treaty provided a potent external source of pressure on Italy to reduce the deficit and debt: many voters blamed these on the Christian Democratic regime. The financial crisis of September 1992 that forced Italy out of the European Monetary System was a traumatic event which brought home how seriously the economy had been mismanaged and how great an effort would be needed to set it right again. The necessary cuts in public spending would undermine the DC's system of patronage and clientelism.

Meanwhile, from below, even before Tangentopoli public opinion was becoming increasingly critical of the corruption and inefficiency of the political system, as the June 1991 referendum limiting the use of the preference vote showed. (The competition for preference votes between candidates on the same party list had been a source of burgeoning campaign spending and hence of corruption). This revulsion among the public crystallized in Northern Italy around the Northern League, a new party which came from virtually nowhere in 1987 to win 8.6 per cent of the vote in the 1992 elections. In the eyes of some observers, the League represented yet another factor contributing to the crisis, a new social group which felt it was not represented in the old political system: the small entrepreneurs of the 'Third Italy', concentrated in the North-East.[20]

Of all these factors, perhaps the most significant was the rising level of corruption that we noted in the last section. If the large enterprises were more easily able to pass on the cost of the bribes and preserve their profit margins through their control of the price they charged, this was not always true for the smaller firms, which were in any case under great pressure to contain their prices because of the 'strong lira' policy pursued until September 1992.[21] As the demands of the politicians increased throughout the last fifteen years of the old regime, these companies found their profit margins squeezed, and eventually abandoned their *omertà* and collaborated with the prosecutors. In addition, the consensus was widespread that the existing political system could not meet the Maastricht criteria for deficit reduction. However, the origins of the crisis of the regime were, in our view, largely endogenous, the result of the rising level of corruption on the one hand and on the other of growing public intolerance of the system, which thereby lost legitimacy at an accelerating rate.

---

b  Multiple occupations:
   i  A parliamentarian who holds a teaching appointment and is also a member of another profession is classified as a member of the other profession unless there is evidence that teaching is the major occupation.
   ii  A parliamentarian who is a member of a profession (including teaching) and an employee of a government agency or company is classified as an employee of that agency or company.
   iii  In all other cases, the occupation held for the longest time is counted.
c  Public-sector workers: Clerks (*impiegati*), workers, and technicians in the public sector are classified as holding subordinate occupations, rather than as managers and functionaries in the public sector.

The most significant single aspect of the political 'revolution' was the disappearance of the DC, which was replaced by three or four fragments, divided between the left and right sides of the political spectrum, and reduced to less than half of the electoral support the old DC had held.[22] The major new force to emerge on the right was Forza Italia (FI), a party created by Silvio Berlusconi in 1993–94 to contest the 1994 election; according to one survey, 73 per cent of FI's voters in 1994 who had voted in 1992 came from the five government parties, and FI inherited the DC's strong base among the self-employed, women (especially housewives), and pensioners, but not among public-sector workers.[23] This party was novel compared to all other Italian parties in two ways. First, it was neither a cadre nor a mass party,[24] but a party of a new type created in a 'top-down' fashion by Berlusconi using the personnel, money, and facilities provided by his companies, particularly Publitalia, the advertising firm (hence the epithet *partito-azienda*, or company-party, sometimes applied to FI). Perhaps the closest analogies are Ross Perot's United We Stand America (later Reform Party) and, earlier, the Swiss Independents, though the personal campaigns of many American candidates for office also present many similarities.

While Publitalia sales agents organized many local Forza Italia clubs (on the model of the fan clubs for Berlusconi's AC Milan soccer team), the national executive was nominated by Berlusconi, with a majority of Fininvest executives, and no national congress was held until spring 1998. Thanks to Berlusconi's television networks and ample funds, FI waged a campaign based on the media and advertising, with little grass-roots involvement. While the trend towards campaigns of this sort, where the media, a small staff of advisers, and the money to pay for them are central, has been noted by many observers,[25] Berlusconi's party represents its *reductio ad absurdum*.

Even more important, FI was the direct emanation of a single capitalist. Poulantzas points out that the capitalist class's hegemony is better secured if it is represented by a party that is not its direct representative; furthermore, one of the reasons he (following the reasoning of Marx in the *Eighteenth Brumaire of Louis Bonaparte*) gives for the difficulty it has in forming its 'own' party in any case is that capitalists are in competition with each other in the economic sphere, and hence have difficulty uniting around a political programme.[26] FI laboured under the handicaps of being an unmediated representative of capital in the eyes of the public and of arousing the suspicion of other capitalists who, apart from the content of his programme, feared that Berlusconi might use his political position to gain an unfair business advantage (the 'conflict of interest' problem, made more acute by the strong evidence that he had entered politics in the first place primarily to protect his three television networks from antitrust legislation and to save himself and his companies from the effects of the Tangentopoli investigations).

While several commentators made the facile comment that Berlusconi's style was 'Bonapartist', in fact he represented instead the phenomenon to which Bonapartism is the antidote: with his business empire, control of a large fraction of the media, and personal political party, he seemed in danger of becoming far more powerful than a single capitalist should be in a competitive market system. Despite these drawbacks, the resources of Fininvest also gave FI considerable advantages, and Berlusconi was able to use his skills as a salesman to address at least the first handicap, presenting himself as a successful self-made man, a model for others who could do the same in the free-enterprise Italy he wished to create, and a capable manager for the country.

In terms of programme, Forza Italia embraced a strong free-market position, advocating a retreat of the state from the economy. Berlusconi himself injected a large dose of ideology into the electoral campaign with his denunciation of the Communist danger (in spite of the transformation of the PCI in 1991). These positions appealed to the petty bourgeois clientele that the party had inherited from the DC. The party favoured privatization and the reduction of the scope of public welfare provision; its ideal appeared to be the Anglo-Saxon form of free-market capitalism, and some of Berlusconi's followers were avowed admirers of Margaret Thatcher.

Another part of the DC's electorate and role, however, was inherited by the successor to the neo-fascist MSI (Italian Social Movement), Alleanza Nazionale (AN, or National Alliance). Under the leadership of Gianfranco Fini, AN sought to shed its connection to Fascism and embrace democracy, thus allowing its legitimation as a potential government party. The party's constituency differs from FI's in that it is more Southern and much stronger among public employees. AN, in keeping with its traditions, is not opposed to state action. In spite of its endorsement of a free-market platform at its 1997 Verona Congress, it wishes to temper the raw free-enterprise model and retains a residual interest in corporatist institutions. While strongly opposed to the three confederal unions, it is not hostile to unions as such, and (unlike FI) has its own 'related' union confederation, the UGL (Unione Generale del Lavoro, previously CISNAL). In its 1994 programme it advocated the revision of the Maastricht Treaty, fearful of the effect of cuts in public spending on its constituency.[27] At the same time, AN is critical of the rigorous policies pursued by the Bank of Italy. While also on the right, the Alliance is solicitous of the interests of those broad elements of its constituency that depend on the state. This has not prevented it from reaching electoral alliances and indeed governing with FI, and many supporters of Berlusconi's party in practice find the Alliance's positions more congenial than those of their own party.

The third major party of the centre-right in the post-1992 period is the Northern League. It emerged in the 1992 election, taking a large share of its support from the DC. Its platform is based on the demand for autonomy for the North (from 1996 to 1998, it demanded outright independence) and a strong hostility to state action, which is identified with 'Rome' and a political system run for the benefit of the South. The League can be seen as a party of protest against both the corrupt political system and the growth of the state; it has often championed protests against taxation. In social terms, it represents in particular the small employers and self-employed of the North, especially the North-East. While in many ways similar to that of FI and AN, the League's electorate tends to be concentrated among the less educated and inhabitants of smaller communes. Like the other two centre-right parties, it is stronger among employees in the private sector, the self-employed, and those who are at least occasional churchgoers.[28] (Naturally, it is confined to the North and a few of the central regions).

In economic policy terms, all three of the centre-right parties demonstrate their dependence on the mass of the self-employed and small entrepreneurs. Hence their strenuous opposition to taxation, often verging on the encouragement of evasion, which gives rise to doubts about the seriousness of their plans to eliminate the budget deficit. (In the 1996 election campaign, AN demagogically proposed to eliminate the deduction of income tax at source for employees, while the Pole – the coalition of AN and FI – proposed restoring the total tax exemption for income from government bonds). And all have been strong proponents of tax incentives for businesses to increase employment. On the currency, they were critical of the Bank of Italy's rigorous policies and tried to induce it to lower interest rates (an important issue for small business in particular). Again, this stance gave rise to the well-founded impression that they were 'soft' on devaluation. With the caveat that AN favours corporatist arrangements in principle, while criticizing the three major union confederations, all three are unsympathetic to the idea of 'concertation', or tripartite bargaining at the national level. (As a Vice-President of Confindustria said, Berlusconi 'doesn't know what concertation is'.[29])

Nonetheless, there are some apparent differences among the three. As we have noted, AN favours a continued significant state role in the economy, and large public expenditures (particularly in the South), while the League and elements of FI want to cut back the state's role and reduce government spending in order to lower taxes. As Revelli puts it:

> Between the tax revolt of the North, the true material basis of the now exhausted electoral mobilization of the League and of the subversive tendencies still present among the possessing classes, and the demand for state assistance of the Southern petty bourgeoisie, which is in its turn the material basis of Alleanza Nazionale's neonationalism, there is an incompatibility which is not only 'cultural' (if we can speak of culture), but structural.[30]

While this is clearly a potential line of cleavage, it will come to the fore only if the different political forces clearly and logically draw the conclusions from their positions. If not, it is possible for both groups to unite in opposition to state action protecting e.g. workers' rights, or against state regulation of their activities, and in favour of particular government measures in their own interests. It has often been pointed out that this schizophrenic attitude to the state is typical of the petty bourgeoisie, which subscribes to free-market, *laissez-faire* slogans as ideology while demanding that the state interfere with the same market to protect them.[31] To a certain extent the electoral programme of the Pole in 1996 achieved this synthesis. Conflicts will arise over particular measures of assistance to one group or another; if these can be presented as general programmes that benefit all (e.g. a reduction in social security contributions for new hires), even these can be papered over. The incompatibility Revelli notes becomes evident only when there is a tight budget constraint that prevents this sort of compromise; otherwise, costs can be shifted to the working class, the inactive population (through, for example, pension cuts), and even large businesses. For this reason, perhaps, the leaders of the centre-right realized that the aim of joining the European Monetary Union with the first group of countries could put excessive strains on their own electoral coalition. In addition, many entrepreneurs of the 'Third Italy' feared, perhaps unduly, that entry into the EMU would reduce their ability to compete on price, while the Southern petty bourgeoisie was basically indifferent to the issue in itself, while hostile to the cuts in public expenditure entry entailed.

A second potential source of division within the centre-right is Berlusconi's position as head of one of the largest conglomerates in Italy. Indeed, the Standa chain, which he owned until 1998, includes many of the large retail outlets that small shopkeepers identify (after the tax authorities) as the source of their problems. Standa is a 'junior' department store, similar to Woolworth's or Marks and Spencer; it emphasizes its supermarkets and clothing departments, but competes in some way with almost every type of small shop, from hardware to stationery. However, Berlusconi's principal political objective is the defence of his television networks, an aim which affects the interests of only a handful of local station owners. He has been successful in keeping this potential conflict of interest with a key part of his constituency in the background.

The three major parties of the centre-right, in sum, are in many ways closer to small business and the petty bourgeoisie than to the largest firms. In this way they are replicating the role of the DC, with even greater attention to this constituency. At the same time, they have lost a large part of the DC's public sector support, in spite of AN's strong showing in Rome, and they no longer have any organic link to a major trade union confederation (if we ignore the UGL). While they have retained much of the Catholic component of the DC's support, the clientelistic element is largely gone.[32] Hence these parties (with a minor caveat for AN) are an even more direct and unalloyed expression of the petty bourgeoisie and small entrepreneurs than the DC was.

Some of the most interesting changes in the party system since the beginning of the crisis have occurred on the left. While the bulk of the Communist Party transformed itself into the Democratic Party of the Left (Partito Democratico della Sinistra, or PDS, now Democratici di Sinistra, or DS) at the Rimini Congress of 1991, a minority left the party to form a new group, Communist Refoundation (Partito della Rifondazione Comunista, or PRC), which rejected what it saw as a move to the right by the PDS and sought to maintain the tradition of the PCI.

The PDS inherited the bulk of the PCI's electorate, becoming the largest single party in 1996 with 21.1 per cent of the vote. It also inherited the PCI's traditional attitude towards economic policy. In spite of initiatives such as the Piano del Lavoro, promoted by the CGIL union in the early 1950s, the PCI had never fully embraced Keynesianism as an approach to economic policy. This is in part because it never shared governmental responsibilities during the post-war boom period, when such policies were both feasible and successful; it preferred to concentrate on plans that operated on the supply side, by reorganizing industrial sectors or promoting small and medium industry, which, until the 1970s, was seen as the victim of the 'monopolies'.[33] Moreover, DC control of the state – to the point of being identified with it – made government action seem not the benevolent, progressive solution it did in other European countries, but a chance for corruption, waste, and inefficiency, so the PCI was less 'statist' than many other parties of the left.[34]

In the mid-1970s, some sectors of the PCI were attracted by the possibility of a 'Manchesterian' alliance with large industry against the parasitic middle classes and public employees. This reversal of the party's traditional anti-monopoly stance, however, bore no fruit as attempts to establish a neo-corporatist arrangement foundered on the competition between different partisan factions in the union movement and the government's inability to deliver the necessary complementary measures. However, during the late 1970s the party was a strong supporter of the austerity measures adopted by the government of national solidarity, which it supported in parliament, in order to right the payments deficit and stabilize the lira.[35] Enrico Berlinguer, the party leader, even theorized an ethical and cultural justification for austerity, appealing to the Catholic and Socialist traditions in Italy. The union movement fell in step, adopting the 'EUR line' of wage moderation in 1978. This period foreshadowed the post-1992 austerity measures adopted to meet the Maastricht criteria.

The PCI's position in the late 1970s had deep roots in the party's history; from 1944, Secretary General Palmiro Togliatti had argued that the Communists must not adopt the position of simple propagandists, critics and advocates of a better order, but propose positive measures short of socialist revolution:

> We cannot be content to criticize or to rail, even if it is in the most brilliant way; we must possess a solution to all the problems of the

nation, we must indicate it to the people at the opportune moment and be able to lead the whole country to achieve it.[36]

This position was a natural outgrowth of the Popular Front strategy adopted by all Communist parties in the 1930s, but applied with particular thoroughness and conviction by the PCI. Togliatti believed the party had to eschew any *attentisme* and forge a coalition that would be able to take power within a bourgeois-democratic context to prevent the resurgence of a fascist threat. Hence the PCI's conscious adoption of the role of a 'national' party, rather than simply the party of one class. During the Cold War, this inclination was reinforced by the party's strong desire to legitimate itself as an acceptable governing party and hence break the *conventio ad excludendum* that kept it out of office.

Furthermore, there was from early in the post-war period a surprising sympathy within the PCI for the current of liberal orthodoxy that dominated in Italian academic economics.[37] Marxist economic thought had never taken deep root in the party, nor had the ideas of J.M. Keynes. The liberal school had prestigious exponents with a reputation for personal honesty who also had distinguished anti-fascist records, such as Luigi Einaudi. This lay, democratic current found its best political expression in the Republican Party. The PCI also appreciated that the Bank of Italy was one of the few institutions that the DC had not succeeded in colonizing, and therefore tended to support the Bank's autonomy: the party's defence of Governor Paolo Baffi when he was forced to resign in 1979 because he had displeased certain elements in the DC[38] typifies its attitude. This was true in spite of the well known connection between central bank autonomy and orthodox monetary policies, and in spite of the Bank's own attempts to pursue a strong anti-inflationary course.

The PCI, in other words, was never a proponent of easy money, inflation, devaluation, and large deficits. It recognized that inflation tended to favour business and the petty bourgeoisie, and that deficits financed, among other programmes, DC patronage schemes. Hence it is possible to understand the PDS's commitment to meeting the Maastricht criteria as the product of the party's history. It is indeed ironic that the PDS demonstrated a firmer resolve on this issue than the parties of the right, which were traversed by the doubts of their constituents about the impact of reaching the criteria on their balance sheets, and feared that monetary union itself could limit their ability to compete. Paradoxically, the PDS and the cabinets it supported in the 1990s, as we shall see, played the role of a 'Bonapartist' government, acting in the long-term interests of capital when capital itself was too short-sighted to do so.[39]

Communist Refoundation, on the other hand, saw its fidelity to the traditional positions of the PCI as a major source of its support. However, it did not, like the PDS, inherit the spirit of the PCI's policy, but instead conceived of its role almost exclusively as the protection of the interests of its constituency (principally the industrial working class). Thus, it typically adopted a defensive position, opposing any reduction in welfare benefits, privatization, tax increases for workers, etc.: it openly opposed the Maastricht Treaty, in view of the sacrifices necessary to meet the criteria. It even called in 1996 for the restoration of the rent control law of 1978 (the *equo canone*), which had been widely evaded in the first place. To deal with unemployment, it supported the creation of jobs by government funding in spite of the problem of the deficit. The PDS, on the other hand, was prepared to consider sacrifices in the interest of broader political objectives. With respect to concertation as well, the leader of the PRC, Fausto Bertinotti, was a former trade unionist who had led the opposition to the July 1993 accord. The party therefore reflected the positions of the left-wing minority faction in the CGIL ('Essere sindacato'); it often outflanked the unions on the left in parliament, creating serious difficulties for the practice of concertation. The PRC's positions appeared to many 'corporative' and trade-unionistic, but this was in part a function of the political situation, in which the previous gains of the working class were under attack and a defensive battle seemed a necessary preliminary to any socialist project.

The former DC, as we have seen, split into three broad groups, the CCD and CDU on the right; the PPI, the Democrats, and the UDEUR on the left; and Democrazia Europea, the party organized by the former trade unionist Sergio D'Antoni, in the centre. The former two are junior partners in the centre-right coalition with FI and AN and have recently (2003) fused, along with D'Antoni's DE, to form the UDC (Christian Democratic Centre Union); the three left-oriented groups have formed, along with Lamberto Dini's Rinnovamento Italiano, the 'Margherita' grouping, which is the second-largest component of the left-wing 'Olive Tree' coalition, after the DS. While much diminished in size, all these fragments have retained many of the DC's political instincts, including a solicitous concern for the petty bourgeois constituency and public employees, a propensity to use government spending for electoral purposes, and hence a reluctance to cut welfare or similar benefits.

The Republican Party found a congenial new alliance in 1996 when Prime Minister Lamberto Dini founded Rinnovamento Italiano (Italian Renewal), a party that reached an electoral pact with the Olive Tree coalition while upholding the traditional Republican emphasis on economic orthodoxy. Rinnovamento was the self-proclaimed moderate wing of the left-wing electoral alliance; it is significant that Dini, a former official of the International Monetary Fund and Director General of the Bank of Italy, should have decided after he had served in Berlusconi's cabinet that the left-wing alliance had policies closer to his own than those of FI and AN. Rinnovamento represents primarily an 'enlightened' wing of the entrepreneurial and professional bourgeoisie, which has no prejudice against the former Communists of the PDS, but has its own programme: it is the party which best reflects the interests and ideas of the major capital-ist groups and the 'good salon'.

In the period after the 1992 election, eight governments have suc-ceeded each other in power: the Amato government, representing the old governing parties but charged with reforming the electoral system and dealing with the economic emergency (June 1992–April 1993); the Ciampi 'technocratic' government (April 1993–May 1994); Berlusconi's right-wing government (May 1994–Dec. 1994); Dini's 'technocratic' government (Jan. 1995–May 1996); Prodi's centre-left government (May 1996–Oct. 1998); Massimo D'Alema's reconstituted centre-left (Oct. 1998–April 2000), which was shuffled once; the same coalition, but headed by Amato (April 2000–April 2001); and the second Berlusconi government, elected in April 2001.

The Ciampi and Dini governments can each be seen as Bonapartist solutions to the problems of government. In each case, parties that represented the ruling class in a more directly political way had proven incapable of governing. Amato's government had been weakened by a series of resignations of ministers under investigation for corruption; Berlusconi had lost the confidence of the Northern League in parliament. As Gramsci wrote, Bonapartism does not require a Bonaparte. These gov-ernments were able to continue the work of reducing the deficit under-taken by Amato, with the support in parliament of the left. (The Dini government depended on the votes of the left, as Berlusconi believed that it should resign and call an election as soon as possible.)

The Prodi cabinet was not a technocratic government, as it resulted from the electoral victory of the left, but there were many elements of con-tinuity between it and the Dini and Ciampi cabinets. Both Dini and Ciampi were members of Prodi's government, which also contained a technical, non-party minister of Justice (Flick), in addition to the party appointments to the other key ministries. And Prodi's cabinet, directed by Ciampi as Minister of the Economy, was determined to continue with the reduction of the deficit in order to bring Italy into the European Mone-tary Union. This is precisely the sort of national task that the representa-tives of capital may not be able to agree to carry out, and that a Bonapartist government, on the other hand, may be able to undertake. In the case of Prodi, the anomaly was that his parliamentary support (like that of Dini) came from the left, while he was opposed by the right.

## The organization of business interests

Not only the party system, but also the configuration of organized interest groups has a major impact on policy-making. Gourevitch considers both parties and interest groups under the single heading of associations, one of the five sets of factors he believes can influence governmental decisions. With respect to the relationship between capital and the state, organizations representing business interests are the most significant, and they shall be the principal focus of the rest of this chapter. The trade union movement, another major actor in economic policy-making, will be dealt with in more detail in Chapter 9.

By far the most significant organization of business interests in Italy is the General Confederation of Italian Industry (Confindustria). It groups private industrial firms only – there are separate organizations for the agricultural, retail, and artisanal sectors, the banks, and public industry. Nevertheless, it has 112,000 member firms with 4,600,000 employees; the firms are affiliated either through one of the 107 territorial associations (each generally corresponding to a province) or through one of the 130 sectoral ('category') associations and federations, or through both.[40] As the largest business organization, it tends to take the lead in most dealings with the government and the unions, and the other associations usually follow suit.

Confindustria is concerned with relations with both the government and the unions, yet its most important function has been to unite the various elements of capital, and particularly small and medium industry, around the leadership of the largest groups, especially Fiat.[41] It has often, in fact, been described as controlled by Fiat, but the situation is somewhat more complex, as was finally demonstrated in 2000 when the organization elected Antonio D'Amato as president in preference to Carlo Callieri, the candidate favoured by Fiat, the first clear defeat the Turinese colossus had suffered in Confindustria. D'Amato promised a more combative neoliberal approach, favoured by many small entrepreneurs, and a *rapprochement* with Berlusconi and the right-wing opposition. It is unclear whether this closer support will survive Berlusconi's second term in office, however;[42] Fiat's critical stance, while softened at the time of Berlusconi's election, persists, and even the Confcommercio, representing small shopkeepers, has broken with D'Amato's hard-line approach to the unions on issues like pensions and employment law.[43] At least down to 2000, while tensions within the organization have been continual, it has, by and large, unified capital quite effectively, given the diversity of Italian industry.

The election of Sergio Pininfarina as President in 1988 is a good example of the complex internal politics of the organization when it was performing this unifying role well.[44] The general problem posed by the choice of the President of Confindustria was to reconcile the interests and claims of the large groups, on the one hand, and the mass membership of smaller firms, on the other. While the former pay the lion's share of the contributions that maintain the organization, and wield tremendous influence, they must be careful not to offend the latter, whose support they need to legitimize and promote their policies. Nor, of course, can the smaller firms ignore the large: in an apocryphal comment, Giovanni Agnelli is supposed to have said 'You can choose a president without Fiat, but not against Fiat'.[45] In 1984 Fiat had exerted all its influence in favour of Luigi Lucchini, a steel manufacturer and charter member of the 'good salon', who was nominated by the executive committee with fifty-four votes in favour, one opposed, and thirty-five abstentions; the abstentions were a sign of the opposition to Fiat among some of the members. In 1988 it was just as determined to secure the election of its own candidate, as it believed it would need Confindustria support to stave off the threat of anti-trust legislation (supported by De Benedetti) and to resolve its continuing problems with the government, especially the Socialists, and respond to an increasingly critical public opinion.

Initially, Cesare Romiti, President of Fiat, was touted as a possible president; with his public profile and considerable personal prestige, he found great favour with many members. Alternatively, Fiat supported Walter Mandelli, the hard-nosed head of the Federmeccanica, the sectoral association of the engineering industry. De Benedetti, Pirelli, and Luigi Orlando, president of the GIM metalworking firm, on the other hand, supported Giancarlo Lombardi, a Piedmontese textile manufacturer who was not acceptable to Fiat, while many of the younger and smaller industrialists favoured Carlo Patrucco, the Vice-President for union relations.[46] Romiti's candidacy, however, was never genuine – Agnelli did not intend to let his most valued lieutenant go. Rather it was a device to solidify support around Fiat's line, which was relatively 'harder' on both the political and the union fronts than either De Benedetti's or the young industrialists'. Agnelli did not realize, however, that the support Romiti garnered because of his personal qualities could not automatically be transferred to another candidate.

Only at the beginning of February, about a week before Romiti's final refusal, did the name of Sergio Pininfarina begin to be discussed. Pininfarina was president of the auto-body maker of the same name, and naturally had close business ties to Fiat. By mid-February he had the qualified support of De Benedetti and Gardini, as well as Agnelli, but there was resistance from the small industrialists, the young industrialists, and some of the sectoral associations, as Pininfarina's candidacy seemed to have been 'imposed' from above by Fiat. It took the diplomatic skills of Carlo Muscarà, chairman of the small industrialists, to secure their support for the new candidate, which their council voted at the end of the month. The powerful regional association of Lombardy, the Assolombarda, was initially hesitant about Pininfarina as well, while Antonio D'Amato, then president of the young industrialists' association, remained opposed because of the method used in promoting him, which seemed to him undemocratic.[47] In the end, Pininfarina was selected almost unanimously.

While the choice of the president of Confindustria may have appeared a simple power struggle, with no clear issues dividing the candidates, it was nonetheless significant because Fiat felt the need to consolidate its hold over the organization in view of the difficulties and political problems which it foresaw. That Pininfarina did his job of uniting industry well was demonstrated by the next presidential election in 1992, when Luigi Abete, owner of a Roman printing firm, was elected with an unprecedented level of support, and chose as his vice-presidents a prominent Fiat manager, Carlo Callieri, and two long-time Fiat allies, Luigi Orlando and Giampiero Pesenti.[48] The divisions reappeared, of course, in 2000, when the D'Amato, disappointed by the 1988 results, was able to take his revenge over Callieri.

Confindustria has a large staff of *c.* 300; it has been described as a small ministry. Its research department (the Centro Studi Confindustria) was intended by Guido Carli (president, 1977–80) to give it a superior position in dealings with the government, just as he had strengthened the Bank of Italy by promoting its research department. Since his time, however, its importance has declined.[49] In addition, Confindustria carries on regular lobbying activities on many fronts, in particular macroeconomic policy issues and other questions affecting industry as a whole, which are largely delegated to it by the firms and sectoral associations. Only Fiat and other large conglomerates promote their own macroeconomic policy line directly with the government. Confindustria also has close connections with the ministerial bureaucracy: its officials maintain contacts with their opposite numbers in the Industry Ministry, and it is traditionally a major source of information for the Ministry. In fact, La Palombara considered it the best example of a *clientela* group, a group which a government department regards as its privileged interlocutor.[50]

Much of the most effective lobbying, however, is carried out by the sectoral associations and individual firms. It is they that pursue the specific concessions and favours that are most valuable for business. Particularly active are associations such as the ANCE (the builders' association), whose members' activities are subject to close governmental regulation. The Federmeccanica also has many lobbyists, and Fiat itself has ten to fifteen. The other conglomerates, such as Olivetti, are also very active, as are numerous medium-sized companies. They also employ lobbying firms when necessary for special projects.

State industry, before the large-scale privatizations of the 1990s, enjoyed a particular, and privileged, position in its lobbying activities. It did not belong to Confindustria: the IRI companies were organized in Intersind, which grouped 329 firms employing 383,000 workers; the ENI companies were represented by ASAP (Associazione sindacale aziende petrolchimiche), which grouped 101 firms.[51] These often followed the Confindustria's lead, but were capable of independent action as well. State companies were at least as actively involved in lobbying as private companies, and retained numerous full-time lobbyists; they saw their public status as legitimizing the favours they provided to parliamentarians (e.g. they often paid the secretarial staff of parliamentary groups and deputies from their own payrolls). Moreover, the political nature of managerial appointments in the public sector meant they could rely automatically on the support of the party or faction to which their managers belonged.

Confindustria, moreover, groups only industrial firms: there are separate employers' organizations for agriculture (the Confagricoltura, which organizes *c.*675,000 of the larger enterprises) and the retail and service sector (the Confcommercio). Financial companies are also separately organized, banks in the Assicredito and insurance in the ANIA (Associazione nazionale italiana di assicuratori). While Confindustria aims to represent all industry, large and small, and has set up a separate National Committee and Central Council for small industry, there is also a rival organization in this sector, the Confapi (Confederation of Associations of Small Industry), with *c.*15,000 members. It was founded in the 1950s as a more 'progressive' alternative to the Confindustria. Much weaker than its larger competitor, Confapi owes what strength it has to its weight in a few provinces where the local situation favours it. In some 'red' provinces, it is an important channel for influencing local government, and hence is particularly strong in the construction industry. In others, such as Milan, it effectively represents the interests of small enterprises as opposed to large, especially in the engineering sector.[52] While not differing fundamentally from Confindustria on most issues of macroeconomic policy, Confapi is active in day-to-day parliamentary lobbying over subsidies, regulations, etc., to ensure better treatment for small and medium firms, which it believes Confindustria often subordinates to its large members.

In spite of this diversity and apparent fragmentation in the representation of business interests in Italy, Confindustria is undoubtedly the principal association, and is typically able to bring the others along with it (but Cf. note 43 above). For instance, during the negotiations for the revision of the cost-of-living escalator from 1982 on, the others subsequently signed agreements with the unions modelled on those already reached by Confindustria; in the later 1980s Confindustria felt that it could safely ignore Intersind and ASAP on macroeconomic issues.

Business lobbyists of all kinds employ diverse methods to attain their objectives. One of the most common, but certainly not the only one, has been money. The Tangentopoli scandal has brought to light a good many of the corrupt dealings of businesses; since 1992, the practice of kickbacks and illegal financing of parties has been considerably curtailed, though not eliminated. This has not led to a marked diminution of business influence on major policy decisions, however, as most corruption aimed at securing specific favours (e.g. construction contracts) or stemmed from politicians' requests. The general power that business derives from its key role in the economy remains untouched.

In spite of their *c.*$90 million annual state subsidy, the parties under the 'First Republic' were constantly in need of cash, as they had very large machines with many offices and permanent employees. While they were required to publish their accounts as a condition of receiving the subsidy, these accounts concealed more than they revealed: they were prepared by auditors chosen by the parties themselves, and did not include the regional, provincial, and local organizations.[53] Furthermore, the system of preference voting for the Chamber of Deputies, whereby each party's candidates competed with each other for preferences in order to be placed at the top of the party's list, required prospective deputies to spend large amounts on their own campaigns. In addition, the factions which existed within some parties, notably the DC, needed money to maintain their own structures.

Businesses did, in many cases, finance the campaign of an individual deputy, though the majority of parliamentarians were not beholden to any one sponsor. They generally supported one or more deputies in their own region (e.g. Fiat in Piedmont). In addition, some deputies who were not indebted for their election to a sponsor acted as paid lobbyists.[54] Often, on the other hand, the initiative came from the politicians' side in the form of requests for kickbacks and other bribes e.g. for public contracts or regulatory favours. As we have seen the Socialist Party, particularly after 1980, carried corruption to new levels. Whereas before 1962 it was sufficient to pay the local Christian Democratic deputy, often at a moderate fixed rate, the formation of the centre-left coalition eventually made it necessary to pay off the PSI as well. The Socialists introduced a new sophistication to the collection of funds, using devices such as front companies.[55] While businesses often willingly paid deputies and supported their campaigns, they also resented the need to pay political 'tolls' when they dealt with the state, and therefore tend to oppose measures that allow the exercise of political discretion.

A graphic illustration of the financial relations between businesses and politicians was provided by the breaking of the Milanese kickback scandal in February 1992. The confessions of one builder to the public prosecutor led to far-reaching revelations of many forms of political corruption, which shook the parties to the very top, and especially the PSI, which had played a major role in the government of Milan, the home town of its Secretary, Bettino Craxi. Most of the transactions involved kickbacks paid by construction companies in return for public works contracts. The contracts in question were let by the Commune of Milan or by municipal enterprises controlled by the Commune, whose boards were politically appointed: the public transit authorities (ATM and MM), the airport authority (SEA), the electric company (AEM), the boards of homes for the aged (Trivulzio and ex-ECA), and other smaller enterprises. They involved the construction of transit lines, stadiums, a theatre, hospitals, and all manner of other public works. Not only construction companies, but also firms providing services, such as school meals, drivers' uniforms, cleaning, and maintenance, were required to pay kickbacks. Further payments were made by businesses which were allowed to purchase property from these enterprises below market value, and by firms that had received planning permission to build on land that had been zoned for agricultural use.[56] In addition, some payments were made by construction industry associations to members of parliament in return for the passage of private bills (*leggine*) favourable to the industry: this was corruption of a different type, in which the initiative clearly came from the business side.[57]

Payments were made in an organized fashion by the firms, which restricted competition among themselves and determined in advance which of them would present the winning bid for each contract.[58] The largest companies, including Cogefar, the largest of all, controlled by the Fiat group, got the lion's share of the work, but the smaller ones formed consortia to participate in the division of the spoils as well. The payments were channelled to all the major parties, whether they belonged to the municipal majority or not: in one case, for instance, a third of the payment went directly to the PSI and the rest to the city secretary of the DC for distribution to the rest of the parties. Generally, one party 'controlled' each municipal enterprise, but the others had representatives on its board: the controlling party supervised the distribution of the funds.

The prosecutors uncovered 150 billion lire (*c.* US$125 million) of payments over the ten-year period 1982–92, and of course some payments remained undetected. The amounts demanded tended to be 5 per cent or less of the value of construction contracts (though for one contract to build new wings for an old people's home the kickback amounted to 6.67 per cent), but rose to 10 per cent for cleaning contracts and as high as 15 per cent for some others.[59] On the politicians' side, there is no doubt that the cost of campaigns had risen considerably over the past twenty years, with the availability of television advertising on private stations, in addition to the traditional posters and newspaper ads. One estimate placed a parliamentary candidate's expenses at 50–60 million lire per day, which would amount to some 2 billion lire for an entire campaign.[60] These figures refer only to the cost of the candidate's personal campaign, which was in addition to that of his or her party. During the period 1980–92, there were ten election campaigns fought in Milan at all levels (municipal to European), and while not all were as costly as a parliamentary contest, they undoubtedly represented a considerable financial burden for the parties and candidates.

A central issue raised by the kickback scandal is the nature of the relationship between businesses and politicians: were the businessmen corrupters or victims? While the payoffs allowed the firms that paid to land lucrative contracts without having to bid competitively for them, and while they could often simply add the kickbacks to the price they charged, so that the taxpayers ended up bearing the burden, they at least claimed that the bribes were also cutting into their profits. As one builder, Beltrami Gadola, stated: 'the entrepreneurs can't take it any longer . . . Because the practice of kickbacks is bringing businesses to their knees. The demands [of the politicians] are so exorbitant that they don't leave margins for profit'.[61] On the other hand, while this may have been the situation of the individual firm, the firms collectively, especially the larger ones, could have called a halt to the practice earlier; evidently, this was not to their advantage.[62] Nor does the argument that the firms were powerless victims hold for the payments made by construction associations in return for favourable legislation.

The relationship could most accurately be described as a symbiotic one, in which both sides saw certain advantages, although it was clearly less essential to the entrepreneurs than to the politicians, and some business-men who felt they would do better in a more competitive environment eventually rebelled against it. The scandal also demonstrates the particu-lar role of the construction industry (and other industries that supply the state sector) in political corruption and party finance, though the involve-ment of construction companies controlled by the largest conglomerates (Cogefar and Sasib, a De Benedetti company) involves further ramifica-tions. This role of the construction industry has often been noted in dis-cussions of Japanese political corruption as well. Moreover, the fact that all parties that had ever governed at the local level (i.e. the PDS [ex-PCI] as well as the DC, PSI, PRI, and PSDI) were involved in the system shows the extent to which a wide-open politics of interests characterized major decisions in this sector. If 150 billion lire had been paid over ten years in Milan, admittedly Italy's richest city, one can only speculate about the total amount collected by the parties in this manner; as total public works spending amounted to some 70 trillion lire per annum, about half spent by the central government and half at the local level, the potential for cor-ruption was immense.

Obviously direct payments were not the only form of support com-panies provided to politicians. As we have noted, state industries might supply secretarial help to members of parliament; other favours, such as travel, might also be provided. Money is not, however, the only tool busi-nesses use to influence politicians, nor, as we have suggested above, may it be the most effective. They also engage in intense lobbying on a large number of issues, presenting information and argument and seeking to build coalitions of supporters in parliament. Sometimes, as we have noted, deputies or party office-holders may act as paid lobbyists. The coalitions of deputies often cross party lines, forming so-called 'transversal parties'. Some are bound together by objective links – e.g. they are from the same city or region – while others are recruited by lobbyists who provide them with background information, of which they are often desperately short: the parliamentary groups frequently work in isolation from the party bureaucracies. Some lobbyists claim the deputies' behaviour can be capri-cious and lack discipline,[63] and that their general cultural level is low. They are therefore open to influence from lobbyists armed with persua-sive arguments. The 'transversal parties' include both government and opposition members, and often operate in committees, which may pass laws if neither a fifth of the committee members nor a tenth of all the deputies request that they be referred to a plenary session of the chamber.

In committee sessions, log-rolling and compromises between the various interests may take place with little public scrutiny.

On larger issues, however, it is necessary to approach not only ordinary deputies but the policy-makers – ministers, their undersecretaries, and their advisers in the parties and the bureaucracy. The same techniques are used, but here the lobbyists face better prepared opposite numbers, who may have their own agendas dictated by the party's electoral interests or ideology.[64]

Considerable lobbying effort is also directed towards the bureaucracy. While the civil service have not supplanted the politicians in policy-making, they may be key sources of policy advice. Furthermore, they are responsible for many regulations and administrative acts of great importance for business, including many major state purchases, and they can neutralize their ministers' efforts by not applying laws or regulations vigorously. Lobbyists complain that, while some senior officials are dynamic and progressive, many are conservative, resistant to change, and culturally limited. The upper ranks of the bureaucracy, recruited mainly from the South and with legal and humanistic training, were traditionally sympathetic to the Christian Democrats, and many owe their promotions to political support rather than professional competence. They are especially opposed to changes that would threaten their jobs or bureaucratic fiefdoms. Therefore, lobbyists often find dealing with the civil service frustrating and even communication with it difficult. On the other hand, civil servants, while not needing large sums for political campaigns, often welcome personal favours such as invitations to conferences, travel, etc. And in spite of their position, they often lack the information, background, or resources they need to do their jobs well, and therefore are glad of the logistical support of an interest group. For example, the Confindustria employees who work at the Ministry of Industry assist the Ministry in communicating policies to the membership; this synergistic relationship described by LaPalombara continued to operate long after his field work in the 1950s.[65]

At the same time, industrialists exercise a more diffuse but no less important influence on political decisions through the mass media, which shape public opinion and directly influence politicians. One of the major groups, Berlusconi's Fininvest, has its principal holdings in the media, including three private television networks and a major daily, *Il Giornale*, but some of the others also have direct links to the communications sector. Fiat owns the only Turin daily, *La Stampa*, which is also one of the major national dailies; it also has a key share in the holding company that owns the *Corriere della Sera*, the largest national daily. The second-largest daily by circulation, *La Repubblica*, was the object of an intense struggle between Fininvest and a group allied to De Benedetti, eventually won by the latter. Many of these outlets are run at a deficit, and therefore subsidized by the parent company. For instance, it has been estimated that business spent *c.*45 trillion lire on communications of all types (advertising, public relations, etc.) in 1988, much of this shaping public opinion directly or indirectly.[66]

These multiple advantages, and the power that derives from its central role in the capitalist economy, should allow business to exercise its influence in a largely physiological, unobserved way. However, Italian capital has, since the end of the DC regime, adopted a progressively more public stance on major issues of economic policy. Its leaders have engaged in more frequent public statements, sometimes openly critical of the government, sometimes lending vigorous support. Confindustria departed in part from its traditional 'governmental' stance in the 1990s, particularly after the centre-left Prodi government took office in May 1996. In April 1997 it held its first 'demonstration' against the government's budgetary policy. With the re-election of Berlusconi in 2001, on the other hand, it took a much more partisan, pro-governmental stance than it had during most of the DC era.

It would be tempting to connect the use of these new, more public political instruments to the end of the privileged channel secured by corruption. However, this conclusion would be too hasty, as the unprecedented demands of the Maastricht criteria and the government's determination to meet them, combined with the pressure on the left against cuts to the social safety net, are sufficient in themselves to account for this new departure in the later 1990s. Corruption was never a major factor in large-scale macroeconomic and budgetary decisions; they involve different actors and a more public and conflictual political process.

## Conclusion

The evidence we have examined suggests that business interests in Italy do not rule directly through a party of their own; government was dominated until 1992 by the Christian Democrats, a 'regime party' with a strong base in the petty bourgeoisie. The second major governing party, the PSI, was less rooted in a distinct social base and therefore more flexible, but was composed of political entrepreneurs whose objectives were often antithetical to those of business. Only two of the smaller coalition partners, the Liberals and Republicans, could be considered unconditionally pro-business. Since 1992 the system has been more complex, but the parties of the centre-right are still close to the petty bourgeoisie, though they have shed some of the old regime's clientelistic appendages and moved closer to small industry than the DC and its allies had been. The strong support for the second Berlusconi government by D'Amato's Confindustria is a reflection of this *rapprochement*. It does not mean that industry as a whole, particularly the largest firms, are prepared to do the same: their show of support for him in 2001 was strictly provisional. The Berlusconi government has shown an overly intransigent attitude towards the unions, has not introduced measures of specific interest to large industry, and, as the events leading up to the resignation of Renato Ruggiero as Foreign Minister in 2002 demonstrated, is insufficiently pro-European for the large firms.

On the other hand, business lobbies are strong and well organized for the pursuit of sectoral advantages – subsidies, a favourable regulatory regime, permits, licenses, and contracts. Here the transversal parties come into play, in a political context that resembles in many ways the American Congress, and has many points in common with Theodore Lowi's 'interest-group liberalism', where key interests exert powerful influence over the committees overseeing their sectors.[67] This interplay of interests, though, does not extend to major decisions of macroeconomic policy, which, as we shall see, is the province of the Bank of Italy and a specialized policy network, or to the social policy and budgetary issues that transcend individual sectors and are bound up with the legitimation of the system as well as economic performance.

# 7 Making Italian macroeconomic policy

In this chapter we shall be concerned with the formulation of macro-economic policy, and in particular with monetary policy – i.e. interest rates and exchange rates. These are closely related to the other aspect of macro-economic policy, fiscal policy: the government's spending, taxing, and borrowing, which is the subject of the next chapter. In the macroeconomic field, it is not always easy to deduce the behaviour of capitalists from their production profile, as the effects of a policy are not immediately obvious; rather, it is filtered through a lens of forecasts, economic theories, and opinions; often factors such as prevailing views or prejudices may intervene. Institutions and ideology affect preferences. International pressures are very strong in this area, first from currency and money markets, and second from other countries and international institutions. Political parties and the rest of the political system have an important role, but their positions are also filtered through the same sort of lens of views and prejudices as the capitalists hold. For these reasons, among others, a strong independent state institution, the Bank of Italy, has been able to exercise considerable power in the field of monetary policy. It has tended, in recent times, to act according to the long-term economic interest of Italian capital, as it has conceived it, regardless of the positions and pressures of the various representatives of business. This behaviour matches well the expectations of the state derivationist approach (see above, Chapter 1).

There have been a considerable number of theories advanced about the determinants of monetary policy, and, in particular, the determinants of Italy's shift from a soft-currency country, with high inflation and a depreciating lira, to a member of the European Monetary Union, with the much 'harder' euro as its currency. Dyson and Featherstone, in their major study,[1] argue that business interests and other 'sectoral groups' had little role in the evolution of monetary policy, because of its esoteric nature, international ramifications, and uncertain policy effects. They stress instead the action of policy entrepreneurs seeking to overcome the immobilism of domestic politics, and the political imperative for Italian leaders of remaining in the 'first division' of European countries. Their account still leaves open the question of why policy entrepreneurs, such as leading civil servants, embraced a view of Italy's economic interests that made European monetary unification a desirable goal.

Thomas Oatley argues against the fashionable thesis that increased capital mobility forced Italy to seek a harder currency, and instead stresses that the long-term goal of policy-makers was to bring about a shift in income from labour to capital, to allow for productive investment.[2] This view is closer to the position argued here, but, while he explores in more depth the political basis of the consensus for monetary stabilization, Oatley also does not relate it to the pressures being exerted by industry. Jeffry Frieden, in a series of articles and books on monetary politics, has laid more stress on the interests of business actors. He has proposed a four-fold division of business interests, suggesting that those involved in international transactions will favour a fixed exchange rate: exporters will want it fixed low, while international investors and bankers will tend, *ceteris paribus*, to want it fixed high. On the other hand, domestic producers who compete with imports will want a cheap and floating currency, while those in the non-tradable sector will want it high and are relatively indifferent to its volatility.[3] This is a very useful starting point for an analysis of business interests; in later work, Frieden has integrated other factors, such as institutions and public opinion.[4]

Walsh also combines a similar analysis of different business groups' interests with institutional factors, specifically the closeness of the links between banks and industry; in the Italian case, his account makes it difficult to explain the decision to enter the EMU, given the identification of the banking sector within industry.[5] In an article that is much closer to the policy-makers' own perspective, Chiorazzo and Spaventa highlight the more technical factors that militated in favour of Italy's entry – in particular, the reduction in interest expenditure by the government as markets came to believe that it would in fact join the euro in January 1999, which allowed it to enter a 'virtuous circle'.[6] Their account tells in favour of a view which stresses the autonomy of state institutions, by suggesting they can perceive and formulate their own goals.

The fundamental division we have identified above (Chapter 3) within Italian capital parallels Frieden's typology in good measure: the large exporting firms, and the banking interests close to them, such as Mediobanca, can be expected to support a fixed exchange rate; given their close relationship, both can be expected to favour a relatively low rate of exchange. On the other hand, smaller firms export and invest less abroad (see Tables 7.1 and 7.2) and their position on the currency is shared by large producers of non-tradables, such as Berlusconi's Mediaset. They tend to rely more on various forms of subsidies and preferences which they fear may be eliminated, either directly or indirectly, by further European integration. In the specific case of EMU, the need to reduce the budget deficit to secure entry naturally led to more critical attention on the part of the government to the problem of tax evasion.

*Table 7.1* Percentage of firms exporting, by size, 1998

| No. of employees | Percentage of firms in size group exporting |
| --- | --- |
| 1–19 | 3.4 |
| 20–99 | 46.2 |
| 100+ | 61.1 |

Source: ISTAT, Statistiche del commercio estero, Tav. 5.1.1, consulted at http://www.coeweb. istat.it, 21 Feb. 2002.

*Table 7.2* Outward foreign direct investment by size of investing firm, 1 January 1994

| No. of employees in Italy | Percentage of total no. of employees abroad |
| --- | --- |
| 1–499 | 11.1 |
| 500–1,999 | 7.8 |
| 2,000–9,999 | 20.6 |
| 9,999+ | 60.4 |
| Total | 100.0 |

Source: Reprint data base, cited in *Previsioni dell'economia italiana*, IX, 1 (June 1995), tav. 44, p. 137.

In the macroeconomic field, however, the form of representation of business interests also shapes those interests.[7] Individual enterprises typically leave the development of policy in this field, and lobbying and pressure for this policy, to Confindustria. In the case of many small and medium firms, this appears in normal times to be an esoteric area where only experts can discern the best course. Confindustria, in turn, attempts to forge a common front of large and small firms, and to mask any divisions within the united bourgeois phalanx, though the influence of Fiat remained predominant down to 2000. It too has a research department, though not nearly as good as the Bank of Italy's. Whatever the technical sophistication of its positions, Confindustria did succeed to a fair degree in keeping small and medium firms 'on side' on issues such as the currency, in part because the large firms also saw the advantage of devaluation and were not won to the more rigorous policies of the Bank of Italy until several years after their initiation: so much so that a spokesperson of Confapi, its rival for the representation of small business, stated the two groups saw eye to eye on these issues.[8]

While Confindustria does represent many firms' views, the largest groups also press their own views directly on the government and the Bank. Fiat is in a particularly strong position, having its own corps of lobbyists as well as predominant influence in Federmeccanica and Confindustria. The large groups have not been restrained in the same way as Confindustria by the need to conciliate the small and medium firms.

Another even more significant institutional factor affecting macroeconomic policy formation was (and remains, in the new context of EMU) the Bank of Italy. This prestigious institution, while not enjoying the broad autonomy of the German Bundesbank, for instance, has more independence from the government than would appear from the formal arrangements that govern it. This autonomy, as we shall see, has grown since the 1970s. Epstein and Schor, in a valuable contribution, argue that the more autonomous a central bank is from the government the more open it is to the influence of capital.[9] This does not appear to be always borne out in the case of the Bank of Italy. The very weakness of Italian capital in the 1970s, and the presence of stronger constraints in the form of a highly mobilized union movement and an unfavourable international conjuncture, reduced the Bank's room for manoeuvre. In the 1980s, the state allowed the Bank greater autonomy; it used this autonomy to pursue policies which contributed to the long-term health of the Italian economy, but were often in contrast with the immediate interests and demands expressed by capital. The Bank was the conduit through which the external constraint of membership in the European Monetary System influenced Italian economic policy; this was no doubt part of the intention of many of the decision-makers involved.

The Bank, founded in 1894, is formally controlled by the 'participants', a group of major banks and credit institutions, who choose the Superior Council. The Governor of the Bank is chosen by the government, but he cannot be removed by it and has no fixed retirement age. Traditionally, there has been little or no political interference in the choice of the Governor, who comes from within the staff of the Bank. Carlo Azeglio Ciampi (Governor 1979–93), for instance, was selected by his predecessor, Paolo Baffi, and Antonio Fazio was selected when Ciampi had become Prime Minister. The Bank's income, furthermore, is derived from its own holdings of government securities of various types. It is therefore not beholden to Parliament for appropriations, and is able to offer high salaries and generous benefits to a large staff. It was under Governor Guido Carli (1960–76) that the Bank paid particular attention to developing a prestigious modern research department. The Bank competed with the universities for the best young economics graduates, and was able to offer substantially better remuneration. The fact that virtually all of these had had graduate training at British or American universities further enhanced the Bank's prestige. Its contacts with the international financial community also gave its views weight. This is one of the reasons for the often noted 'intellectual subjection' of the Ministry of the Treasury to the Bank.

The Bank's prestige is further enhanced by its reputation for integrity and stance above party politics. Appointments are not politically controlled – some senior Bank officials were Communists, even before they entered the parliamentary majority in 1976. The PCI, as we have noted, was surprisingly supportive of the Bank and its autonomy, because it perceived that it was one of the few state institutions independent of the DC. It did this even in spite of the often deflationary direction of the Bank's policy. When Paolo Baffi was accused of corruption because the Bank of Italy, in the exercise of its supervisory duties, was impeding some of the banks' risky salvage operations in the chemical sector, the PCI sprang to his defence. One Communist parliamentarian suggested Baffi was under attack because he was resisting the clientelistic manoeuvres of Christian Democratic bankers.[10] The DC, however, often supported the Bank because it agreed with its policies. The Socialists were perhaps more prepared than others to criticize the Bank openly, as Craxi did while Prime Minister in 1985.[11] More recently, the first Berlusconi government attempted in August 1994 to impose an outsider as Director-General, because it was opposed to the Bank's recent decision to raise interest rates. This attempt failed, but the next in line for the job, Tommaso Padoa Schioppa, was passed over in favour of the junior deputy, Vincenzo Desario (see below, p. 140). This has remained a unique instance of political interference.[12] Similarly, the Bank does not welcome open lobbying from interest groups, though of course it maintains contacts on an ongoing basis with bodies such as Confindustria, so that exchanges of views and proposals occur constantly.

Several institutional developments of the early 1980s further increased the Bank of Italy's autonomy. The most noteworthy was the 'divorce' of the Bank from the Treasury in July 1981. This eliminated the rule that the Bank was obliged to buy all government bonds that had not been sold at the reserve price on the open market. When the Bank bought bonds, it was in essence financing a part of the government deficit by printing money. The divorce was therefore an important step towards a policy of tighter money and higher interest rates. The Bank pressed for this step, which would both promote its policy goals and increase its institutional autonomy. According to some observers, it felt compelled to do so to preserve its autonomy after the 1979 attacks which had led to Baffi's resignation.[13] At the same time, the Bank has attempted to reduce its use of administrative controls for which it required the approval of the Ministry of the Treasury – such as the *massimale*, or limit on the growth of banks' loans. It increasingly relied, throughout the 1980s, on open market operations over which it has complete control, such as the sale and purchase of Treasury bonds and foreign currencies.[14]

The Ministry of the Treasury also plays a role in setting macroeconomic policy: it must formally agree to the administrative measures adopted by the Bank (e.g. the *massimale*) and the discount rate on deposits by the banks. Generally, in the 1980s, its power was eroded. Only when there has been a capable Minister in office (e.g. Beniamino Andreatta or Giuliano Amato) has it exercised a major influence.

Monetary policy since 1973 can be divided into four major phases. In the first, from the oil shocks to 1981, Italy attempted to deal with the consequences of high inflation as best it could, and was forced to follow a policy of devaluation. From 1981 to 1992, the Bank of Italy was able, with the more or less willing support of the government, to follow a 'strong lira' policy, tightening monetary policy to counterbalance the rising government debt, and devaluing only when necessary to avoid loss of competitiveness on world markets. This kept the currency within the European Monetary System but eventually led to such a severe overvaluation that it was forced to leave the EMS by a speculative attack in September 1992. From then until 1996 the lira was allowed to float towards a more realistic level, with various fluctuations. In the fourth phase, it rejoined the EMS in December 1996, as part of Italy's effort to enter the European Monetary Union in the first group of countries, and objective which it achieved in 1999. From that point, Italy has ceased to have an independent monetary policy – the Bank of Italy is represented on the board of the European Central Bank, but as one of eleven member countries.

This chapter will be principally concerned with the three latter phases; we shall examine the influence of the various factors we have discussed on the formation of monetary and credit policy in Italy.

## The 'strong lira' policy (1981–92)

In the 1980s, the policy of the Bank of Italy was conditioned by a series of international constraints very different from those of the 1970s. In particular, Italy's joining the European Monetary System (EMS) in March 1979 placed serious limits on the degree to which it could use the instrument of devaluation to achieve payments equilibrium. Instead, given the government's inability to use fiscal policy for macroeconomic goals, the Bank was impelled to keep interest rates relatively high in order to prevent a fall in the value of the lira.

The EMS was an agreement between a group of European states (in the early 1980s, West Germany, France, Italy, Belgium, the Netherlands, Denmark, Luxemburg, and Ireland) to allow their currencies to fluctuate only within a limited range *vis-à-vis* the other currencies in the system. The decision to enter the EMS, taken in December 1978, owed more to the political situation of the time than to technical economic considerations, or even the pressure of capitalists, workers, and their interest groups. The prevalent opinion among experts, including the Bank of Italy, was that Italian entry was at least premature, and that certain conditions needed to be negotiated to account for Italy's special needs.

The issue, however, was seen by the political right as a good one on which to provoke the end of the already dying coalition of 'national solidarity', by forcing the Communists to vote against the government in Parliament. The Liberals, Republicans, and Social Democrats, as well as the right wing of the Christian Democrats, were strongly in favour of immediate entry for this reason. The President of Confindustria, Guido Carli, apparently came around to the same view at the last minute (this is an interesting and not atypical example of the ambiguity of the business position on the currency). The rest of the DC and the Socialists wanted a 'gradual' entry, while the Communists were not opposed in principle, but wanted stronger guarantees before Italy joined.[15] There was also pressure on the government for Italy to join at once so as to be seen as a full participant in European integration, and this factor weighed heavily on Prime Minister Giulio Andreotti.

Although the Bank of Italy's viewpoint did not prevail, this episode illustrates well the autonomy of political institutions as a whole in this field of economic policy-making. While firms had begun to restructure in 1976, they were still not healthy enough by 1978 to embark whole-heartedly on a risky enterprise such as joining the EMS. The political right, however, was less cautious, and believed that the contest for political power was ultimately more important than the current state of firms' balance-sheets. However crude their motives, their political instinct was in this case sound. In addition, of course, Andreotti and his advisers foresaw that entry into the EMS would eventually bring external pressure to bear on industry to control wage costs, and on government to control its deficit. While this was an underlying factor, it was not, as we have seen, the only or the determinant one in the decision.

The permitted range of fluctuation around each currency's 'central parity' in the EMS was $+/-6$ per cent for the Italian lira and Irish punt, and $+/-2.25$ per cent for the other currencies. If the exchange rates were in danger of exceeding these limits, the central banks intervened in the market to keep them within the agreed bounds. Periodic realignments of the central parities were also permitted in the early years: from March 1979 to January 1987 there were eleven such re-alignments, and the central parity of the lira in terms of the deutschmark fell by 36.5 per cent. However, from 1982 on these re-alignments were the result of negotiation, rather than unilateral action by the countries involved, and this led to a certain amount of co-ordination of national economic policies.[16] From 1987 on, there were no more re-alignments until Italy's exit from the EMS in 1992.

Since Italy experienced a higher rate of inflation than most of the other members of the EMS during this period, the real rate of exchange of the lira appreciated. That is, in spite of the re-alignments, Italy was not able to compensate entirely for its inflation rate by devaluing its currency. This led the Bank of Italy to pursue more restrictive policies than it otherwise would have had to do in order to control inflation. Furthermore, the leading country of the EMS was West Germany, which followed a consistently conservative monetary course, putting stability of the currency, the control of inflation, and balance of payments equilibrium ahead of growth. The West German Bundesbank, the central bank, is notably autonomous from the political authorities, and this made it easier for it to pursue a restrictive course. This policy was then transmitted, via the EMS, to Italy and the other member states.[17] Its negative effects on the lira were partly alleviated, however, by the rise in value of the American dollar *vis-à-vis* all the EMS currencies in the period 1981–85.

The external constraint represented by the EMS provides the most important explanation for the restrictive policies, particularly the high interest rates, followed by the Bank of Italy in the 1980s. Domestic interest rates had to be kept sufficiently high to attract foreign capital (and prevent outflows of Italian capital) so that the exchange rate could be kept high (the current account was in deficit for six of the first nine years of Italian membership in the EMS). Furthermore, they also had to be kept high to brake domestic inflation; while an independent policy objective of the Bank, this also became necessary to ensure the competitiveness of Italian exports, since continual devaluation was no longer an option. The alternative view that the principal reason for high interest rates was the governmental deficit is implausible, as there is little evidence of 'crowding out' of private borrowers by the state, and the rate of saving by both families and businesses was notably high. The public debt could have been financed even at lower real rates of interest, particularly in view of the range of administrative controls available to the Bank and the Treasury. Even the aim of controlling inflation may no longer be well served by high interest rates, as they lead to the injection of more purchasing power into the economy through the interest paid on the public debt, which, at high real rates, may nullify the depressive effect of tight money on business expansion and consumer spending. This is especially the case when, as in the later 1980s, firms have become cash-rich, consumer credit is relatively underdeveloped, as it is in Italy, and bonds are widely held by people of relatively modest incomes with a high propensity to spend. The inescapable conclusion is that Italy's external monetary relations were the primary reason for high real domestic interest rates.[18]

As Table 7.3 demonstrates, real interest rates, which had been negative throughout the later 1970s, became positive in 1981 and increased throughout the decade. Because of the 'exchange risk', as well as the inflation differential, Italian rates rose higher than West German ones.

The role of macroeconomic policy in the restructuring of Italian capital in the 1980s has been the subject of some debate. Throughout the period, the Bank of Italy's relatively restrictive course kept real interest rates high and allowed the lira to appreciate in real terms against other currencies (see p. xi, above): while the nominal effective exchange rate fell by 30 per cent, the real exchange rate of the lira (taking account of differences in inflation) rose by 15 per cent. The disadvantages of this policy for many businesses are obvious, but there are also grounds for believing that some capitalists benefitted from it, and in many cases were aware that they would benefit. There were clearly divisions within the capitalist class on

*Table 7.3* Real long-term interest rates, 1970–99 (percentages)

| 1970 | 0.8 | 1980 | −4.4 | 1990 | 3.9 |
|------|------|------|------|------|------|
| 1971 | −0.1 | 1981 | 0.8 | 1991 | 5.1 |
| 1972 | 0.3 | 1982 | 2.0 | 1992 | 8.3 |
| 1973 | −4.3 | 1983 | 2.8 | 1993 | 7.0 |
| 1974 | −7.9 | 1984 | 3.6 | 1994 | 6.8 |
| 1975 | −6.3 | 1985 | 4.4 | 1995 | 6.8 |
| 1976 | −4.6 | 1986 | 3.3 | 1996 | 3.9 |
| 1977 | −3.7 | 1987 | 4.3 | 1997 | 4.3 |
| 1978 | −0.6 | 1988 | 3.6 | 1998 | 2.2 |
| 1979 | −2.4 | 1989 | 5.1 | 1999 | 3.2 |

Sources: 1970–83: OECD Economic Outlook, *Historical Statistics 1960–1983* (Paris: OECD, 1985), p. 102; 1984–91: OECD Statistics Directorate, *Historical Statistics 1960–1994* (Paris: OECD, 1996), p. 108; 1992–99: *OECD Historical Statistics 1970–1999* (Paris: OECD, 2001), p. 94. Real interest rates are defined as rates on long-term government bonds deflated by the GDP price deflator.

these issues; furthermore, as Offe and others have pointed out, the long-term best interests of capital are unknowable in any case.[19] These divisions and the particular difficulty of determining the interests of capital in a field that can be well understood only by those with considerable expertise allowed the Bank to act with considerable autonomy from the capitalist class. The government, in the 1980s, played a secondary role, with the political institutions acting mainly as the channel for the pressure of some elements of industry opposed to the Bank's policy of economic rigour.

There is a large body of opinion which credits the 'strong lira' and tight money policy of the Bank of Italy with providing a powerful stimulus to the renaissance of Italian business in the 1980s.[20] Unable to rely on devaluation, firms were forced to become more efficient, shedding unnecessary labour and adopting new cost-saving machinery and processes. They became more resistant to wage demands as well. This process of restructuring occurred with considerable governmental assistance, particularly in the form of the reduction in social security contributions and legislation permitting early retirements in industry. An alternative approach to the erosion of firms' price advantages was the improvement of quality; this path was taken by some, but the attempt to contain costs was the primary response. Hence investment in cost-reducing machinery increased in the 1980s, and productivity grew rapidly. In this way the long-term restructuring of Italian industry was favoured by the Bank's policy.

There were other, more particular benefits for various sectors of industry that flowed from the relatively high exchange rate. Raw materials and food imports, mostly priced in dollars, became relatively cheaper. This was a general benefit to the whole economy, which was augmented by the fall in the world price of oil in 1986. The financial sector benefitted from a stable exchange rate, and investment abroad became more attractive for firms.

On the other hand, the evidence is strong that capitalists themselves did not fully foresee or appreciate the benefits of a stronger currency. Many sources refer to industry as the 'party of devaluation', and when I pointed out to one member of Parliament that large firms and Confindustria said they were opposed to it his response was 'Shameless lies!'[21] Business representatives were readier to admit that devaluation was favoured more strongly by small companies, especially in traditional sectors such as clothing and leather goods.[22] These are the sectors which send the largest shares of their exports to the United States and other dollar-area countries. Other industries, like automobiles, appliances, and machine tools, rely primarily on the European market; the EMS prevented them from suffering from a rise in the nominal value of the lira. However, large industry also often urged devaluation, and periodically generated pressure for it.

Yet another reason why industry was unhappy with the 'strong lira' policy initiated in 1981 was that currency instability and frequent devaluations provided the opportunity for speculative profits, especially for large firms with extensive operations abroad and therefore large amounts of foreign currency at their disposal. Indeed, some economists believe that large industries purposely unleashed attacks on the lira in order to provoke a devaluation.[23] Italy's entry into the EMS did not put an end to devaluations, but it did restrict their size and frequency. Some speculative attacks were resisted and beaten back by the Bank: e.g. in August 1987.

While the Bank's tight money policy and 'strong currency option' flowed from Italy's membership in the EMS, we can date the former from the credit squeeze of March 1981 and the latter from February–June 1982, when the lira was allowed to appreciate in real terms to its highest level since 1975. The available evidence points to business opposition to this policy in the first half of the 1980s. After 1985, this opposition softened as most firms' positions improved and many realized the long-term benefits that flowed from the Bank's policy.

In June 1980, shortly after Italy's entry into the EMS, Umberto Agnelli of Fiat gave a famous interview to *La Repubblica*, asking for both the devaluation of the lira and permission to reduce the work force by means of massive lay-offs.[24] In fact, the firm was already about to begin preparations for the September lay-offs which marked a turning point in Italian industrial relations. In spite of intense lobbying, however, the Bank refused the request for devaluation. It was especially offended by the manner in which Agnelli had attempted to exercise pressure on it; however, the very choice of a newspaper interview demonstrates that in this situation even the Agnellis had no special, more discreet channels when it came to major issues of policy.[25]

This incident was perhaps the most striking illustration of capitalists' general opposition to the Bank's restrictive policies in this period. When the Bank did devalue in March 1981, this was accompanied by an increase in the discount rate from 16.5 to 19 per cent and other restrictive measures. Confindustria was strongly critical of the government's new policy, arguing that wage restraint was the only remedy needed by the economy. Vittorio Merloni, the President, was attempting to play to small and medium industry, but this line was not unwelcome to Fiat, either. Textile manufacturers, on the other hand, were 'euphoric' about the devaluation, as they were so dependent on export markets.[26] When the lira, along with the French franc, was devalued by a further 3 per cent in October, however, Franco Mattei, the Vice-President of Confindustria, criticized Mitterand for drawing Italy into a further devaluation by his expansionist policies.[27] This demonstrates that some of the more far-sighted business spokespeople realized that restrictive policies could bring significant benefits. Finally, as late as July 1985 (on the eve of a further 6 per cent devaluation), Confindustria produced an economic policy document which warned against a credit squeeze, which would hurt industry, and stated that using only monetary policy and the strong currency option 'is a vain and harmful operation because it penalizes the productive structure'.[28] The document instead called for structural changes, such as a reduction of the state deficit, to promote growth and deal with the country's problems. While another devaluation did follow the writing of the document, the Bank did not abandon either the tight monetary policy or the strong currency option for the long term.

The policy of tight money and high interest rates, inaugurated with the credit squeeze of 1981, also had a positive side for some other important interests in Italy. While the banks were relatively unimportant as a political pressure group, and saw their own interests as tightly bound up with those of manufacturing industry, as Walsh points out,[29] they drew large and easy profits from this policy. Many Italian banks were rather unwilling, or perhaps unable, to evaluate the risks involved in industrial credit, and preferred to act as intermediaries placing depositors' funds in safe state or blue-chip bonds. In this capacity, they have functioned as the representatives of the large mass of small savers who hold government bonds and derive great benefit from a high interest rate policy. As the banks are the sole bidders at the auctions of state bonds, they can act as a cartel to keep rates fairly high. In this way the savers, who would normally be an atomized and relatively powerless group, have acquired a certain amount of influence over the credit market.

These small savers also have a considerable amount of political power: most of them belong to the traditional clientele of the DC, the petty bourgeoisie. As the peasantry declined in numbers, this group of rentiers stepped in to fill the gap in the Christian Democratic power bloc. They are used to paying little or no tax on their income (cf. the tax-free status of state bonds until 1986, and the low rate imposed since then), and the DC was also aware that the high-interest policy generates consensus among them. Therefore, they had as their political representatives not only the banks, but also the DC and many members of the other governing parties as well. Over half of state bonds are in the hands of these small savers (see Table 7.4, which excludes short-term bonds, where small savers predominate), and much of the capital invested in them by financial intermediaries, such as mutual funds and banks, is derived from their savings as well. In 1991, over half of all the investments of families (excluding cash and deposits) were in state and other public sector bonds.[30] Pressure from these investors was an added incentive for keeping interest rates high, even though it led to the inflation of the public debt.

As they became more cash-rich as the 1980s progressed, more and more firms also invested in state bonds; the high rates of return made them exceedingly attractive. Banks and other financial companies were of course able to profit from high rates. Furthermore, the largest companies benefitted from special low interest rates offered by the banks, such as the well-known 'Fiat rate', 1–2 per cent below prime. This cushioned them from the worst of the high rates. Indeed, they could make an easy profit investing these borrowed funds in state bonds! The same large companies also could borrow abroad, where rates were considerably lower, assuming the 'exchange risk' themselves. In addition, the interest on corporate borrowings is, of course, tax-deductible. The large firms, in a word, were able to use their superior market power to cushion themselves against the effects of tight money and even profit from it, just as they had profited most from speculation against the lira in the 1970s.

The tight money policy followed by the Bank, then, favoured all those who owned money capital, and were thus able to profit from the high rates. In the longer perspective, it also promoted the centralization and 'financialization' of Italian capital, allowing the cash-rich to take over the cash-poor, often driven to the wall by the high cost of loans. Its impact on the structure of the Italian economy, as we have seen in Chapter 3, has been significant.

On balance, then, the policy of tight money, while promoting improvements in productivity, harmed the economy as a whole by holding back economic growth. In the face of high rates of return for safe bond

*Table 7.4* Placement of Italian state bonds (medium- and long-term), 1990

|  | *Percentage* |
| --- | --- |
| Families | 47.1 (est.) |
| Firms | 10.4 |
| Institutional investors | 11.0 |
| Central bank | 6.3 |
| Banks and other financial institutions | 22.4 |
| Other | 2.8 |

Source: V. Conti and R. Hamaui, eds, *Il mercato dei titoli di Stato in Italia* (Bologna: Il Mulino, 1993), p. 321.

investments, any project with any risk involved must promise an even higher rate of return to be undertaken. However, as Kalecki pointed out,[31] capitalists are not always in favour of growth at any price. While complaining of the results of tight money, they were also satisfied with the change in the economic and social climate in their favour as the 1980s progressed. At one level, they appreciated the value of the Bank's course. Therefore, their criticisms of it were typically ambiguous. In the July 1985 document quoted above, the Confindustria blamed the state deficit rather than the Bank for high interest rates, and called for its reduction as a precondition for bringing them down.[32] Obviously, from the point of view of Confindustria, a governmental austerity programme would create the climate in which a tight-money policy would be less necessary.

Nonetheless, many firms, especially small and medium-sized ones, found the high interest rate policy extremely costly and constricting for their expansion plans. It also drained purchasing power from the domestic market, and diverted much money from consumption to saving. The administrative controls on lending, such as the *massimale* or limit on the expansion of the volume of loans, hit small firms worst because banks were unwilling to refuse their largest customers. The Confindustria was compelled to polemicize with the Bank throughout the 1980s over interest rates, but, as we have suggested, its complaints did not carry the full force that they would have had if Fiat and other large groups had been truly suffering from the Bank's policy.

The biggest 'loser' from the policy of high rates, though, was not capital, but the state. Because it was by far the largest borrower in the 1980s, many observers refer to it as a 'monopsony debtor'. In 1987, the public sector accounted for 78 per cent of increases in net liabilities and at the end of the year it accounted for 63.5 per cent of the total net liabilities of the various sectors (see Table 7.5). As many observers pointed out, the rise in interest rates was one of the main reasons for the growth of the total public debt. Cavazzuti suggests that the debt grew because the state did not wish to raise taxes, because taxes would be redistributive, and therefore preferred to finance its expenditure by borrowing.[33] Borrowing, of course, redistributes income upwards, to the holders of bonds from ordinary taxpayers. That the state has played this perverse redistributive role is very indicative of the balance of power in Italy. It is not simply a question of the political power of the petty bourgeoisie and their representatives, the banks; the Governor of the Bank of Italy, along with many other economists, also believed that a high level of saving by households is an essential structural strength of Italy's economy, and was therefore pleased to see savers rewarded (while at the same time criticizing the government deficit). The pro-rentier bias of policy was therefore also a matter of economic theory.

*Table 7.5* Net financial position of different sectors of the economy, 1987 (assets minus liabilities, billions of lire)

| Sector | Change in 1987 | Stock at end of 1987 |
|---|---|---|
| *Surplus sectors* | | |
| Households | +131,753 (91.0%) | +1,141,291 (87.5%) |
| Banking system | +5,966 (4.1%) | +136,828 (10.5%) |
| Overseas | +1,286 (0.9%) | +12,735 (1.0%) |
| Balancing item | +5,772 (4.0%) | +13,571 (1.0%) |
| Total | +144,777 (100%) | +1,304,425 (100%) |
| *Deficitary sectors* | | |
| Firms | −31,865 (22.0%) | −475,481 (36.5%) |
| Public sector | −112,912 (78.0%) | −828,944 (63.5%) |
| incl. central govt. | −102,518 (70.8%) | −732,761 (56.2%) |
| Total | −144,777 (100%) | −1,304,425 (100%) |

Source: calculated from Banca d'Italia, *Relazione del Governatore sull'esercizio 1987* (Rome, 31 May 1988), vol. II (Appendix), Tables aD37 and aD38, pp. 206–11.

## From the 1992 crisis to the return to the EMU

Eventually a combination of capital inflows and inflation generated by wage settlements in the non-tradable-goods sectors, especially the public service, made the strong lira policy increasingly punishing for Italian business by the early 1990s.[34] In spite of the mounting pressure on the lira, governments doggedly attempted to keep it within the EMS as long as possible. When French voters approved the Maastricht Treaty in a referendum by only 51 per cent to 49 per cent, however, confidence in the European Monetary System rapidly eroded and speculative movements against its weaker currencies intensified. Between the beginning of June and mid-September 1992, a total of forty-eight billion dollars was spent to attempt to prop up the lira at its parity within the EMS, but by early September signs of a lack of confidence in the currency were appearing within Italy as well as on the international markets: at the end of August, the treasury bond auction failed to sell 3.3 trillion lire of bonds, and customers were beginning to withdraw funds from banks in fear of extraordinary measures by the government. In this situation, the Bank of Italy raised interest rates and the lira was devalued by 3.5 per cent, but these steps were not enough to calm the markets, and finally on 15 September the lira was forced out of the range allowed by the EMS; it was not to return to it for four years.

The government and the Bank, after the crisis of September 1992, loosened monetary conditions and allowed the lira to fall: by the end of the year, it had lost *c.*20 per cent *vis-à-vis* the German mark, and 1993 saw a further small decline. These policies provided a welcome relief to businesses, which were able to increase their exports and profits as a result. The merchandise trade surplus rose from 3,852 billion lire in 1992 to

51,989 billion in 1993, an increase equal to 3 per cent of the GDP. After reaching an historic low in 1992, profit margins also recovered, slowly in 1993 and decisively in 1994.[35] These policies were accepted on all sides as a necessary adjustment after the trauma of September 1992; during the period 1992–94, moreover, the rate of inflation continued to decline, as consumer demand fell after the austerity measures announced by the government: the consumer price index reached a low of 3.7 per cent in October 1994 before beginning a new rise. This extremely fortunate conjunction of declining inflation and devaluation was what allowed exports and profits to boom. The wage moderation guaranteed by the various accords between unions and employers, particularly the July 1993 accords, played a major role as well in this export-led recovery.

However, during the first Berlusconi government this virtuous pattern was already beginning to change. In May the US Federal Reserve increased its discount rate, and a flight from weaker currencies, such as the lira, began, fuelled also by the wrangling within the new government coalition. In spite of the rise in Italian interest rates, capital continued to leave the country and the lira continued to fall. These developments, along with a temporary rise in the inflation rate in July 1994, were taken by the Bank of Italy as a signal of impending problems (which eventually did emerge, in 1995). The Bank also took into account the continuing instability of the political situation, as the three principal governing parties did not display a consistently united front, and believed that the combination of devaluation and recovery would eventually have a negative effect on the price level. Therefore, in August it raised the official discount rate from 7 to 7.5 per cent, interrupting a long series of cuts that had begun in September 1992, and took steps to limit the expansion of the money supply. This led to serious protests from within the governing coalition, with many accusing the Bank of hostility to the government, and one member of parliament suggesting an international plot against Italy, manoeuvred by the 'Jewish lobby'.[36] The government deputies were concerned about the end of devaluation and easy money.

As a result, relations between the government and the Bank cooled, and the governing parties opposed the choice of Tommaso Padoa Schioppa as Director General of the Bank, proposing instead an external candidate. Padoa Schioppa was considered too close to Carlo Azeglio Ciampi, the former Governor and Prime Minister. The candidate chosen by the Superior Council of the Bank must be ratified by the cabinet. The Governor, Fazio, defended the Bank's autonomy, and in the end a compromise candidate was chosen, Vincenzo Desario, an internal candidate but not closely identified with Ciampi.[37]

While 1994 had seen a further devaluation of the lira by nearly 10 per cent, the real monetary crisis was to come in the next year; by March, the mark had risen from 1050 to 1274 lire, and on 17 March the Italian currency lost 5 per cent of its value in one day. There was a capital flight

similar to that of September 1992. The primary reason for this instability
was the uncertain political situation, in which the Dini government lacked
a guaranteed majority and suffered from the repeated attacks of the right-
wing opposition, which insistently demanded the dissolution of parliament and a fresh election. On 16 March, Dini had secured approval of his
budgetary manoeuvre in the Chamber only because Communist Refoundation split on the issue. From the point of view of the financial markets,
this was not a firm base on which the cabinet could rely.

Another reason for the renewed crisis of the lira was the increasing
instability of international financial markets; movements of capital were
becoming extremely rapid, and hence less responsive to changes in interest rates or other manoeuvres by central banks. Instead, expectations of
future movements came to dominate, so that political instability had an
even stronger negative effect on the markets.

The actions of the Bank of Italy and the passage of the Dini government's budgetary package, with some 21 trillion lire of spending cuts and
tax increases, eventually stabilized the situation, and by the end of Dini's
term, the lira was stronger than it had been at the beginning. For the rest
of 1996, it continued to appreciate, returning to the levels of mid-1994 by
the end of the year, when it rejoined the EMS at a central parity of 990
lire to the mark, only about 1 per cent above the market quotation. An
increasingly restrictive monetary policy and the decline of inflation had
both contributed to this result, which, however, required firms to
struggle to maintain their competitive advantage. On the occasion of the
lira's re-entry into the EMS, the Confindustria stated that it would have
preferred a parity of 1050 to the mark, and the Chairman of Fiat, Cesare
Romiti, concurred. Nevertheless, this was the best rate that Ciampi, now
Minister of the Treasury, could negotiate with the other EMS members;
France, in particular, had been insisting on a higher rate for the lira,
such as 950.

In the 1992–96 period, the international exchange markets had the
greatest influence on monetary and interest rate policy, as the lira was
buffeted by strong speculative currents. In 1992 and early 1995, the
markets responded to perceived weaknesses in the political system and
the way it was addressing economic problems; from April 1995 on, they
registered the results of the struggle against inflation and the measures to
contain the government deficit, as well as the positive trade balance.
While the monetary policy pursued by the Bank of Italy, sometimes in
conflict with the preferences of the major capitalist groups, contributed
to this result, it was not the principal factor. The role of the government
in monetary policy was limited, though it was able to intervene decisively
in certain moments, such as the decision to re-enter the EMS at 990 lire
to the mark.

## Conclusions: the Bank's new role after the EMS entry

The relative weight of the various actors in the determination of macro-economic policy has changed significantly over time. Under Governor Guido Carli, the Bank of Italy was relatively autonomous from direct pressure by capital. The birth of the centre-left shifted the political centre of gravity to the left, and the nationalization of electric energy in 1962 eliminated the traditional hegemonic bloc of Italian capitalism. Carli sought to create a favourable climate for the economic plans of the centre-left, while at the same time doing everything to promote the profitability and growth of large private industry. He served the interests and goals of the government by, for instance, allowing the growth of the special credit institutions which gave loans on the basis of criteria laid down by the political authorities (economic planning, regional development, etc.). He also allowed the increase in the value of bond issues by various state and para-state institutions in the 1960s; these issues were partly responsible for the withering of the stock exchange, as they proved more attractive to savers. In return for these services to the government, Carli claimed the right to advise it on economic policy as a whole, and at the same time put the profitability of industry even ahead of the struggle against inflation, as the credit expansions of 1962 and 1973 demonstrate.

In the 1970s, the relative weakness of capital in the political sphere was reinforced by its increasingly difficult economic situation, after the growth of union power triggered by the Hot Autumn and the first oil shock. The Bank, paradoxically, found itself more constrained by this new situation, its autonomy reduced by the need to take emergency measures to protect the lira and stem accelerating inflation. Already, the power of the international money markets was beginning to make itself felt. In early 1976, the Bank was forced to take the unprecedented step of suspending the official quotation of the lira for forty days (20 January–1 March). The very weakness of capital in this conjuncture made the Bank less autonomous. Baffi, the new Governor, began to draw back from Carli's role as 'counsellor of the Prince' and concentrate on the specific responsibilities of the Bank, laying the groundwork for the increase in its autonomy that followed on the 'divorce' in 1981. Baffi's choice was made easier because the government failed to provide a clear framework of economic policy, as the centre-left governments had attempted to do in the 1960s with the chimera of economic planning.

The entry into the EMS was a primarily political decision which helped provide the missing policy framework for the Bank of Italy. Henceforth it was set on a more restrictive, 'neo-Einaudian' course (after the Liberal Treasury Minister of the late 1940s, who pursued an orthodox deflationary policy); while their training and socialization may have given the Bank's staff a propensity to follow such a course in any case, they needed an 'anchor' like the EMS in order to withstand pressures for a laxer policy. As this chapter has demonstrated, capital in the 1980s was divided on issues of macroeconomic policy; while small and medium firms pressed strongly for a more permissive stance, many larger capitalists were pulled in both directions. This division within the ranks of capital allowed the Bank considerable autonomy again, especially after 1979, once the worst of the economic emergency was over and Italian firms were in a less precarious financial position. This is the most important and interesting conclusion stemming from our discussion of this period. Moreover, as the recovery turned into a boom more capitalists began to believe that there were long-term benefits of the Bank's restrictive policy. And an important factor at the back of their minds was the influence of this policy on industrial relations: the deflationary climate permitted, indeed forced, firms to shed labour and control labour costs, weakening the unions, and forcing them to moderate their policies if they wished to reach an accommodation with the employers. The Bank therefore indirectly seconded the offensive against union power in the factory.

The autonomy the Bank had won in the early 1980s under Ciampi was used to effect in the early 1990s, particularly when pressures on the lira began to mount in 1994 and the Bank had to pursue a course that was unwelcome to the Berlusconi government. Here, however, the Bank was once again exposed to the pressure of the international money markets. Having lost the reference point of the EMS, the lira was subjected to the full weight of speculative pressure, and many of the Bank's decisions were almost obligatory, if it wanted to prevent an excessive and inflationary depreciation after the very successful devaluation that followed the September 1992 crisis. Clearly the Bank had the long-run interests of capital at heart in allowing the lira to fall after the crisis, but it was not prepared to heed what it considered short-sighted objections to its tightening of monetary policy from the summer of 1994 on. This tightening, and the eventual appreciation of the lira, were gradual but no less inexorable. That the balance of payments did not suffer, but continued to improve, demonstrates that the Bank's policy did not truly damage Italian capitalism, in spite of the protests. The Bank, acting autonomously, once again kept in view the long-term interests of capital better than capital itself.

# 8 The politics of budgets and public debt

In the period since 1992, the question of the government deficit has frequently occupied centre stage in Italian politics. While the situation was already grave by the middle and later 1980s, the signature of the Maastricht Treaty suddenly made the solution of the issue urgent. The high Italian governmental debt is rooted in the same general circumstances that produced similar debt problems in most of the major industrialized countries, but the factors peculiar to Italy which explain why the country has a total governmental debt second only to Belgium's in relative importance are mainly political, and largely related to the policies followed by the Christian Democratic regime in building support for its rule. The massive effort to solve the debt problem since 1992 has involved cuts in spending and tax increases in many areas; for the first time, they have been directed in part at the beneficiaries of the DC regime, such as the petty bourgeoisie, while public employees and workers in general have not been particularly targeted, as has been the case in many other episodes of fiscal consolidation. Nor have business interests suffered especially (other than from the general tax increases). This Italian route to fiscal consolidation is explained by the fact that it was carried out by governments with a strong non-partisan 'technical' flavour, or by the centre-left Prodi cabinet, while the right, during its brief period in office, actually showed less enthusiasm for meeting the Maastricht deficit-reduction target.

## The significance of the debt problem

Total state sector debt reached a maximum of 124.3 per cent of GDP in 1994, after which it began to decline very slightly (see Table 8.1). In 1993, the interest on the debt reached 12 per cent of GDP, a record for the industrialized world.[1] Such a large debt had several negative consequences, though they were perhaps not as serious as some commentators implied. At the popular level, government deficits are held to fuel inflation, which is particularly unwelcome to wealth-holders and rentiers. In fact, inflation is by no means a necessary consequence of high deficits, as the recent experience of Japan proves; theoretically, inflation can be controlled by

*Table 8.1* The debt–GDP ratio in Italy, 1970–97

| Year | | Year | |
|------|------|------|------|
| 1970 | 34.2 | 1984 | 73.3 |
| 1971 | 38.4 | 1985 | 81.1 |
| 1972 | 42.7 | 1986 | 85.3 |
| 1973 | 44.0 | 1987 | 89.9 |
| 1974 | 44.1 | 1988 | 92.7 |
| 1975 | 49.9 | 1989 | 96.0 |
| 1976 | 48.7 | 1990 | 98.7 |
| 1977 | 51.2 | 1991 | 101.9 |
| 1978 | 57.0 | 1992 | 108.6 |
| 1979 | 56.6 | 1993 | 115.9 |
| 1980 | 54.8 | 1994 | 124.3 |
| 1981 | 57.7 | 1995 | 123.8 |
| 1982 | 62.7 | 1996 | 124.0 |
| 1983 | 68.4 | 1997 | 121.6 |

Source: Banca d'Italia, quoted in Dino Pesole, *I debiti degli italiani* (Rome: Editori Riuniti, 1996), p. 29 (1970–95), and Banca d'Italia, *Relazione del Governatore sull'esercizio 1997* (Rome, 1998), p. 161. The debt is that of the 'state sector' (which excludes local and regional government and social security agencies) until 1995, then the debt by the EU definition, which is higher by *c.*0.5 per cent.

monetary policy, as suggested by the Mundell-Fleming model.[2] High government debt, in the second place, is held to 'crowd out' private investment in productive projects by pre-empting savings and/or pushing interest rates up.[3] Whether this effect is really produced depends on several other variables, including the rate of saving of households, the demand for capital by business, and the degree of monetization of the deficit. Furthermore, the internationalization of the economy has meant that it is more difficult for 'crowding out' to happen on the national level, though it may occur on a world scale. In the third place, the fear that the debt will have to be serviced and eventually paid off with higher taxes may act as a disincentive to businesses and consumers, leading them to invest and buy less (the so-called 'Ricardian' effect). Fourthly, the growth of debt leads to instability in the currency and securities markets, because of fears of a future 'debt crisis', and possible monetization, default, or tax increases on bondholders. This can lead to higher interest rates, as investors require a risk premium to invest in the country.[4] In addition, it can, in certain circumstances, lead to the depreciation of the currency and hence to inflation, hence increasing interest rates even further. Finally, from a directly political point of view, government debt makes public spending easier, and, to the extent that business opposes public spending, it will oppose deficits to finance it. On the other hand, government debt transfers income from working taxpayers to bondholders, who are on average wealthier (and older): it is an income-transfer programme for the well off (if older, they may also have a

lower propensity to save). If much of the debt is held abroad, these transfers can also generate balance of payments problems.

From the point of view of capital, these consequences are not all uni-
formly negative. Larger firms, at least, are able to escape the effects of any
'crowding out' by borrowing abroad. The instability of the currency
markets may provide an occasion for speculative gains, though internationally oriented businesses nevertheless prefer stability. And the income transfer involved in high debt may well be advantageous to many businesses that
themselves own bonds, and to those whose customers hold them. Nonetheless, after a certain point the advantages of high debt begin to be overshad-
owed by the disadvantages, especially when the fear of inflation and higher
future taxes begins to take hold. From the point of view of workers, the
short-term stimulus arising from deficit spending is welcome, but most of
the longer-term consequences of high debt are negative insofar as they
depress the economy and limit the growth of employment; workers generally do not have the compensation of bond interest or the ability to borrow
outside the country. The petty bourgeoisie may have some bond income,
but otherwise suffer the same negative consequences as the workers.

Of course, these theoretically informed expectations are not always
borne out in reality. For example, the experience of the recent past may
have led many Italians to expect monetization and/or inflation rather
than tax increases to deal with the debt problem, and in any case many
firms and petty bourgeois expected to evade much of the future tax
burden. Nor were the depressive effects of the debt on the economy clear
or unequivocally present: while currency instability undoubtedly discouraged foreign investors and was a problem for internationally oriented
firms, the consequent devaluation of the lira provided desperately needed
oxygen to the exporting sectors. And, until the early 1990s, only a small
portion of the debt was held abroad; even by 1997, most estimates put the
foreign-held portion of the debt at *c.* 15 per cent (see above, p. 87)).

These varying positions on the debt issue were also reflected in the
debate during the years in which the debt accumulated. But the interests
of domestic actors were not the only factor involved. International trends
and the positions adopted by the parties and interest groups were also
very significant components of the dynamic that led to the debt problem.

## Causes of the debt problem

First and foremost, Italy's public debt explosion stemmed from the same
international economic factors that were at the root of the growth of
government deficits in the entire industrialized world. These international
trends, which originated outside the Italian economy, affected government policy directly and through the interests of domestic actors. Above
all, the slowdown of economic growth after 1973 led to a structural
increase in unemployment, and hence greater expenditures, while at the

same time reducing the tax base relative to the population (see Table 8.2). In Italy, unemployment began to increase significantly in 1977, when it nearly doubled compared to the previous year. From 1973 to 1983, the ratio of unemployed to the population increased by 91 per cent, while the amount spent by the Cassa Integrazione Guadagni (Unemployment Compensation Fund) increased by 727 per cent as a percentage of the GDP.[5]

The welfare state was designed to operate as a safety net in an economy close to full employment, and could not function in the same way in the face of permanently high levels of joblessness. Ironically, Italy had just significantly enriched its welfare state (but without reaching the level of welfare provision of its more northerly European neighbours). The increase in unemployment benefits (which was, of course, only the most direct impact of the downturn on government expenditures) was greater than the growth of unemployment because those who lost their jobs were more heavily concentrated in the core sectors of the economy that were covered by the Cassa Integrazione, and because employers and unions pressed the government to respond to the crisis with more generous assistance to facilitate the restructuring of industry (the 'Extraordinary' Cassa Integrazione, financed entirely from general government revenues). This is a good example of the action of international economic forces through domestic actors' interests and demands.

At the same time, the shift of the major central banks towards tight-money policies, beginning in 1978, raised the cost of government borrowing and hence compounded the effects of the deficits that had been building up in the previous five years and subsequently increased. Even when primary surpluses were restored in 1992, high real interest costs, in excess of the growth rate of the economy, ensured that total government debt would continue to mount. The fall in inflation that these tight-money

*Table 8.2* Unemployment rates in Italy, 1971–95 (percentages)

| | | | |
|------|------|------|-------|
| 1971 | 3.2  | 1984 | 9.3   |
| 1972 | 3.7  | 1985 | 9.3   |
| 1973 | 3.5  | 1986 | 9.9*  |
| 1974 | 2.9  | 1987 | 10.2  |
| 1975 | 3.3  | 1988 | 10.5  |
| 1976 | 3.7  | 1989 | 10.2  |
| 1977 | 7.2  | 1990 | 9.1   |
| 1978 | 6.8* | 1991 | 8.6   |
| 1979 | 7.2  | 1992 | 8.8   |
| 1980 | 7.1  | 1993 | 10.2  |
| 1981 | 7.9  | 1994 | 11.3  |
| 1982 | 8.5  | 1995 | 12.0  |
| 1983 | 9.2  |      |       |

Source: *OECD Economic Survey: Italy,* various years.

Note
*New data series begins.

policies eventually induced also had another effect on government debt: the nominal GDP did not grow as fast as it would have had inflation remained high, and hence the debt–GDP ratio increased more quickly. (One might suppose that with a higher rate of inflation interest rates would have risen, thus producing the same effect, but this would not have been an automatic result, especially given the very high rates that obtained in any case in this period). In addition, of course, the tight-money policies compounded the problems of unemployment and slow growth that had begun to emerge in 1973: the severe world recession of 1981–82 was in large measure induced by these policies.

Finally, the build-up of government deficits, caused by spending increases without balancing increases in taxes, was facilitated by another major event in the international economy, the end of the Bretton Woods exchange-rate system in 1971. The relatively fixed exchange rates of Bretton Woods acted as a brake on deficit financing, as governments needed to maintain confidence in their currencies through prudent budgetary policies. With this limitation gone, governments were freer to let their currencies sink in value. This occurred dramatically in the case of the lira, which had remained pegged at 625 to the dollar for over twenty years, but sank to 870–880 by early 1977 (while the debt–GDP ratio had risen from 38 per cent to 51 per cent, admittedly only one of the factors in the currency crisis).

These essentially exogenous factors were not, however, the only explanation of the explosion of government debt. There is a consensus in the literature on state spending that there are two types of causes of the growth of government expenditure in the past century: structural and political. The first term refers to those expenditures that are necessitated by the development of the capitalist economy – for example, the growth of large cities requires urban transportation systems, and (though more controversially) the end of the rural household economy and the break-up of the extended family create the need for some form of assistance for those unable to work because of unemployment, injury, ill health, or old age. The second term refers to expenditures that result from the political pressure and struggles of their potential beneficiaries: for example, workers' struggles for improved unemployment benefits, or job-creation schemes for particular categories of workers. Under the second heading we can also place the decision on how to finance increased expenditure – through higher taxes or borrowing. Italian governments opted for the latter in large part because of the political resistance to raising taxes.

These two broad types of causes are not, of course, completely separate: political struggles may be, indeed often are, necessary even to introduce 'structural' changes. These do not occur automatically simply because they are functional to the capitalist economy, and states may fail to introduce reforms that would enhance capital accumulation significantly. This is the essential point raised by the historical derivationist approach (see Chapter 1). Furthermore, the crucial details of the administration of government programmes, including whether provision shall be entirely public or not, benefit levels, etc., are also subject to political decision.[6] In addition to these different reasons for the initiation of a programme, there may be specific, 'technical' reasons for an increase (or decrease) in the amount of money it requires: e.g. the ageing of the population, or expensive advances in medical technology. Though they may be quantitatively very significant, these may be considered subsidiary because they do not explain the origins of the programme, but only changes in its cost.

In Italy, both structural and political causes contributed to the growth of government spending and the deficit, but, if we focus on the deficit as our *explanandum,* the latter were definitely more important. While the pension system was below the European standard before 1969, and school attendance was below it until the mid-1970s, after that time increases in spending did not reflect economic needs so much as political pressures combined with technical factors that pushed up pension and other expenditures. The primacy of political causes is particularly evident if we consider the failure to increase tax revenues to match expenditure growth, especially in the 1970s.

Of the political factors increasing public expenditure, most were manifestations of long-term trends rather than responses to cyclical or structural crises of the capitalist economy. One of the most important trends was the expansion of public employment, which increased continually from 1960 to 1990.[7] In 1960, there were 1.6 million public employees (not counting state-owned industries), or 7.6 per cent of the employed labour force, while in 1990 there were 3.665 million, or 15.5 per cent of the employed labour force. While much of this increase was the natural result of the expansion of the state's activity, there were many signs of the operation of a political dynamic as well. A case in point is the educational system, which had 1.15 million employees in 1991. Education spending by the state rose from 2.1 per cent to 3.7 per cent of GDP from 1960 to 1990; during this period, the number of students in the state school system increased from 12.1 per cent to 16.4 per cent of the population (with a peak of 18.7 per cent in 1977), thanks to longer attendance at school. But at the same time, the teacher:student ratio grew by 70 per cent, from 1:15.6 to 1:9.2, a figure higher than that of any of the other major industrialized countries.[8] This increase was not the result of a conscious decision to improve the quality of education, but rather of a series of partial measures to satisfy the demands of various categories of teachers.

To confirm this interpretation, we note that in the same period the ratio of non-teaching staff to students increased four and a half times (!),[9] indicating the presence of an even stronger political dynamic. The decision-making process was theoretically centralized in the cabinet, Parliament, and the Ministry of Education, but in practice many principals and provincial superintendents of education were involved in hiring new teachers on temporary contracts; these teachers then constituted a lobby group of *precari* (untenured teachers) who pressed for permanent status, with the aid of the competing unions in the sector. Politicians were concerned about the general problem of graduate unemployment, and at the same time were susceptible to the particular pressure being exerted on them in their own constituencies and by national interest groups.

An even more striking example of the same phenomenon can be seen in the case of hospitals, where the ratio of employees to patient/days increased fivefold from 1960 to 1990.[10] (In the same period, the number of patient/days per capita actually declined, while the cost of public hospitals rose from 1.1 per cent to 2.5 per cent of GDP). Much of the increase in staff occurred in the period 1969–72, when the hospitals were allowed to set the rates they charged the social security funds. After that, along with attempts to reduce the number of hospital beds, the government provided for the regularization of the *precari* in the sector (1985), and set new staffing standards that led to an increase in employment (1988), for a total of some 145,000 new staff as a result of these two initiatives.

As in the case of education, the increases of the earlier years brought levels of quality closer to the standards of other industrial countries, while those of the later period went beyond that point, though whether the increase in personnel resulted in higher quality is very doubtful. Here decision-making was even more decentralized, as the regions, rather than the central government, were directly responsible for managing the hospitals. (The central government, however, continued to make broad regulations and provide funding). Decisions were often taken by individual administrators who in some cases treated the jobs as political patronage.

A third significant example of expenditure increases caused by political factors is old-age pensions, which became the central focus of the debate on the welfare state in the mid-1990s. Old-age and survivors' pensions increased without interruption from 1961 on, rising from 3.3 per cent to 10.3 per cent of GDP by 1990; at the same time, disability pensions rose from 1.5 per cent to 3.6 per cent of GDP, with a peak of 3.8 per cent in 1983.[11] A part of this large increase (*c.*9 per cent of GDP) can be accounted for in strictly political terms: the concession of disability pensions to large numbers of applicants, particularly in the South, functioned as a disguised form of unemployment relief. Proof of this is the large difference in the percentage of recipients in the different regions. Similarly, in the early 1980s the law was changed to facilitate early retirement on full pension by workers in companies that downsized. This was in the first place a political concession to the companies engaged in restructuring.

Another example was the extension of the system to various categories of self-employed workers, with low contribution levels that did not cover the benefits paid out. However, much of the increase in pension expenditure was due to the operation of rules and institutions that already existed in 1960, but that became much more costly as the pension system matured. For example, the retirement age was already set at sixty for men and fifty-five for women in the private sector, and a series of special provisions allowed many to retire on a full pension earlier than that. As the number of retirees, and the proportion of them covered by the public pension system and entitled to a full pension, increased, these rules operated to increase pension costs significantly. What needs to be explained politically is the inaction of governments in the face of these rising costs in the two decades from 1975 to 1994.

Increases in pension costs were also due to structural changes, and in particular the ageing of the population: those over sixty made up 13.7 per cent of the population in 1960, and 20.2 per cent in 1990. Nevertheless, this factor alone does not account for the 182 per cent rise in old-age pension expenditure as a percentage of GDP.[12] For this, political factors, including the failure to amend existing rules, have to be invoked.

All in all, the above factors can account for a large part of the growth of public expenditure in Italy. The relative lack of productivity increases in many public services – often cited by conservative scholars[13] – was not a major cause, except in the education sector. It did not enter into the spectacular increase in pension expenditure, and productivity gains were achieved in health care. Even in education, a political dynamic leading to an actual increase in the teacher:student ratio was at work, rather than simply a failure to cut that ratio through productivity improvements.

While social policies, and particularly welfare state policies, are the product of an attempt by the governing parties to construct a system of class alliances, industrial policy, including state assistance to industry and specific sectoral policies, is the subject of the interplay of interest groups and lobbies. These two logics differ from each other. The interests which take part in the bargaining over industrial policy are already established interests, primarily capitalist, and the bargaining process serves to reflect and confirm the positions of power which they already occupy thanks to their market strength, rather than their electoral significance. This logic in turn contributed to the government deficit by allowing business interests to secure favourable spending and taxation decisions.

As Pasquino has pointed out, 'the whole institutional circuit – representation, decision, execution – is fully open to the influence of interest groups and lobbies'.[14] Lobby groups develop inter-party coalitions of supporters – the so-called 'transversal parties' described above (p. 122) – which promote their laws and projects. These coalitions were favoured by the absence of any alternation in government: the DC and its allies being permanently in power, and the PCI and certain other parties (MSI, Greens, Radicals, etc.) being permanently in opposition, the intensity of partisan divisions was to some extent diminished because the stakes were not as high. This situation contributed to the 'consociational' features of Italian democracy, noted by authors such as La Palombara.[15] It is no surprise that *c.*87 per cent of the minor laws passed in committee by Parliament were supported by both government and opposition.[16] Party lines, while not as fluid as in Washington, were therefore considerably more relaxed than at

Westminster, and allowed for the sort of inter-party coalitions that can form, for instance, within specialized committees of parliament. Even during the 'Second Republic', some of the same habits have persisted.

It would be a mistake to view these coalitions, however, in the same light as the 'iron triangles' described in the literature on US politics.[17] First, their influence is restricted to a particular range of policies within an issue area, and coalitions tend to be constructed *ad hoc*. Second, the influence of the parties is stronger in Italy. Third, the groups that are able to exercise this sort of influence are mostly capitalist groups of one sort or another, very often single firms, and they operate within a framework of major policies which is already significantly biased in their favour. By and large, the effect of this interest-group activity, then, is to reinforce and replicate the existing structure of power, as determined principally by the market. Far from being an illustration of the autonomy of the state and politics from society, as Linda Weiss has suggested,[18] Italian industrial policy demonstrates the inability of the state to significantly alter the existing constellation of forces. In other spheres, the state does demonstrate a degree of 'autonomy'. But the most striking feature of its industrial policy has been a radical subordination to 'civil society'.

A striking feature of Italian industrial policy is the prevalence of general, indiscriminate measures as opposed to precisely targeted forms of assistance. As Cipolletta has noted, policies intended to deal with particular economic conjunctures have served as unintended industrial policies.[19] These policies are the result of lobbying efforts and political pressure by industry in general and its representatives, such as Confindustria. While they are available to all firms, the principal beneficiaries are often the largest companies, who are usually in the best position to take advantage of them. What appear, then, as unfocussed interventions with no element of planning behind them tend to reinforce the existing tendencies of the economy.

One of the most important forms of general assistance to industry has been the so-called 'fiscalization' of social security contributions – i.e. the assumption by the state budget of a portion of the employers' contributions. General fiscalization is akin to a tax cut for industry, one which reduces the disincentive to employ labour. In addition, some forms of fiscalization have been restricted to certain firms or types of workers: for instance, additional fiscalization was made available in the late 1970s for Southern firms and for newly hired women workers.

Another significant form of state aid, which was equally effective in promoting the renaissance of Italian industry, was financial support for the reduction of the industrial labour force. Laying off large numbers of unionized workers is not easy politically, and in some cases illegal, so that assistance in this process was most welcome. The two major forms it took were early retirement provisions implemented by the social security administration, and extraordinary payments from the Cassa Integrazione made on a case-by-case basis to workers laid off by particular firms. The

Interministerial Committee on Industrial Policy selected the sectors to benefit from the latter.

These two forms of aid accounted for the largest share of all state aid to industry. In 1983, total aid reached a maximum of 3.1 per cent of GDP (revised series), falling to 1.7 per cent in 1987. In 1983, the special fiscalization for the South accounted for 28 per cent of all aid other than capital grants to the state sector, and early retirements and the CIG for 31 per cent. In 1987, the comparable figures were 26 per cent and 36 per cent.[20] This left a relatively small proportion of the funds for targeted, promotional assistance: the fiscalization was a generalized benefit for all industry located in the South (though firms evading their social security contributions could not take advantage of it), while the early retirement and special CIG benefitted principally the heavy industrial sectors which needed above all to shed workers (steel, chemicals, and engineering). Traditional sectors, such as food, clothing, textiles, and wood products received far less than their share of special CIG payments.[21]

In addition, several other types of assistance to industry are in effect general subsidies: the Sabatini law (no. 1329, 1965) and a 1976 presidential decree (no. 902), for instance, remained in force for years and provided assisted credit for the purchase of new machinery and equipment.

At the same time, there have been attempts to provide state subsidies to particular industrial sectors, or to small and medium industry. In general, these attempts have failed; while the state has lavished many benefits on the petty bourgeoisie, it has not been successful in extending direct aid (as opposed to tax relief or tolerated evasion) to small industrialists and entrepreneurs. Instead, funds originally targeted for this and other groups have ended up in the coffers of the largest firms. This apparent paradox can be explained by the greater lobbying capacity of the large firms, their familiarity with bureaucratic procedures, and their natural tendency to think in terms of expansion of capacity.

For instance, the major industrial assistance law, no. 675 of 1977, by 1984 supported 9,287 billion lire of investment, 80.5 per cent of which was in the steel, automobile and chemical sectors, dominated by large firms.[22] Special funds set aside for small and medium industry, with the support of all parties in parliament, went unused, so that the residue was diverted in 1981 to large industry. Finally in 1984 the remaining money was transferred to a new, largely unrestricted fund that could be used to purchase any type of advanced machinery (law no. 696).[23] Similarly, the major fund of 4.7 trillion lire set up in 1982 under law no. 46 to support applied research went largely to the electronics sector, again dominated by the big firms; the same was true of the Innovation Fund administered by the Ministry of Industry and the applied research fund controlled by the parapublic financial institution, IMI.[24] Discussion in parliament on law no. 46 centred on whether the funds would be disbursed by the Ministry of Industry or IMI, with opposition senators arguing that the former was less efficient and more open to 'clientelistic' pressure. The law was strongly backed by Confindustria, and Ministry of Industry officials went so far as to publicly criticize parliament for its slowness in passing it.[25] The law's passage was in fact supported and furthered by the major industrial groups that were to end up as its major beneficiaries.

In contrast to the above ostensibly general measures, state purchasing policies and special laws relating to particular companies or sectors of the economy are openly tailored to individual situations. These are the areas in which not only lobbying and political pressure, but also bribery and corruption, are the most intense and frequent, as the 'Tangentopoli' investigations revealed. They also represent a considerable drain on the state's budget.

The industries most dependent on state purchases are the construction industry, office machinery, and industrial and electrical machinery and equipment. In construction especially, the practice of requesting kickbacks in return for contracts is widespread at all levels; and, while often represented by companies as a 'tax' imposed by the parties on them, is more the result of a collusive bargain (see above, pp. 121–122). The firms tend to form consortia which assign projects to their members, largely on the basis of historical shares of the market, and rig the bidding to secure the desired result. The kick-backs to the parties may be viewed as the price they pay for this protected, oligopolistic situation, in which they can more than recover the cost of the payments by managing their prices.[26] The result, of course, is a transfer of money from taxpayers to both politicians and firms. This was the pattern not only in much of the construction industry, which receives contracts from all levels of government, but in other normally more or less competitive sectors such as military uniforms or railway matériel; the latter deal exclusively with the national government and its agencies.

In other fields, a single supplier has enjoyed a monopoly, without the necessity of bidding – e.g. Fiat in the provision of automobiles to the government and police, Olivetti in telex machines for the post office. These arrangements cannot be explained by a lack of competing firms, for in sectors such as computers and telephone equipment the state has not favoured the one or few Italian suppliers but opened bidding to foreign firms as well (though some of them, such as IBM, have large subsidiaries in Italy). In a few cases, foreign firms have also become part of consortia which divide work on the basis of historic shares.[27] As recent investigations have shown, bribes have often, though not invariably, been paid for by these large contracts as well. While academic commentators may deplore these procurement systems which are costly and do not allow the state to undertake any real economic planning or direction, they are generally profitable to the businesses involved, at least in the short term. Even in the longer term, they may allow some firms, such as Fiat, the stable financial basis for longer-term corporate planning.

The state is also involved with individual firms as regulator, market actor, or source of funds. Here the scope for lobbying, pressure, and corruption is greatest. For example, when the Ferruzzi group sold back the ENI chemical assets to the state after the failure of the 'Enimont' merger with its Montedison holdings, the price was inflated above market value in return for kickbacks to the governing parties. This was one of the most egregious scandals uncovered by the Tangentopoli investigations: a straightforward corrupt bargain leading to a transfer of state funds to Ferruzzi, which was already in serious financial difficulty. The state in this case was being called on to salvage a conglomerate through an irregular form of subsidy.

The other major set of political decisions that account for the deficits Italy accumulated from 1970, aside from social policy and industrial policy, concerns the taxation system. The country moved rapidly in the post-1968 period to the level of expenditure of the other advanced European democracies, but the level of taxation did not keep pace. As Table 8.3

*Table 8.3* Government revenue and expenditure, Italy 1970–94 (percentages of GDP)

| Year | Revenue | Expenditure | Deficit |
|------|---------|-------------|---------|
| 1970 | 30.4 | 34.2 | 3.8 |
| 1971 | 31.1 | 36.6 | 5.5 |
| 1972 | 30.9 | 38.6 | 7.7 |
| 1973 | 30.4 | 37.8 | 7.4 |
| 1974 | 30.6 | 37.9 | 7.3 |
| 1975 | 31.2 | 43.2 | 12.0 |
| 1976 | 32.9 | 42.2 | 9.3 |
| 1977 | 34.3 | 42.5 | 8.2 |
| 1978 | 36.0 | 46.1 | 10.1 |
| 1979 | 35.7 | 45.5 | 9.8 |
| 1980 | 37.8 | 46.1 | 8.3 |
| 1981 | 39.3 | 51.2 | 11.9 |
| 1982* | 41.5 | 53.7 | 12.2 |
| 1982# | 36.2 | 47.8 | 11.6 |
| 1983 | 38.1 | 49.0 | 10.9 |
| 1984 | 37.9 | 49.7 | 11.8 |
| 1985 | 38.5 | 51.3 | 12.8 |
| 1986 | 39.2 | 51.1 | 11.9 |
| 1987 | 39.3 | 50.6 | 11.3 |
| 1988 | 39.7 | 50.7 | 11.0 |
| 1989 | 41.4 | 51.7 | 10.3 |
| 1990 | 42.3 | 53.6 | 11.3 |
| 1991 | 43.3 | 53.9 | 10.6 |
| 1992 | 44.0 | 54.0 | 10.0 |
| 1993 | 47.1 | 57.1 | 10.0 |
| 1994 | 44.9 | 54.4 | 9.5 |

Sources: Calculated from OECD, *National Accounts*, vol. II, 1984 and 1996.

Notes
*Old system of national accounts.
#New system of national accounts.
Capital transfers are excluded from revenue, and expenditure is expressed net of them.

demonstrates, expenditure rose rapidly in the first half of the 1970s, from 34 to 43 per cent of GDP, but revenue did not begin to rise significantly until 1976. From that time on, its growth continually lagged that of expenditure. In part, this matched the general trend in industrialized countries: in times of economic downturn, revenues grow more slowly than expenditure. But the unwillingness of governments to adjust income to expenses was also clearly politically motivated, prompted by the resistance of many constituencies to increases, especially in the light of the inequities of a system that made the burden on those who actually paid the taxes particularly heavy relative to that on the large number of evaders.

## The attack on the debt problem

While several previous governments had announced their intention to reduce the deficit, and that of Ciriaco De Mita (1988–89) had planned to eliminate the primary deficit by 1992, it was only with the first Amato government (June 1992–April 1993) that a serious attack on the problem was undertaken. Amato came to power at the end of the so-called 'First Republic', when the Tangentopoli scandals had started to take their toll of the old parties and personnel. This was the primary factor that enabled him to act more independently of the pressure groups and electoral lobbies that had impeded changes in the past. While his cabinet was composed principally of party politicians, his was understood to be a temporary government, with the job of reforming the electoral law, rejected implicitly by the voters in a referendum, and then dissolving Parliament. In other words, internal political developments of a seemingly autonomous origin (the Tangentopoli investigations) were crucial in facilitating Amato's serious attack on the deficit/debt question.

However, international pressures also converged at this point with domestic politics. In January, Italy had signed the Maastricht Treaty, which, as we saw in Chapter 5, committed it to reducing its deficit to 3 per cent of GDP by 1997. The Italian ministers who signed the treaty realized that this was an unrealistic target, but believed the country could not remain outside the new European currency. Furthermore, when Amato took office, the lira was already being targeted by speculators, who saw that by remaining so long in the EMS it had become seriously overvalued. Eventually, in September, the speculative pressure led to the major crisis in which the lira (along with the pound sterling) left the EMS and was devalued by *c.*16.6 per cent. Speculation continued to drive the currency downwards for the rest of the year. The experience of September 1992 traumatized public opinion as well as the political elite, and made both ready to accept tougher measures.

Capital and its representatives were clearly supportive of the elimination of the state's deficit, which they perceived as a source of the high interest rates and shaky state of the lira. Of course, some exporting industries that favoured a low exchange rate for the lira may not have been wholeheartedly behind the public pronouncements of their organizations, such as Confindustria. And Confindustria considered, naturally, that the deficit should be eliminated by spending cuts, particularly to pensions and health, not by tax increases. In fact, in February 1994 it suggested a plan in which the deficit would be eliminated in five years while fiscal pressure was simultaneously reduced by half a per cent of GDP per year.[28] Small businesses and the petty bourgeoisie had the same general attitude to deficit reduction, but had stronger motives for caution in their support. First, they were even more opposed to the tax increases which, realistically, any deficit reduction plan would include; many were far less able to pay, given their precarious financial position. Second, they did not see the immediate advantages of European monetary union that the large exporting firms did. And while they were more concerned about the level of interest rates than the large firms, they were not convinced of the long-term benefits of monetary union in this sphere.

Unions, along with businesses, were concerned about the recessionary impact of tough budgetary measures on the economy and employment, but they accepted the need for fiscal 'consolidation' as well. Naturally, they did not wish to see this at the expense of workers, or of cuts in the welfare state, such as those envisaged by Confindustria.

Among the political parties, the leading forces of the old regime, the DC and the PSI, had demonstrated their inability to deal seriously with the deficit issue for the previous eleven years. While the deficit had peaked in 1985, at 12.6 per cent of GDP, it had only been brought down to 10.2 per cent by 1991. Both parties were afraid of arousing the ire of their electoral clienteles with either cuts or tax increases, such was the fragility of their support. The CDU/CCD and the PPI, successors of the DC, retained a good deal of this mentality. (Polling data show that the 'centre' in 1994 – essentially the PPI – had twice as much support among public employees as among the rest of the population[29]).

On the right, the National Alliance (AN) was in many respects similar to the centre in its often more demagogic defence of the welfare state and government spending. Forza Italia was more consistent, in that it supported the business programme of deficit reduction through spending cuts, but even it had to deal with segments of its own clientele who benefitted from spending, and others who were the beneficiaries of high interest rates on government bonds. For the Northern League, the deficit and debt were yet another sign of 'Rome''s misgovernment, and their economic philosophy supported smaller government, but the League was prepared to treat these issues as a function of its broader political strategy, aimed at autonomy for the North. Hence its willingness to use the pension reform issue to defeat the Berlusconi government, deserting the coalition in opposition to the cuts he proposed.

Among the left-wing parties, the Democratic Party of the Left (PDS), the principal successor of the Communist Party, while committed to supporting the welfare state, was also committed to a 'responsible' stance towards the debt/deficit issue. This position, unusual in a left-wing party, was rooted in the long-standing mentality of the PCI, which, from Togliatti's Salerno speech of 1944 onwards, was oriented to finding positive solutions to the country's problems rather than simply denouncing the errors of the capitalists and their governments.[30] As we noted above (see p. 113), the PCI and its leadership had always had an affinity with the liberal wing of the intelligentsia that was critical of the oligarchic, closed character of Italian capitalism and looked to the Anglo-Saxon democracies and their freer markets as models. This affinity was far deeper than simply a tactical convergence of views during the 'anti-monopoly' phase of the PCI's strategy; it was related to the intellectual prestige of liberal economists and intellectuals, and to wartime links forged with many of them who fought in the Action Party.

Two representative examples of this liberal tendency in the immediate post-war period were Ugo La Malfa, leader of the Republican Party, and the group that formed around the weekly *Il Mondo* in the 1950s, some of whom later founded the influential daily *La Repubblica* in 1976. In view of the connivance they perceived between government and the business elite, this group did not see state action as a panacea, nor did Keynesianism fully penetrate it. Lacking a group of qualified Marxist economists, the PCI was to some extent left with the liberal economics of this group as the most readily available alternative. This goes a long way towards explaining the positions adopted by the PDS in the 1990s; it was not only the party most able to secure social consensus for deficit reduction, it was in many ways the one that was intellectually and politically most in sympathy with this objective. In 1996, Prime Minister Lamberto Dini, a former Director General of the Bank of Italy, founded Rinnovamento Italiano, a party which allied with the left-wing Olive Tree coalition, including the PDS: Rinnovamento carried on the tradition of the Republicans, preaching fiscal rigour while refusing to ostracize the major party of the left.

The smaller, more left-wing successor to the PCI, Communist Refoundation (RC), had a more traditional leftist attitude to budgetary issues. It was concerned above all to defend, in a rather trade-unionistic fashion, the acquired rights of workers, and in particular their rights to pensions and other forms of social wage. Many of its leadership, including its Secretary, Fausto Bertinotti, had been prominent in the left-wing minority faction of the CGIL union confederation, Essere Sindacato. Nonetheless, RC as well had inherited some of the PCI's mentality, and, above all, like trade union negotiators, its leaders were capable of compromise.

## Deficit reduction in retrospect (1992–97)

Italy's reduction of the governmental deficit was indeed spectacularly rapid, and belied the expectations of most informed observers, including the ministers who signed the Maastricht Treaty. In six years, under five different governments, it fell from 9.5 per cent to 3 per cent of GDP, a major achievement, particularly in view of the significant potential for resistance. Between July 1992 and the end of 1996, measures worth nearly 360 trillion lire were announced to reduce the deficit, and some 330 trillions' worth were implemented, divided roughly in half between increases in revenue and expenditure cuts, including *c.*19 trillion from privatizations and nearly 12 trillion in reclassifications of expenditure to conform to European Union accounting practices.[31] A large number of these measures (approximately 40 per cent of the total amount) were one-time or of limited duration, rather than permanent[32] (the 'Euro-tax' imposed in December 1996 would even be reimbursed, the government promised); some of the predicted revenues and savings did not materialize; and each year the dynamic of public expenditure and revenue tended to widen the gap between income and expenses, so that a 'corrective manoeuvre' was always necessary in any case to prevent an increase in the deficit. Hence the long-term impact of the deficit-cutting measures was only 6.5 per cent of GDP, one third of the much higher figure that 360 trillion represents. This was still a very significant cut, which hit especially hard in a period when the economy was already weakened by the international downturn, and contributed significantly to the depth of the recession in 1992–94.

The most significant cuts were imposed by the Amato government at the beginning of this period: 30 trillion in July 1992, and a massive 92.3 trillion in September, the largest single deficit-reduction package ever introduced in Italy. There was an emphasis on revenue generation (slightly over half of the two *manovre*), and privatizations were supposed to bring in several trillions. Moreover, *c.*80 per cent of the revenue-generation measures were permanent, while over half of the cuts in expenditure were only temporary. As a 'non-political' emergency government, Amato's cabinet felt that it did not have the political strength to impose even more severe cuts in public spending. Among the most note-worthy of the Amato measures were increases in income taxes amounting

*Table 8.4* Corrective manoeuvres 1992–96 (totals in trillions of current lire)

|  | *Permanent* | *One-time* | *Total* |
|---|---|---|---|
| Tax increases | 99 | 54 | 153 |
| Privatizations | – | 19 | 19 |
| Spending cuts | 91 | 56 | 147 |
| Reclassifications | 12 | – | 12 |
| Totals | 202 | 129 | 331 |

Sources: See note 31.

Note
Figures not inflation-adjusted.

to some 24 trillion lire. This included 7 trillion to be raised from a new 'minimum tax' on the self-employed, based on a presumptive calculation of their income; the government was later forced to drop this proposal under pressure, but shopkeepers and artisans were also required to pay social security contributions on their whole income. This and other measures in Amato's packages, such as a differential increase in social security contributions, began a pattern that was to persist over the following six years: the singling out of the self-employed for extra increases, a policy justified by the fiscal privileges they had hitherto enjoyed. A further 16.5 trillion was raised from one-time levies on various forms of wealth: bank accounts, real property, and company assets. The introduction of deductibles and charges for health care and the end of some forms of pension indexation accounted for some 12.5 trillion, over half of the permanent spending cuts. The measures affecting public employees, it should be noted, were mostly of a temporary nature, but there was a freeze on increases in their salaries.

The government of Carlo Azeglio Ciampi, which succeeded Amato's in April 1993, was even less political: Ciampi was not a member of Parliament, but rather had been the Governor of the Bank of Italy, and he chose his cabinet without reference to the political parties. In one year in office, he imposed 43.7 trillion lire in cuts and higher taxes (12.4 trillion in an emergency package in May, and 31.3 trillion in the regular budget in September), plus an extra 6.7 trillion in taxes introduced at the end of 1993 to make up for the possible failure of some of the previous measures to materialize. Ciampi's 'manoeuvres' were not as heavily weighted to the taxation side as Amato's, though with the two emergency packages included taxation still predominated. This led to a favourable reception by markets and analysts, who saw the September budget, which included almost exclusively spending cuts, as containing structural provisions that would permanently reduce the deficit. Health costs and government purchasing were two of the larger items singled out for savings. Ciampi's budget was supported in parliament by the PDS as well as the former governing parties. In this, the party was demonstrating its responsibility and commitment to repairing the state of public finances.

The seven-month government of Silvio Berlusconi (May–December 1994) is the most interesting of the whole period 1992–97. It was a political government (the first for two years) of the right, led by one of the country's major entrepreneurs and committed to a *laissez-faire*, pro-business, and anti-communist platform. Yet, paradoxically, its budgetary policies were judged by the financial markets and much of the business community to be too weak, and its commitment to deficit reduction was seriously questioned. As Marx pointed out in the *Eighteenth Brumaire*, the bourgeoisie has difficulty in itself occupying the leading roles in government: personal economic interests, very much in evidence in Berlusconi's case, prevent individual bourgeois from taking account of the needs of their class as a whole.

In the first place, Berlusconi's commitment to the construction of Europe, and specifically to monetary union, was in serious doubt. As Foreign Minister he appointed a 'Eurosceptic', Antonio Martino, a member of the Bruges Group of supporters of Margaret Thatcher's critical position on European unification. This was taken as a sign that the new government lacked the political will to reach the Maastricht parameters on time – indeed, Martino criticized them as 'arbitrary and incomprehensible'.[33] Furthermore, many members of Berlusconi's coalition, particularly Alleanza Nazionale and former members of the DC, were closely tied to the public sector and reluctant to see cuts to the spending that maintained their supporters. Berlusconi, on the other hand, had, as an advocate of neo-liberal, market-oriented solutions, promised that he would introduce no new taxes. Hence it appeared unlikely that his government would give the highest priority to deficit reduction and meeting the Maastricht criteria, even though these objectives were regarded as central by major business spokespeople, including Confindustria and the *salotto buono*.

As we saw in Chapter 3, Berlusconi was, indeed, always an outsider to the Fiat/Mediobanca core group of Italian big capital. His relations with Enrico Cuccia had been only sporadic, and indeed his media interests were quite distant from the industrial concerns of the *salotto buono*. He personally had less need of further European integration and currency stability for his own enterprises, and was therefore more able to appreciate the concerns of those capitalists who feared they would not be able to compete in Europe without the assistance of periodic devaluations, or were apprehensive about the tightening regulation and enforcement of laws that further integration would bring.

In fact, the Berlusconi government's budget, presented in September, included 50 trillion lire in cuts and tax increases, which the markets judged to be the indispensable minimum. On the revenue side, the new government had already introduced tax incentives for the creation of new jobs – the Tremonti decree, which was very well received by business but did not bring the net increase in revenue that was expected. Much of the new revenue foreseen in the budget (*c.* 11.5 trillion lire) was to come from an offer of an amnesty for unpaid taxes, under which taxpayers could settle their accounts with the state on very favourable terms, paying *c.* 10 per cent of the outstanding sum. The next largest amount (6.9 trillion) was to be generated by an amnesty for buildings erected without permits, in return for the payment of fines. After being reduced several times during the parliamentary debate on the amnesty, these fines were also relatively low. So Berlusconi kept his promise not to increase taxes, and furthermore raised revenue by offering advantages to those who had flouted the law in the recent past.

On the expenditure side, by far the most controversial of Berlusconi's proposals was to institute reduced pensions for those who retired on the basis of their seniority (35 years' contributions entitled workers to a full pension) before the normal retirement age, and to lower the value of all pensions relative to pre-retirement earnings. These measures, which would produce their full effects only in the future, were the most bitterly criticized; the government also proposed to block retirement on seniority pensions for a year and to postpone the cost-of-living adjustments to existing pensions, in order to generate immediate, if temporary, savings. These pension proposals provoked the immediate and vigorous opposition of the unions, with whom the government had failed to negotiate a pension reform; on November 12th, 1.5 million people demonstrated in Rome against the budget, and against the pension proposals in particular. The Northern League, one of the government parties, voted against the pension cuts in parliament, and Berlusconi was forced to negotiate again with the unions. On December 1st, they and the government agreed to suspend retirements on seniority pension for six months, and to negotiate a pension reform package by the middle of 1995. Nevertheless, 8.6 trillion of the savings in the budget finally approved by parliament came from pensions, and another 6 trillion from health.

The budgetary measures of the Berlusconi government, then, were weighted in favour of its own constituency: the self-employed were the principal beneficiaries of the tax amnesties, while employed workers and pensioners suffered most under the pension and health provisions. This proved to be too biased a manoeuvre, and even the Northern League, which represented in the first place small manufacturers and other bourgeois groups, could not support the pension proposals; in truth, the League had had serious doubts about a governmental coalition with Berlusconi from the outset, and the pension issue was the most inviting one on which to break up the cabinet. In addition, other forces within the government, especially ex-Christian Democrats such as the Minister of Labour, Clemente Mastella, and some members of Alleanza Nazionale, had opposed the line of economic 'rigour' from the beginning.

Berlusconi was succeeded by a second 'technical' government, this one led by his Treasury Minister, Lamberto Dini, a former Director General of the Bank of Italy. Dini received parliamentary support from the centre-left and the Northern League, while Berlusconi and his allies abstained at first, while continuing to call for the dissolution of parliament and new elections as soon as possible. Dini was forced to bring in an emergency mini-budget (*manovrina*) in February, containing *c.* 21 trillion lire in new taxes and spending cuts: the largest amounts came from increases in excise taxes on energy and the value added tax. Dini's own budget for 1996 included 34.1 trillion lire in total deficit reduction (including 1.6 trillion in lower interest charges): 22.6 in revenue and 11.5 in spending cuts. While the revenue measures were many and various, firms were hit with a new tax on their assets (3.45 trillion), and the self-employed with new presumptive bench-marks for income tax (4 trillion); at the same time, increases in social security contributions were to generate another 6.65 trillion. Unlike Berlusconi, then, Dini spread his net broadly, with the greater burden falling if anything on enterprises large and small. Finally, in December 1995 the government had to make up for overly optimistic predictions by introducing a further *manovrina* consisting of 1.5 trillion in cuts and 3.8 trillion in taxes, partly sales taxes and partly further new 'parameters' for assessing the incomes of the self-employed.

After winning the election of April 1996, the centre-left government of Romano Prodi set about finishing the task of meeting the Maastricht criteria. In sharp contrast to Berlusconi, Prodi's cabinet and coalition appeared completely committed to reaching the goal of a deficit of only 3 per cent of GDP in 1997. Having no real business interests of their own or direct ties to business interests, the ex-Communists of the PDS considered this an essential test of their ability to govern in the national interest, of their credibility and trustworthiness. Of the other coalition parties, Dini's Rinnovamento Italiano was even more committed to financial rigour: it occupied the right wing of the governing coalition, representing business interests in somewhat the same way as the Republicans had under the DC regime. The ex-Christian Democrats of the PPI were a potential problem, but could be managed by Prodi himself. Communist Reconstruction (PRC) had formed an electoral alliance with the other parties, but had not subscribed to a common programme and did not enter the government, maintaining its freedom of manoeuvre; the government, however, depended on it for its majority. The PRC chose not to frontally oppose Italy's entry into the monetary union, but rather to exert pressure on the means adopted by the government to qualify, bargaining in trade union fashion to mitigate the impact on its own constituency, the industrial workers and the poorer strata in general.

In fact, Prodi's measures were second only to Amato's in their severity: in a July *manovrina* and then the 1997 budget, a total of 78.5 trillion lire were cut from the deficit. Of *c.* 32.8 trillion in new taxes, 11.5 trillion were to be raised by a unique new 'tax for Europe', which, Prodi promised, would not only be temporary but would be refunded to taxpayers once Italy was part of the monetary union. The other tax adjustments fell somewhat more heavily on firms than individuals. Of the many spending cuts, the largest single items were transfers to the railways, the post office, local governments, and the highways administration, totalling some 12 trillion lire. In addition, the government was able to obtain the approval of the European statistical agency, Eurostat, for the re-classification of *c.* 15.8 trillion that it had previously counted as government expenditure: debts of the state railways, interest on postal savings, and liabilities arising from Constitutional Court decisions in pension cases. All these complex measures were superintended by Carlo Azeglio Ciampi, who had agreed to enter the Prodi government as Treasury Minister.

The Prodi government, in other words, was prepared to take drastic action to enter the EMU in the first group of countries, while not touching the interests of its own constituency too severely. So much so that the opposition, led by Berlusconi, not only opposed the budget in parliament, but organized a mass demonstration against it in Rome in November 1996, condemning the government for its tax increases.

Overall, the fiscal retrenchment of the period 1992–97 was a major success, reaching the Maastricht criterion when most observers had judged that Italy could not. The methods used touched on some, but not all, of the structural causes that had generated the debt in the first place. Many of the tax increases were general, such as the higher income tax rates introduced by Amato or Prodi's 'Euro-tax', but some targeted the self-employed in particular and aimed to at least reduce, if not eliminate, the privileges they had hitherto enjoyed. On the expenditure side, the hotly debated pension cuts produced savings, and there were a series of reductions in the health budget, but by and large public sector workers bore only a small share of the burden. Many of the cuts were instead to transfers to other agencies or purchases of goods and services.

The non-political governments and Prodi's centre-left cabinet had also proved to be better able to pursue the policy supported by major business interests, confirming again Marx's intuitions on Bonapartism. While not imposing the brunt of the retrenchment on public employees and private-sector workers, they were not as tender with another element of the DC coalition, the self-employed; they also made some inevitable cuts in pensions and health, but not to the extent that Berlusconi or the right had demanded, so much so that in 1997 demands for a revision of the Dini reform led to a more rapid phasing-out of the seniority pensions.

While the governments of 1992–98 were an excellent example of Bonapartism – government by an alternative leadership where the bourgeoisie cannot rule more directly – the theory of Bonapartism does not account fully for the content of their policies. Apart from the details of implementation and the distribution of burdens, the objectives they pursued were indeed those of Italian capital, especially its dominant fraction, and they pursued them more effectively than the 1994 right-wing government did.

# 9    The state and industrial relations

The central political and economic relationship in a capitalist economy is ultimately that between capital and labour, and its regulation poses particularly delicate problems for the state. While, at the beginnings of the labour movement, governments often appeared to act as tools of business interests against labour, such a naked instrumental relationship has not existed in Europe or Italy for decades. Even at the height of the Cold War, the Catholic CISL unions often enjoyed the favour and protection of the Italian state, as they were seen as more moderate than the Communist-dominated CGIL. While the internationalization of the advanced industrial economies and the growing popularity of the Anglo-Saxon model of capitalism have led many governments to encroach on unions' power over the past two decades, this process has been uneven and has never led to a return to the situation before unions were recognized at all. An instrumentalist view of the state's role must therefore be rejected. Similarly, an attempt to derive the state's function purely from the economic logic of capitalism would suggest that it should oppose the creation of a counter-power to that of the employer in the workplace. This simple derivationist approach does not fit the facts either.

Nicos Poulantzas' framework appears to offer a better explanation of contemporary state policy in the industrial relations arena. He suggests that the principal role of the capitalist state is political, and that its primary objective *vis-à-vis* the dominated classes, such as the workers, is to weaken and disorganized them politically, if necessary through economic concessions, keeping their struggles at a stage of 'economic isolation'. At the same time, it unifies the capitalist class, which is also divided and isolated in the economic sphere.[1] Poulantzas' approach, however, must be modified in two major respects. First, as the historical institutionalists such as Skocpol have stressed, the state must operate within the constraints dictated by history. Institutions and practices, as well as attitudes and ideologies, are some of the most important historical legacies which limit the state's ability to pursue the long-term political interests of capital. While they reflect the balance of class forces at a previous moment in history, they nevertheless exercise a real power in the present.[2] While Poulantzas' concept of 'décalage' (differential temporality) could accommodate these historical legacies, he does not in fact develop it very far in this direction. Second, the object of struggle between the classes is itself defined by the economic logic of capitalism: the major issues are those that are crucial to the accumulation of capital, and any concessions that are given to the working class are concessions with respect to the policies which are held to be optimal for that accumulation.[3] To this extent, the derivationist approach is also a necessary element in any explanation of policies affecting the dominated classes, including industrial relations. Hence, a Poulantzian approach must be inserted within a context of legacies and issues furnished by history and the dynamic of capital accumulation.

## Legacies and problems

The framework of Italian industrial relations is a product of a long historical evolution, but much of it reflects recent history, in particular the Hot Autumn of 1969 and its aftermath. Because it was part of the formative period of many union leaders and militants, and because it led to significant institutional innovations, the effect of this unprecedented strike wave continues to be felt to the present day, and is at least as important as that of deeper-rooted historical legacies.

The basic structure of collective bargaining in Italy originated in the last decades of the nineteenth century, when workers formed industrial unions which came to negotiate sector-wide contracts. The practice of industry-wide bargaining remains: there are currently well over a hundred national contracts, covering different sectors ranging from the metalworkers, who include workers in the auto industry and engineering, to employees of aerial photography companies.[4] (In some sectors, there may be more than one contract, if the employers are represented by two or more associations – e.g. Confindustria and Confartigianato, the artisans' association.) Very few workers are not covered by a national contract. These are generally applied in all workplaces in the industry, except for the significant number in the 'black' or 'grey' economy.[5] While plant-level agreements supplement them in a third, at most, of all companies, the industry-level contracts remain more important.

Because of the national industry-level contracts, unions do not require or seek formal legal recognition from individual employers. In addition, the unions have traditionally had clear political affiliations, so that membership took on, in the eyes of many, a political significance. This was particularly so in the Cold War, when the Communist-dominated CGIL unions competed with the Catholic CISL and the Social Democratic/ Republican UIL. For these reasons, a plurality of unions have generally been present in any large plant, divided on political lines rather than occupationally, as in Great Britain. Hence union membership or dues-paying has never been compulsory (indeed the idea of compulsory membership is associated with the Fascist regime), and this situation has allowed so-called 'autonomous' unions that are not affiliated to any of the three major confederations (CGIL, CISL, and UIL) to gain a foothold in many workplaces, especially in the public sector, and provide disgruntled supporters of the three large 'confederal' unions with an alternative.

In the 1960s, as the union movement became stronger, the practice of supplementary plant-level bargaining began to spread: it was originally promoted by the CISL unions in particular, in imitation of the American model. Plant agreements covered matters specific to the individual work-place which the national contract could not, such as employer-furnished transportation, but also provided for bonus payments and other wage sup-plements. At the end of the decade, long-contained wage demands com-bined with the difficult situation of Southern workers who had emigrated to the North and the speed-up of production to produce an unprece-dented explosion of militancy, the Hot Autumn. As a result, real wages increased by 26 per cent in two years, and, perhaps even more signific-antly, union membership increased by 16 per cent; in addition, plant-level organization spread with the formation of factory councils composed of shop delegates. Hence, plant-level bargaining also became more wide-spread. Much of this militancy was of a grass-roots variety, and explicitly critical of the confederal unions; they were, however, able eventually to place themselves at its head and channel it, with a resultant gain in strength and bargaining power. The formation of a federation of the three confederations in 1972 further added to the unions' ability to defend their members' interests. The effects of the Hot Autumn con-tinued through the early 1970s, with real wages rising a further 30 per cent in 1970–73, and union membership a further 19 per cent.[6]

The unions are often presented as living off the 'rent' of the strong position they held in the early 1970s, a position which has since been eroded. The weakening of the economy in the late 1970s, under the impact of the oil crises, led to a crisis of major industry, to which it responded with restructuring and an offensive against the workers' shop-floor power. The symbolic event of this period was the 1980 strike against mass lay-offs at Fiat, which was defeated after the so-called 'march of the 40,000' technicians, foremen, and other pro-company workers.[7] From this point on, the unions gradually lost members, both absolutely and relat-ively, falling from 49 per cent of employed workers in 1980 to 39 per cent in 1987, then remaining relatively steady until 1994–96, when a further decline of *c*.2 per cent occurred.[8] The high rate of inflation made the automatic cost-of-living escalator clause negotiated at the national level between the confederations and Confindustria increasingly vulnerable. The 1983 'Scotti accord', named after the Minister of Labour of the day, was a triangular agreement in which the unions agreed to limit its effect in return for reductions in tax rates and increased family allowances. However, in 1984 the unity of the three confederations came to an end over the government's decree-law suspending the operation of the escalator for a period. The Communists subsequently collected the signatures necessary for a referendum to abrogate the law, but the referendum failed by a vote of 54.3 per cent to 45.7 per cent (Cf. p. 102 above).

More generally, changes in the economy and the labour market that began in the 1980s were weakening the unions' structural position in the economy. The number of industrial workers had begun to decline, though later than in most other advanced economies, and so did the proportion in large workplaces; in spite of their efforts, the unions were weaker in smaller plants and in the growing service sector. In both of these, the black and grey employment markets were important.

Despite these setbacks, the unions' position remained strong enough that they had to be considered in the formulation of economic policy, and in the factories they often engaged in 'micro-corporatism' as firms restructured, reaching agreements on early retirements and the reorganization of work. While they had lost some members and bargaining power, they remained in the early 1990s a force to be reckoned with, capable of mobilizing millions of workers in critical situations. With the revolution in the party system set off by the *Mani pulite* investigations of 1992, furthermore, the principal reason for the division of the union movement was in part removed: the parties with which the confederations were identified split, disappeared, or transformed themselves, loosening their ties with the unions in the process. Changes in the party system also left the unions, paradoxically, with an even more important political role, as defenders of the broad interests not only of workers but also of pensioners. Their successful opposition to the Berlusconi pension reforms in 1994 was the most striking demonstration of their political role – a role which the parties lacked the legitimacy and unity to perform.

Of course, the unions, and particularly the confederal unions, are not synonymous with the working class. On the one hand, they are a social movement which represents interests that go beyond the industrial working class, embracing many members in the public sector, services, etc., as well as pensioners, the unemployed, and others affected by government policies on which the unions have exerted influence. On the other hand, there is often significant shop-floor opposition to the confederations' policies, which is sometimes reflected in support for the 'autonomous' unions.

The state in this context acts, from a Poulantzian perspective, to unite the capitalist class. The economic needs of capitalists, however, compel it to take account of the unions' strength and to bargain with them to achieve the most satisfactory outcomes possible. Following this logic, the Italian state has not directly attacked or weakened the union movement, but rather sought to tame it, bringing it to reach agreements that smooth the further accumulation of capital. As we shall see, these actions by the state may indeed, in certain circumstances, weaken the unions. For instance, in the negotiation of the pension issue the unions were able to protect the rights of older workers, while sacrificing some interests of the younger and those not yet in the labour force. And the agreements themselves weakened the unions' support on the shop floor, as many of the more radical workers opposed any concessions. So an indirect consequence of the government's action has been to jeopardize the unions' position as representative of the workers, at the same time as other agreements have confirmed or strengthened their institutional presence.[9]

The capitalist class has not had a united approach to labour relations issues, and therefore the state's role has been particularly necessary. In the private sector, the most notable differences are between the larger and smaller firms; the former not only have no hope of evading the provisions of the national sectoral contracts, but also have a strong union presence on the shop floor so that they are compelled to engage in the 'second tier' of bargaining at the firm level as well. Hence they are forced to deal with the union movement, and cannot embrace the same outright anti-union positions as many of the smaller employers. In certain regions, notably the South and the North-East, plant-level bargaining in small firms is less common than elsewhere, and the owners tend to take a more anti-union stance. There are also significant differences between industries: in the chemical sector labour costs are a much smaller fraction of the price of the product than in, for instance, the metalworking industries; hence, the chemical employers' association is less likely to assume a rigid bargaining position than the Federmeccanica, representing metalworking employers. The public sector, as well, traditionally took a more conciliatory line with its unions; until 1993, public-sector companies were not members of Confindustria, but bargained their own national contracts through their own organizations, Intersind (IRI) and Asap (ENI).

The commonly employed division between large and small firms must be qualified in other ways as well. For example, Fiat, the largest private sector firm of all, took the lead with its 1980 lay-offs when the other large companies were sceptical or opposed to confronting the unions; as its president of the time said, 'The most benevolent considered us wishful thinkers'.[10] Support came from the small and medium-sized firms instead. Fiat, in fact, has often adopted hard-line positions *vis-à-vis* its own work force, and involved the union only formally in its changes in the organization of work, circumventing union rules wherever possible.[11] At the same time, at the national level it has supported collaboration with the unions over broad economic policy issues, recognizing the considerable differences and tensions between the local Turinese militants and the national leadership.[12] And Fiat is the largest member of Federmeccanica.

Industrial relations are also part of firms' broader strategies. The larger companies, not always led by Fiat, aim at a 'modern' capitalism inserted into the global economy, with a leaner state, a reduction in welfare expenditure, and reduced government debt. As we have seen, their interests are

financial as well as industrial, and hence they support 'orthodox' monetary and fiscal policies. But they are also forced to take a broad, strategic
view of their problems. In return for the unions' collaboration in this
project, they are prepared to make some concessions, especially on the
political front, for instance by recognizing their role in economic policy-
making. The smaller firms may share the rhetoric of a scaled-down state,
but their concrete goals of tax cuts, easier credit, and a more competitive
currency are not in fact the same as those of the 'modern' wing of capital.
Having these goals, which can be achieved without direct negotiation over
the welfare state and similar issues, and which are indeed not opposed by
the left, they do not need to seek compromises with the unions, and in
any case they have a narrower, firm-level view of their situation in which
they do not seek to construct grand alliances on the national political
scene.[13] This attitude is shared both by the dynamic, export-oriented small
firms of the North-East and by more backward, small and medium firms in
the rest of the country. Even large companies such as Fiat have occasion-
ally given their support to elements of this programme – e.g. when Romiti
suggested Italy might delay its entry into the European Monetary Union.
Confindustria has traditionally had to balance the views of both the larger
and the smaller companies; the growing economic importance in the
1990s of the small and medium firms, symbolized by the North-East, has
made this even more delicate and difficult, and increased the potential for
division among different segments of capital. Whereas in the 1970s and
1980s Fiat could in the end assert its hegemony over the whole capitalist
front, after 1990 this was less and less a foregone conclusion.[14]

In the years before the political revolution which began in 1992 with
the first *Mani pulite* investigations, the Italian state was not able to provide
leadership to unify the various segments of capital. While the Scotti
accord of 1983 had been negotiated thanks to the efforts of a Christian
Democratic labour minister, with the St. Valentine's Day decree of 1984
suspending the cost-of-living escalator and the subsequent referendum the
Craxi government effectively nullified whatever progress towards a form of
tripartite concertation had been made by that pact. The governments of
the so-called 'CAF' (Craxi-Andreotti-Forlani) era were unable to choose to
support any particular economic strategy, whether that of the 'moderniz-
ers' or that of the 'populists', the proponents of cheap money and government largesse. It was indeed in the last months of the CAF period that
Italy signed the Maastricht Treaty, ushering in EMU; however, the ministers who participated in the conference admitted that they considered the
conditions for joining the monetary union impossible for Italy to fulfil.[15]

## The *scala mobile* and the Agreement of July 1993

Throughout the 1980s, Italy's inflation performance remained worse than
that of the rest of the G7, and in most academic and popular discussions

of it a major causal role was assigned to the automatic cost-of-living escalator clause (the *scala mobile*) which had been established by an agreement between the union confederations and the employers' organizations dating from 1945. In 1975, its role had been reinforced by the equalization of the cash value of a percentage point of inflation for all wage levels, so that it also took on a redistributive function. As with pensions in the 1990s, the *scala mobile* was a constant refrain from large segments of business and the press, who held the unions' 'conservatism' on the issue responsible for the ills of the nation's economy. The unions, for their part, saw it as a fundamental right which workers could not sacrifice. After the agreement of 1983 and the decree of 1984, the mechanism was changed so that on average roughly half, instead of three quarters, of the increase in the cost of living was automatically added every six months to workers' wages.[16] The issue remained unresolved, however, as the employers sought more freedom to pay workers increases on the basis of their qualifications and productivity, instead of an automatic escalator. Finally, in June 1989 Confindustria threatened that it would unilaterally rescind the agreement on the escalator.

Throughout 1990, conflict on the issue intensified as Confindustria tried to slow down the signing of the national sectoral contracts until the unions would agree to deal with the *scala mobile*; eventually, in June, concerned by signs that parliament would extend the escalator and by a small upturn in inflation, it formally rescinded the agreement. The unions, for their part, requested Parliament to pass a law extending the life of the escalator clause for two years. Finally, on 6 July 1990, a tripartite agreement between the government, the unions, and Confindustria provided for a non-renewable extension of the *scala mobile* by law to the end of 1991, and the beginning of negotiations for a complete reform of the structure of compensation. Throughout this phase, the government's role was that of mediator between the two 'social partners', and often the unions were able to receive substantial support within the governing parties and in parliament.

No agreement was reached during two more years of negotiations, which were difficult and frequently interrupted. However, from the beginning the solution of the issue of the *scala mobile* was bound up with that of a general reform of the structure of collective bargaining. From the unions' perspective, the escalator clause limited their freedom to negotiate because so much of the money available for wage increases was absorbed by this automatic mechanism. The reduction in inflation coverage above the minimum level in 1984 made the mechanism even more egalitarian; hence it further undermined traditional skill differentials to which the unions were committed. The employers not only wanted more flexibility to reward skill and productivity, but also saw that, with the lira pegged to the deutschmark in the European Monetary System while Italy's inflation rate continued to outpace the other members of the EMS, they needed to take radical steps to contain their costs.

Confindustria therefore proposed not only the abolition of the *scala mobile*, but also the elimination of the two-level system of bargaining. Their proposal, however, was rather byzantine, reflecting the divisions and perplexities on the employers' side: both types of bargaining would be permitted, but if a plant-level agreement was signed it would take the place of the national sectoral contract.[17] Of the union confederations, only the CISL was ready to renounce the *scala mobile* completely, while the proposals of the other two union centrals involved some form of *ex post* recovery of inflation by workers.[18]

In this conjuncture, the role of the state was crucial in breaking the impasse. The outbreak of the corruption scandals and the April 1992 election led to the formation of a new government by Giuliano Amato on 28 June 1992. Amato, a Socialist, was an academic who had been on the staff of the CGIL and subsequently served as a long-time adviser to Craxi; his own opinion was that drastic measures were necessary to confront the deficit, which was threatening the stability of the lira and its place in the EMS, as well as, in the longer term, standing in the way of Italy's entry into the EMU. As a former union official, Amato used his insider's knowledge to help bring the confederations to an agreement: he threatened to resign unless the social partners could reach a negotiated solution. This would have had serious consequences for the nation's economy, as international confidence would be shaken in an already difficult situation: Danish voters had just rejected membership in the EMU, initiating a period of extreme turbulence on the foreign exchange markets.

The very precariousness of the Amato government's own situation, given the impact of the corruption scandals on the parties which supported him (DC, PSI, PSDI, PLI), made his threat all the more credible: it was not clear who would be able to replace him. The country's serious economic situation was not sufficient in itself to force the unions and employers to agree to a new wage structure: the state played a crucial intermediary function in bringing the widely separated parties together; in the end, the long-term goal of capital, the abolition of the *scala mobile*, was achieved.

The agreement reached on 31 July between the unions, Confindustria, and the government (in its dual role as largest employer and policymaker) finally ended the *scala mobile*, and also declared a moratorium on wage increases negotiated at the plant level for 1992 and 1993. At the same time, the parties agreed to resume negotiations on the reform of the structure of collective bargaining, having established certain points of departure: the preservation of two levels of bargaining, the idea of a target inflation rate set by the government as a reference point for wage bargaining, and the principle that workers should receive partial inflation protection if any time elapses between the expiry of one collective agreement and the signing of the next. All of these principles were eventually put into practice in the July 1993 agreement.

In the immediate, the 1992 agreement appeared to seriously weaken the unions' position with their rank and file. Many criticized the confederations for failing to consult their memberships before signing the 31 July agreement (many factories had closed for the summer vacation); as an alternative, Bruno Trentin, secretary general of the CGIL, had offered his resignation for failing to follow the mandate he had been given. The executive committee refused to accept it, endorsing his course of action *ex post.* Nevertheless, during the autumn, while the confederations waged a vigorous campaign against some of Amato's budget cuts, rank-and-file workers and some factory councils, composed of shop delegates, sharply criticized the union leadership. Even within the CGIL executive, the left-wing faction 'Essere sindacato' ('being a union') was joined by some others in opposing the agreement. This was a warning the unions took to heart in their subsequent negotiations.

The crisis of the lira in September 1992 and the government's austerity package of 93 trillion lire had temporarily distracted the parties from the reform of collective bargaining. In early 1993, however, the Amato government began work again on the problem, attempting to link it with the regulation of the labour market and other issues that were in dispute between the parties. It failed to produce an agreement, but it laid the groundwork for its successor: in April 1993, as the corruption scandals eroded the governing parties' positions even further, Carlo Azeglio Ciampi, Governor of the Bank of Italy, was asked to form his 'technical' government. With a Socialist academic expert on industrial relations, Gino Giugni, as Minister of Labour, Ciampi soon produced a tripartite agreement on 3 July. This time, the unions did hold a referendum among their members, which produced a majority of *c.* 2/3 in favour, in spite of the continuing opposition of 'Essere sindacato' and other radical groups.

The July agreement has often been presented as an example of a 'new phase' of neo-corporatism, where unions seek, in return for wage moderation, organizational support and legitimacy rather than concrete benefits such as guarantees of full employment.[19] The explicit *quid pro quo* of the earlier phase of corporatism has been replaced by a recognition of common goals, in particular, in the Italian case, the need to meet the Maastricht parameters, which are cited in the preamble of the July accord. The agreement has several significant features:

1   The unions and the employers' associations (the 'social partners') and the government are to meet formally twice a year (in May–June and then in September) to jointly define economic policy objectives, including the target inflation rate, economic growth, and employment growth, in the context of the government's budgetary objectives. The parties agree to act coherently with these objectives (particularly the inflation target) in their bargaining, pricing, and other policies. The government may act to 'correct' actions that are not coherent

with these objectives, through competition policy, taxation, or the revision of social security contribution rates.[20] These policies will act both to offset and to 'dissuade' excessive wage and price increases.

2   The two levels of bargaining are maintained, but their roles are clearly distinguished and defined, in response to the employers' concerns. The national contracts will provide for wage increases to protect workers' incomes from inflation, but this is not to be an automatic mechanism: other factors, including the general economic situation and the competitive position of the country and of the specific industry, must be taken into account. The non-economic provisions of the national contracts will remain in effect for four years; the wage clauses will be re-negotiated every two years. The plant-level contracts (or territorial contracts, which cover several smaller enterprises in a district) will concern 'subjects and provisions that are different from and do not overlap with the compensation clauses assigned to the national collective agreement'.[21] They can, that is, provide for wage increases that reflect productivity improvements in the plant in excess of those needed to fund the increases set out in the national contract. Their duration is set at four years, and the agreement provides that they may be regulated by the national contract. As before July 1993, firms are not required to enter into plant-level agreements, and in fact only a third, at most, of workers are covered by them.

3   A new form of plant committee, which will be authorized to conclude plant-level contracts, is established: the RSU (*Rappresentanza sindacale unitaria*, Unified Union Representation). Two thirds of its members are elected by the workers, voting for lists presented by the union confederations and any other unions with significant support in the plant; one third are chosen by the three confederations.[22] This latter provision, which reinforces the confederations against their shop-floor rivals, such as the 'rank-and-file committees' (*Cobas*), was inserted at the insistence of the *employers*, who wanted to be sure that their opposite numbers at plant-level negotiations were the same as those at the national level – a further guarantee against the danger that the two levels would lead to excessive and unco-ordinated wage increases resulting from the summation of the two contracts.

4   Many clauses of the agreement concern various measures to increase employment, from vocational training to research and development.

5   Finally, the government agrees to respect the inflation targets in setting its own fees and prices, and in its bargaining with its own employees (which it had not done in the recent past). At the same time, the agreement contains provisions reinforcing the new private-sector model of collective bargaining for the public service.

The July agreement did indeed initiate a new phase in Italian industrial relations, formalizing and guaranteeing many union rights which had existed only as a matter of practice. (It even included a commitment by the government to legislate the application of national contracts to all workers in a sector). The preservation of the two contractual levels could be seen as a major union victory. However, institutionalization also brought with it a certain 'taming' of the unions, in their acceptance of the goal of inflation control and indeed of the overall economic policy of the government, and more specifically in their endorsement of a framework which *de facto* protected the core industrial work force in large firms, while offering much less to those in small plants, the service sector, and the black and grey labour markets. In fact, the provisions for the weaker segments of the labour market, such as easier apprenticeships for youth and more vocational training, were of uncertain effect. Over the long run, the taming of the union movement limits its ability both to hold the loyalty of some of its existing base and to expand into the most dynamic sectors of the work force. This result is a partly unintended consequence of the Ciampi government's policy: much of the content of the July accord flowed naturally from previous negotiations or proposals by the parties themselves, such as a March 1991 agreement between the confederations on the new RSUs. The government's major contribution was to provide the impetus for the conclusion of an agreement, including the various promises of legislative changes and spending on economic development which helped bring the two social partners to sign it.

## The July accord tested: the metalworkers' contract of 1997

The first round of contract negotiations after the July accords, in 1993–94, was very smooth: for the first time in many years, the metalworkers' contract was signed without any time lost due to strikes, and only five days after the expiry of its predecessor.[23] Two years later, however, the renegotiation of the wage provisions of the national contracts did not go as easily. While the chemical workers signed a contract providing for increases of 228,000 lire per month, the central metalworkers' contract proved much more difficult. Although both sides agreed that increases were necessary to cover the planned inflation level of the coming two years, the unions requested a further amount to make up the difference between planned and actual inflation in 1994–96, the period of the previous agreement, during which wages had been geared to the inflation target. The July protocol referred to this inflation difference as a 'further point of reference' in setting new wage levels, along with such factors as general trends in the economy and the labour market, the competitive position of the sector, and the objective of preserving the purchasing power of wages; it was also to be evaluated in the light of changes in the country's terms of trade and trends in [total] compensation.[24]

The Federmeccanica, representing the employers in the private sector, believed that general economic conditions did not permit the recovery of past inflation. It argued that, except for 2 per cent imported inflation, it had in fact already been recovered through wage drift, particularly through plant-level agreements. It also pointed out that the weight of social security contributions and income taxes was such that workers' take-home pay was less than half of the employers' labour costs, suggesting that the government should do something to raise workers' purchasing power. In fact, the increase in the value of the lira after the steady devaluation from September 1992 to March 1995 had made Italian exports considerably less attractive, with their price competitiveness index falling *c.* 19 per cent by October 1996.[25] (This appreciation of the currency was, of course, the result of the Dini and Prodi governments' efforts to prepare the economy for entry into the EMU).

The decision by the Prodi government, on 25 November, to re-enter the EMS at the level of 990 lire to the deutschmark, *c.* 1 per cent above its recent market level, simply reinforced the employers' determination to contain salary costs. These were the real motives for their resistance to the unions' wage demands; while commentators usually suggest that smaller employers, especially in the growing North-East, are the most anti-union, in this round of negotiations they were in fact more willing to reach a compromise with the unions than the large firms. This was principally because they were receiving new export orders in spite of the higher value of the lira, and wanted to secure labour peace to take advantage of them.[26] The large firms such as Fiat, however, feared the new competitive climate and pressed for some kind of relief, either on wage costs or in the form of government assistance. These divisions within the employers' front were partly responsible for Federmeccanica's inability to arrive at a positive proposal until very late in the negotiations (mid-November) and for its raising a whole series of other demands and preconditions concerning general government policy, assistance to the industry, etc.[27]

The government's role in the course of the negotiations was noteworthy: early in the nine-month process, the unions called on it to provide an authoritative interpretation of the July accord, hoping that, as a centre-left coalition, it would endorse their position on the recovery of past inflation. The government, however, kept out of the fray for over six months. In mid-November, in the face of a long hiatus in the negotiations, the leaders of the parliamentary caucuses of the governing coalition signed a motion requesting it to intervene as 'guarantor' of the July accord. More significantly, this is the point at which the employers' front began to crack: Alessandro Riello, a major manufacturer of electrical appliances and a former president of the Young Industrialists' organization of Confindustria, publicly criticized the Federmeccanica's approach to the negotiations,[28] and he was representative of many of the most dynamic firms in the North-East. As a centre-left coalition, the government did not aim to weaken the unions; on the other hand, it did seek to tame them by finding a solution that was both negotiated and compatible with its own objective of meeting the Maastricht criteria. Hence it did not endorse the unions' view on the recovery of past inflation: the Minister of Labour, Tiziano Treu, stated that the July accord 'does not speak of the automatic and total recovery of inflation'.[29] As the secretary of the CISL, Sergio D'Antoni, stated after the agreement was reached: '[Prime Minister Prodi] always tells me, "don't worry, we're friends", while I always reply, "that's just what worries me, because otherwise everything would be clearer"'.[30] (Prodi and D'Antoni share their Catholic and Christian Democratic background as well as a generally progressive stance). The government's concerns were to obtain a settlement that preserved labour peace, was compatible with its overall economic policy, and avoided an irreparable split in the employers' front. Although a centre-left cabinet, it acted in many ways as Poulantzian theory would predict.

Just before Christmas, the government proposed a compromise solution involving an increase of 200,000 lire per month, a figure closer to the unions' position, which had been reduced from 262,000 to 215,000, than to the employers', which had risen from 120,000 to 138,000–139,000.[31] Evidently it shared the view of Riello and the more moderate wing of the employers that Federmeccanica's stance was too intransigent. The proposal was accepted by the unions, but rejected by Federmeccanica. At this point, some observers on the union side speculated that Confindustria's real objective was to bring down the government, and that the metalworkers' contract was being used as part of its campaign. Fossa, the President of Confindustria, had concluded a withering attack on Prodi's economic policy by saying, 'If the government doesn't change, it will be swept away'.[32] In the end, however, a solution was reached with the direct participation of the Minister of Labour and Prodi himself as mediators in a typical marathon bargaining session. While accepting the figure of 200,000 lire, Federmeccanica managed to have the increase paid gradually in three stages, and secured the extension of the contract from 24 to 30 months and an agreement that no plant-level increases would come into effect in 1997. The contract also clarified further that the plant-level agreements were to award increases only on the basis of productivity and the economic performance of the firm, thus addressing one of the employers' long-standing complaints. But the unions received an increase that amounted to 7 per cent, or 1.5 per cent more than the inflation target, and hence could claim that much of the ground lost to inflation in the previous two years had been made up.

The long struggle over the metalworkers' contract in 1996–97 seemed to put the July 1993 agreement in question. The employers appeared, from the unions' perspective, to be repudiating the link between wage increases and inflation and attempting to subvert the two-level system of bargaining. In the end, however, their motives were more short-term and conjunctural: as suggested above, some of the major industries in the sector, in particular automobiles, were in difficulty because of the stronger lira; once the government subsidy for scrapping older vehicles was announced at the end of the year, prospects improved and opposition to the metalworkers' demands weakened. The same could be said of the doubts expressed by Romiti about Italy's entry into the EMU: business leaders' views on major issues tended to reflect short-term considerations to a surprising extent (in spite of the often voiced criticism that they were concerned more with politics than with business[33]). The government, on the other hand, kept in view the objectives of social peace and Italy's entry into the Euro zone. To a certain extent, these stances reflected an unconscious division of labour between Federmeccanica/Confindustria and the government, with the former in particular relying on the latter to do its part. The final agreement brought a return of unity to the employers' front, while provoking significant divisions within the union: only 67 of the 128 members of the executive of the CGIL metalworkers' union, the FIOM, voted in favour of acceptance, the rest judging the increases insufficient.[34]

## Union organization on the plant floor

The conclusion of the metalworkers' contract still left for the future the promised review of the July 1993 accord, originally planned for 1997. The Confindustria was still unhappy with the existence of two levels of bargaining, but divided as to which to eliminate. Those with plant-level bargaining preferred to do without a national contract, but the small employers without a plant contract feared the generalization of that system to their firms if the national level were eliminated. In the absence of agreement on the employers' side, the government's defence of the two-level system represented a logical point of equilibrium.

Another major aspect of the July 1993 accord, the formation of the RSUs, aimed to revitalize the plant-level representation of workers while at the same time linking it to the national unions. In December 1993 a further agreement between the union confederations and Confindustria set out further characteristics of these new organisms. Detailed provisions for the election and functioning of the RSUs were included in the first national contracts signed after the accord; by the end of 1996, approximately two million workers, or one seventh of all employed workers, had elected some 10,300 RSUs with approximately 50,000 members. The new organisms were found principally in larger industrial plants, and especially in the metalworking and chemical industries. Despite their relatively slow diffusion throughout the country, the elections to the RSUs demonstrated a surprisingly high degree of support for the three major confederations, which obtained 95.5 per cent of the votes. Turnout was also relatively high, at 72.8 per cent.[35] While the 'autonomous' unions did not participate in many workplaces, especially in the public sector, this result nevertheless showed that the July accord had if anything reinforced the unions' links with the rank and file and their capacity to represent them. Rather than weaken them, the new system, despite its limitations, had strengthened them. Indeed, it aimed at incorporating them in 'concerted' decision-making rather than breaking them.

In view of the different perspectives of the CISL and UIL, who were more ready to play this role, and the CGIL, whose willingness to do so was questionable, despite the moderate background of Sergio Cofferati, its secretary general, this strategy involved a certain risk (note that the CGIL received *c.*49 per cent of the votes in the RSU elections). This risk was limited by an awareness that if the unions were rent with serious divisions this would considerably weaken their voice and most likely their support among the rank and file as well. However, the establishment of the RSUs themselves contributed to the taming of the union movement because of their continuous involvement in direct negotiation with the employers over issues such as productivity bonuses: these negotiations usually bring the parties together around the common objectives and problems of the firm. At the same time, the links with the confederations through the 'reserved third' of seats would, in the minds of the employers, serve to restrain the more radical plant activists.

## Unemployment and the labour market

Another major theme in the relations between unions and governments has been the creation of employment and the regulations governing the labour market. The unions naturally aimed at reducing unemployment; from the employers' side, tremendous pressure was exerted to achieve more 'flexibility' in the labour market, through a relaxation of the laws governing hiring and employment contracts and of the minimum wage levels prescribed by the national contracts. Confindustria and other business groups argued that these measures of flexibility should be introduced particularly in the South, where unemployment was far more serious than in the rest of the country; they would encourage firms to establish there and to hire more workers. The CISL and UIL were prepared to make concessions of this type, while the CGIL remained sceptical, contending that special dispensations for the South were simply the first step in an attempt to lower wages and employment standards throughout the country.[36] In addition, many workers and unionists remembered that it was only in the early 1960s, and after bitter struggles, that they had secured the abolition of the system of separate wage zones which provided for lower pay for Southern workers. They perceived this as a major conquest of the labour movement.

While the traditional 'exchange' between wage moderation and full employment was not possible, given the Maastricht limits on macro-economic policy, nevertheless the July accord contained a series of micro-economic and 'supply-side' measures aimed at combating unemployment (e.g. promoting vocational training). The one clause with a Keynesian flavour dealt with the acceleration of the approval of public works, which had been blocked by the discovery of widespread kickbacks and cartels by the *Mani pulite* investigations.[37] On the other hand, several provisions, such as the extension of apprenticeships and 'training' contracts, the licensing of temporary work agencies, and the reference to the possibility of negotiating wages below the contractual levels in zones hit by economic crisis, embodied parts of the employers' programme. The one limit was that much was left to future negotiations between the parties, or to legislation by the government. Other more neutral measures to promote economic growth generally, such as aid to research and development, improved export credits, and lower taxation of risk capital, were also accepted by the unions because of their supposed job-creating potential.

All parties recognized that the July accords provided only a framework in this field, and the Prodi government, as a centre-left administration, was determined to do something on the unemployment issue. Negotiations in September 1996 led to the signing of a 'Pact for Work' (*Patto per il Lavoro*) by the government and thirty-two unions and employers' associations. It included more detail on education and training, including commitments from the government to raise the school-leaving age and promote technical and co-operative education and study leaves. It regulated temporary work and temporary employment agencies more precisely, limiting them to jobs requiring high or intermediate skill levels. Part-time work was encouraged by an increase in social security contributions if hours worked exceeded 36 per week. In addition, to encourage the 'emergence' of black and grey market jobs, employers were allowed to regularize their workers gradually, taking up to five years to reach the contractual minimum wages.

Perhaps the most controversial aspect of the Pact were the 'local contracts' (*contratti d'area*) which the unions and employers' associations, in concert with local governments, could sign in zones of economic crisis. These would involve government and EU subsidies for development initiatives, but could also include special labour market measures, including wage policies, designed to encourage economic growth. However, when the law implementing the Pact was discussed in Parliament, Communist Refoundation and the Greens added an amendment which stipulated that the national minimum wage levels had to be respected; the CISL and UIL (and, naturally, Confindustria) protested against this legislative intervention, which they claimed limited the freedom to bargain of the unions and employers.[38]

The government's involvement in labour market policies was in part motivated by a desire to accommodate, at least by an expression of intention, the unions' aim of job creation. At the same time, it offered incentives, such as subsidies for zones in crisis, to encourage greater labour market flexibility. Its efforts in this direction, however, were less than successful, as the fate of the local contracts demonstrates. In fact, much of the entrepreneurial activity in the South involves the use of black and grey labour in any case, so that it is difficult to assess the real impact of the measures the employers are pressing for; the problem of unemployment has no simple or straightforward solution.

In the labour relations field, the state was constrained by the historical legacy of Italian labour relations, including both the structure of collective bargaining and the attachment of the unions and workers to certain institutions and practices. It was also limited by the immediate imperatives of capital accumulation – e.g. the metalworking employers' need to contain costs in 1996–97. Within these boundaries, its actions tended both to unite the capitalist front, or at a minimum avoid major splits within it, and to bring the unions into a form of co-operative negotiation that was functional to the needs of capital. Given the divisions in the union movement itself, this was an uncertain enterprise, but the government considered it more prudent to bank on a strong and moderate union movement rather than a divided and weak one. In this it was able to represent the long-term interests of capital, as it perceived them, better than the capitalists themselves, as in the case of the 1997 metalworkers' contract. Its role seems to confirm in a modified form the Poulantzian interpretation of the role of the state in capitalist society; but this interpretation has to be inserted into a framework of capital accumulation and institutional legacies.

# 10 Conclusion

## The limits of the state's autonomy

In the previous chapters, we have seen that somewhat different logics appear to apply in different policy areas. While the approach favoured in the Introduction, German derivationism, did indeed account well for the monetary policies of the Bank of Italy, we called on the concept of Bonapartism, a centrepiece of Poulantzas' theory of the capitalist state, to explain the eventual resolution of the issue of government debt, while a version of his approach modified to include institutional and economic factors also best fitted the facts of industrial relations policy. Bonapartism, furthermore, appears to do justice to the historically autonomous role of the state in Italy. Does this mean that theoretical eclecticism is the only possible stance to take *vis-à-vis* the Italian political economy? Is the search for a unified theory a hopelessly modernist endeavour anyway? Or can the different threads be woven together into a coherent whole?

In fact the derivationist approach is open enough to accommodate our findings with respect to budgetary policy and industrial relations, as well as monetary policy. Joachim Hirsch, who has already been quoted in the Introduction, attempts to base his derivation of the state on the nature of exploitation under capitalism, and in particular on the non-coercive form of that exploitation.[1] This implies a sensitivity to the need to secure the consent or acquiescence of both capitalists and non-capitalists for the policies of the state. Hence a Poulantzian element is built into Hirsch's theory from the beginning: the objective tendencies determined by the law of value and the capital relation assert themselves through the mediation of concrete political movements and processes, class struggles and conflicts between individual capitals and groups of capitals on a national and on an international level.[2] Hirsch, like Poulantzas, envisages conflicts between capitals[3] and also the fragmentation of the state apparatus into different institutions operating with different logics in response to pressures from distinct fractions of capital and from non-capitalist classes:

> It necessarily falls apart into a conglomerate of relatively unconnected part-bureaucracies, because it must, in a contradictory manner, relate to and support itself on competing individual capitals having, under

the conditions of competition on the world market, extraordinarily different valorization interests, *and* on opposing classes and class fractions – not least because certain measures which secure the reproduction of capital in the long term can regularly be implemented only under the pressure of non-capitalist classes and against the resistance of individual capitals and groups of capitals. Already from this it follows that under capitalist conditions there can be no unified interventionist strategy.[4]

This version of derivationism, then, can account for the way in which the Italian state operated according to seemingly different logics in different policy areas; a purely economic theory is insufficient to explain the actions of the capitalist state. It is not just a question of taking account of ideology and institutions, which shape actors' perceptions of their economic interests, as suggested in the Introduction.[5] The nature of capitalist relations of production means that there is a political element included in the economic from the outset:[6] just as the relations of exploitation in a slave-holding society may impose limits on the economic options of slave-owners, making, for example, industrial production unattractive for essentially political reasons,[7] so capitalist relations of production impose constraints on the ability of the capitalist state to act in what would be the best interests of capital in a purely economic sense.

The above approach does not imply indeterminacy, since the political constraints on the state can in theory at least be specified *ex ante*. Unlike Poulantzas' framework, it postulates that there is pressure for the state's action to conform to the economic logic of capital (as indicated for example in Chapter 9); unlike a crudely derivationist theory, it sets political limits to the operation of the state. Again in distinction to Poulantzas, our approach does not postulate that the political limits to the fulfilment of the economic interests of capitalists consist only of the concessions that must be made to secure overall social harmony and stave off revolutionary activity: they also operate within the economy itself, within individual workplaces, and not always as part of a conscious political strategy of capital. Interestingly, these political limits may often take the form of institutions or ideologies, as in the case of industrial relations – institutions and ideologies which embody a view of the way in which industrial relations ought to be conducted that is only partly shared by different social classes. In the Italian case, we saw that it is more strongly embraced by the unions than by the employers, whose acceptance of it is usually pragmatic rather than normative.

It is also worth reiterating, again in opposition to a crudely derivationist approach, that there is no unique best solution to the problems facing capital in its self-expansion. For instance, Italy's entry into the EMS and the Bank of Italy's pursuit of a more restrictive policy in the 1980s were not necessarily the best strategy for Italian capital – more expansionary alternatives were also available, that might, especially in different political conditions and with a different industrial relations situation, have proved at least as profitable. So derivation in the sense of reading off the state's policies from the objective demands of capitalist expansion is not possible. On the other hand, if an institution such as the Bank pursues a policy that is in its view conducive to the long-term interests of capital, even if it must act in the face of the opposition of a large segment of the capitalists themselves, then it can be said to be acting according to a broadly derivationist logic, as opposed to an instrumentalist or Poulantzian one.

The role played by the governments of the 1992–98 period in solving the debt problem can be called Bonapartist in the sense that the normal political representatives of capital were replaced by technical governments and later by a centre-left one. Again, the broad logic is derivationist in that the goal of debt reduction and the objective of entry into the EMU can be seen as a strategy (though not the only possible one) conducive to the expansion of Italian capital. The Bonapartist aspect, stemming from the inability of the hitherto governing parties, the DC and its allies, to undertake the necessary policies, demonstrates again that measures in the objective interest of capital do not flow automatically from the political system. It would be possible to argue that the Bank of Italy played a similar Bonapartist role in one policy area (monetary policy); while Louis Napoleon derived his prestige from his name and the legacy of his uncle's regime, the Bank drew on a different mystique, but one equally potent in economic circles.[8] This point does not, however, contradict the argument made above that the content of the Bank's policies reflected its view of the long-term interests of Italian capital.

Finally, in the area of industrial relations the function of the state in maintaining the consent of the dominated class is central – this can be accommodated within Hirsch's approach as a political limit on the action of the state (see above). Even here, however, the need to maintain consent interacted with the goals of Italian capital as dictated by the economic conjuncture. The nature of capitalist relations of production limited the economic choices available both to capitalists and to the state.

Derivationism, in other words, can explain well the content of state actions in the various policy areas we have considered. On the other hand, concepts derived from Poulantzas' work, such as Bonapartism, can account for the fact that these policies, potentially in the interest of Italian capital as whole, were actually adopted – i.e. the conjunction of political forces that allowed them to be implemented. Poulantzas' theory, taken alone, would suggest that budget deficits should be run to conciliate different classes and interests, and that concessions to the working class may be necessary in industrial relations, without giving sufficient weight to the economic imperatives of capitalist accumulation. The tendency towards Bonapartism for Poulantzas stems in the first place from the conflicts between fractions of the bourgeoisie, and in the second from the need to conciliate the working class and other non-capitalist classes. In the Italian case, the dominant position of the 'good salon' over other fractions of capital was scarcely challenged during the period of this study; while concessions had to be made to the needs of small and medium capital, the overall shape of policy was always more consonant with the interests of Fiat, Pirelli, and Mediobanca, even when it diverged from their first preferences. The need to conciliate the petty bourgeoisie (whose interests are typically similar to those of small capital) and, at times, the working class was more serious; yet the need for Bonapartism arose from the economic situation that Italy was faced with, and the reluctance of all classes and class fractions, in varying degrees, to undertake policy initiatives such as entry into the EMS and deficit reduction.[9] This is where Poulantzas' approach is seriously deficient.

International factors played a key role in structuring the choices available to the state, and to the various fractions of capital, for that matter. Italy's joining the EMS was not in the interest of Italian capital, at least in the short run and as it saw it. However, the availability of this option made it possible for political parties to use it for their own purposes in the struggle against the left. Similarly, the shift in the climate of ideas in Europe towards monetarism, and the influence of the Bundesbank's tight money policy, transmitted through the EMS, determined the Bank of Italy's policy of the 1980s.[10] And of course the need to control inflation in view of Italy's intention to rejoin the EMS was a powerful stimulus to the conclusion of the July accord on collective bargaining in 1993. None of this is meant to suggest that Italy was inevitably locked into a policy pattern imposed by Germany's monetary stance. It was certainly possible for the Italians to stay out of the EMS in 1979, and the consensus of informed opinion was against their joining the EMU in the first group until at least autumn 1996. But the international factor powerfully tilted the range of options available in one direction. In Italy in particular the widespread support that European integration has enjoyed at both the elite and the mass level has exercised a strong influence in the same direction. International influences in their turn, while often transmitted through markets, are typically also the product of political decisions, whether by national institutions such as the Bundesbank or by international bodies.

It is worth while at this point to compare the above analysis with some of the other major approaches to the study of economic policy-making.[11] We have already shown both the value and the limitations of a Poulantzian approach; more traditional instrumentalist Marxist explanations, which see the state as a tool of the capitalist class, responsive to its expressed policy preferences, fare even less well in the face of the evidence concerning monetary policy, on which the Italian capitalist class was reluctant to follow the Bank of Italy until the later 1980s. Furthermore, the divisions within capital over industrial relations, and its opposition to the methods of the governments of the 1990s in reducing the deficit, if not to their goal, make a straightforward instrumentalist explanation of these policies difficult to sustain.[12] *A fortiori*, a pluralist approach, which views policy as the outcome of the push and pull of a myriad of interest groups, of which the various groups of capitalists are only a fraction, cannot account for the monetary policy, which was generally unpopular to the extent to which it was understood. While the bargaining and concessions to different interests around deficit reduction and industrial relations approximates the pluralist model better, the basic thrust and content of these policies is not very well explained by pluralism.

Furthermore, as Hall points out, the groups' interests are not an automatic reflection of their objective social situation, but are influenced by cultural, ideological, and institutional factors.[13] For the same reasons, rational choice theory, applied to the actions of societal actors, does not provide a satisfactory explanation of their behaviour. When applied to governments, it explains neither their tolerance of the Bank of Italy's restrictive policies, which indeed harmed the DC in the 1980s, nor the deficit reductions of the 1990s. Neither of these policies enhanced the electoral appeal of the parties responsible.[14]

When we turn to Skocpol's own preferred state-centred theory, it seems to reflect the historical pattern of Italian politics, characterized by a politically weak capitalist class and an active, strong state. On further examination, however, it is quite inappropriate for the Italian case. While, in her seminal article on interpretations of the New Deal, she correctly pointed out that actors in the state had autonomous influence on policy, and that institutional structures of power such as political parties shape and limit the possibilities of public policy, this does not provide us with a theory that explains the actual course that the state adopted. And it is difficult to conceive of Italian political leaders as an autonomous state elite pursuing their own self-aggrandizing projects. For instance, the personnel of the Bank of Italy are surely among the prime candidates for membership in anyone's listing of the Italian state elite; yet the EMU project led to the Bank's losing its most important functions to the European Central Bank.

Any state-centred theory would have to be at a minimum seriously revised to take account of the EU's supplanting the nation-state in many roles.[15] Similarly, theories such as Fred Block's,[16] which posit that state managers are autonomous from the capitalist class but are structurally driven to promote capital accumulation in most circumstances in their own self-interest, are undermined by such seemingly non-self-interested actions. In addition, Block's theory cannot account for decisions that are motivated primarily by partisan rivalry, such as the Italian entry into the EMS.

Finally, we must also consider the neo-institutionalist analysis developed by Peter Hall.[17] It differs from Skocpol's focus on state institutions and the autonomous agency of state elites: for Hall, institutions are more akin to conventions of behaviour, with a strongly interpretivist, even Wittgensteinian, aspect. Institutions, as Hall recognizes, are essentially rules of action. He writes that 'they have a more formal status than cultural norms but one that does not necessarily derive from legal, as opposed to conventional, standing',[18] but the concept of an institution that he uses throughout *Governing the Economy* is in fact quite elastic, encompassing for instance the structure of markets for British goods (Chapter 2). It would not be unfair to say that for him institutions are a particular type of cultural norms, though they may be norms shared and understood by only a particular group of the population (e.g. the conventions of parliamentary behaviour). Seen in this light, Hall's approach has some of the same defects as cultural analysis: while it is often a good way of explaining differences between nations or cultures, it is not as good at explaining change within a culture. For this, it must often draw on other forms of analysis. For instance, in the case of Italian industrial relations, the policy area where institutional/cultural factors have the most obvious role, these factors cannot account for the impetus to change that led to the end of the old *scala mobile* and the conclusion of the July accords in 1993.

A strong case can also be made that the institutional position of the Bank of Italy was a necessary condition for its pursuit of a tight money policies in the 1980s and after; yet, again, it had held this privileged institutional position since the war, but began to pursue these policies only in the 1980s. Hall, like Skocpol, is right to lay emphasis on the institutional factors that give the state the capacity to act (or deny it that capacity); yet whether these capacities are exercised, and for what ends, cannot generally be explained by the institutional analysis itself.

To summarize very briefly, the above explanations are all limited by their near exclusive focus on political or institutional factors. On the other hand, an analysis of economic policy-making must begin from the economic structure and the dynamic of capital accumulation. There is no single path laid out *ex ante* for accumulation; we have seen the crucial role of international factors in privileging certain paths, by enhancing the opportunities they seem to offer. These international factors no longer operate solely through the preferences of domestic actors, as Gourevitch's analysis implies.[19] They also operate on the state itself; Italian capital, even its more internationally oriented dominant fraction, was more hesitant about much of the direction of policy. In Italy over the past two decades, the state has led the country along a path of internationalization, the same path chosen by the leading fractions of capital in virtually all the developed world in the post-1973 period. The USA has been the driving force behind the much discussed process of 'globalization'; Canadian business decisively adopted an international strategy after 1985, supporting the drive for North American free trade; the leading fraction of British capital, finance and banking, had always been strongly internationalist in its orientation. Elsewhere in the European Union, German capital had also come to the conclusion that further internationalization was essential after the oil shocks of the 1970s,[20] and Germany was of course the dominant state within the EU. The new model has brought vastly increased profits and freedom for businesses and investors, while many of the previous gains of the working class have been rolled back. However, it is still evolving, and as it evolves resistance to it is also growing, in Italy and throughout the world.

# Notes

## 1 Introduction: capital and the state

1 See note 5 below.
2 Even accounting conventions are not neutral reflections of an underlying objective economic reality: see Norman Macintosh, *Accounting, Accountants, and Accountability: Poststructuralist Positions* (London: Routledge, 2002), especially Chapter 6.
3 See Peter Hall, *Governing the Economy* (New York: Oxford University Press, 1986), p. 19, for a distinction between institutions and cultural norms.
4 See Bob Jessop, 'Regulation Theories in Retrospect and Prospect', *Economy and Society*, 19, 2 (1990); I am indebted to Marcus Pistor for this reference.
5 Ithaca, New York: Cornell University Press, 1986; see pp. 55–60 on production profiles. Gourevitch recognizes the limitations of this approach to some degree: 'The ambiguity of interests causes problems: preferences may derive from situations, but what if situations are unclear?' (pp. 59–60). In truth, situations are *never* clear. His approach to production profiles is itself somewhat 'ambiguous' in that it is consistent both with a form of rational choice theory (collective actors act in their own interests) and with a Marxist economic interpretation of politics.
6 See especially *Pouvoir politique et classes sociales* (Paris: Maspéro, 1968) [English translation: *Political Power and Social Classes* (London: New Left Books, 1974)].
7 See John Holloway and Sol Picciotto, eds, *State and Capital: A Marxist Debate* (London: Edward Arnold, 1978), especially the editors' introduction and Hirsch's essay, 'The State Apparatus and Social Reproduction: Elements of a Theory of the Bourgeois State'.
8 See the discussion of Offe in Martin Carnoy, *The State and Political Theory* (Princeton, New Jersey: Princeton University Press, 1984), pp. 130–140; this book provides a useful summary of the Marxist debate on state theory up to that time.
9 See *Pouvoir politique et classes sociales*, p. 221 (English ed.: p. 204].
10 Rudolf Hilferding, *Finance Capital: A Study of the Latest Phase of Capitalist Development* (London: Routledge and Kegan Paul, 1981) [1910]; V.I. Lenin, *Imperialism, the Highest Stage of Capitalism*, in *Selected Works*, vol. I, part 2 (Moscow: Foreign Languages, 1952) [1917]; Karl Kautsky, 'Ultra-imperialism', *New Left Review*, 59 (Jan.–Feb., 1970) [1914].
11 'On the Analysis of the Bourgeois Nation State within the World Market Context', in Holloway and Picciotto, eds, *State and Capital*.
12 This is also one of the insights of the 'world-systems' approach: see Immanuel Wallerstein, *The Modern World-System* (New York: Academic Press, 1974), p. 348:

'Capitalism has been able to flourish precisely because the world-economy has had within its bounds not one but a multiplicity of political systems'. Cf. also Michael Mann, *The Sources of Social Power*, vol. 1 (Cambridge: Cambridge University Press, 1986), especially Chapter 15.

13 *States and Social Revolutions* (Cambridge: Cambridge University Press, 1979), p. 14.

14 E.g. K. McNamara, *The Currency of Ideas* (Ithaca, New York: Cornell University Press, 1998), especially pp. 144–151.

15 For one contribution to such an analysis, see Robert Brenner, *Uneven Development and the Long Downturn: the Advanced Capitalist Economies from Boom to Stagnation 1950–1998* (*New Left Review*, 229, May–June 1998: Special Report).

16 See Chapter 4 below.

17 See Chapter 2 below for a historical discussion of Italian capitalism.

18 See Chapter 6 below.

19 See Chapter 5 below.

20 See Chapter 3 below on the structure of Italian capitalism.

21 'The State Apparatus and Social Reproduction: Elements of a Theory of the Bourgeois State', in Holloway and Picciotto, eds, *State and Capital*, pp. 83–85.

22 See Grant Amyot, *The Italian Communist Party: The Crisis of the Popular Front Strategy* (London: Croom Helm, 1981), for a discussion of the PCI's strategy down to the end of the government of 'national solidarity' in 1979.

23 See Chapter 9 below on industrial relations.

24 See Chapters 7 and 8 below.

25 Cf. Antonio Gramsci, *Selections from the Prison Notebooks*, ed. Q. Hoare and G. Nowell Smith (London: Lawrence and Wishart, 1971), p. 220, where J.R. MacDonald's Labour governments are described as Bonapartist.

26 Chapters 7 and 8, below.

27 Chapter 9 below.

## 2 The growth and development of Italian capitalism

1 See G. Ingham, *Capitalism Divided? The City and Industry in British Social Development* (Basingstoke: Macmillan, 1984), and Michio Morishima, *Why Has Japan 'Succeeded'?: Western Technology and the Japanese Ethos* (Cambridge: Cambridge University Press, 1982).

2 Maurice Aymard, 'La transizione dal feudalesimo al capitalismo', in *Storia d'Italia*, Annali, vol. I (Turin: Einaudi, 1978), pp. 1174–1178.

3 Philip Jones, 'Economia e società nell'Italia medievale: la leggenda della borghesia', in *ibid.*, especially pp. 291–308.

4 E.g. *Quaderni del carcere*, ed. Valentino Gerratana (Turin: Einaudi, 1975), vol. II, p. 1039.

5 *Ibid.*, pp. 1361–1362.

6 Aymard, 'La transizione', pp. 1160–1162.

7 Piero Ugolini, 'Tecnologia ed economia agrarie dal feudalesimo al capitalismo', in *Storia d'Italia*, Annali, vol. I, p. 402.

8 Cf. R. Brenner, 'The Origins of Capitalist Development: a Critique of Neo-Smithian Marxism', *New Left Review*, 104 (July–Aug. 1977), and B. Moore Jr., *Social Origins of Dictatorship and Democracy: Lord and Peasant in the Making of the Modern World* (Boston: Beacon Press, 1993 [1966]), especially pp. 421–423. It is Moore who lays the greatest stress on the importance of a transition to commercial agriculture for future democratic development; seen in his framework, eighteenth-century Italy resembles pre-revolutionary France in many respects,

and future Italian history gives some clue as to what might have happened there had there been no Revolution.

9 See e.g. John Cammett, 'Two Recent Polemics on the Character of the Italian Risorgimento', *Science and Society*, XXVII, 4 (Autumn 1963), and E.M. Capecelatro and A. Carlo, *Contro la 'questione meridionale'* (Rome: Samonà and Savelli, 1972).

10 On the definition of capitalism, see Jairus Banaji, 'Modes of Production in a Materialist Conception of History', *Capital and Class*, 3 (Autumn 1977).

11 See e.g. *Quaderni del carcere*, vol. III, pp. 2010–2014.

12 John Gooch, *Army, State, and Society in Italy 1870–1915* (London: Macmillan, 1989), pp. 12–13.

13 Ministero dell'Interno, Direzione Generale dell'Amministrazione Civile, Servizio Elettorale, *Compendio dei risultati delle elezioni politiche dal 1848 al 1958* (Rome: Istituto poligrafico dello Stato, 1963), pp. 12, 15, and 400.

14 R.A. Webster, *Industrial Imperialism in Italy 1908–1915* (Berkeley: University of California Press, 1975), pp. 15 ff.

15 See Hilferding, *Finance Capital*.

16 See Alexander Gershenkron, *Economic Backwardness in Historical Perspective* (Cambridge, Massachusetts: Harvard University Press, 1962), pp. 76–77.

17 Peter Gourevitch, *Politics in Hard Times* (Ithaca, New York: Cornell University Press, 1986), pp. 94–103.

18 Antonio Gramsci, 'La situazione italiana e i compiti del PCI' (the 'Lyons Theses'), in *La costruzione del Partito Comunista 1923–1926* (Turin: Einaudi, 1972), pp. 491–493.

19 See Grifone, *Il capitale finanziario*, pp. 7–10, and Gerschenkron, *Economic Backwardness*, pp. 88–89; cf. Valerio Castronuovo, 'La storia economica', in *Storia d'Italia*, vol. IV, part 1 (Turin: Einaudi, 1975), pp. 115–117, for a different view.

20 Grifone, p. 12.

21 See above, note 15.

22 Giampiero Carocci, *Giolitti e l'età giolittiana* (Turin: Einaudi, 1971), pp. 36–37 and 41–43.

23 Antonio Gramsci, 'Alcuni temi della quistione meridionale', in *La costruzione del Partito Comunista*, p. 146, and 'La situazione italiana e i compiti del PCI', *ibid.*, pp. 492–494.

24 See Webster, *Industrial Imperialism*, pp. 150 ff. and Giuliano Procacci, *History of the Italian People* (New York: Harper & Row, 1970), pp. 326–327; cf. Carocci, *Giolitti*, pp. 37–41.

25 Procacci, *History*, p. 332.

26 Nicos Poulantzas, *Fascism and Dictatorship* (London: NLB, 1974), pp. 114–117.

27 See later in this chapter, p. 22 for an explanation of 'Fordism'.

28 Grifone, pp. 99–106.

29 *Ibid.*, pp. 106–107.

30 See Castronuovo, 'La storia economica', p. 314 n1 and p. 316.

31 Eugenio Scalfari and Giuseppe Turani, *Razza padrona* (Milan: Feltrinelli, 1974), pp. 19–22, and A. Martinelli, 'Organised Business and Italian Politics: Confindustria and the Christian Democrats in the Postwar Period', in P. Lange and S. Tarrow, eds, *Italy in Transition* (London: Frank Cass, 1980), p. 74.

32 Scalfari and Turani, *Razza padrona*, p. 22.

33 *Ibid.*, p. 86.

34 Michele Salvati, 'The Impasse of Italian Capitalism', *New Left Review*, 76 (Nov.–Dec. 1972), pp. 7–10.

35 Martinelli, 'Organised Business', p. 73.

36 See Joseph La Palombara, *Interest Groups in Italian Politics* (Princeton, New Jersey: Princeton University Press, 1964), pp. 267–270.

37  See Eugenio Scalfari, 'Un "corsaro" al servizio della repubblica', in Francesco Rosi and Eugenio Scalfari, *Il caso Mattei* (Bologna: Cappelli, 1972), and Scalfari and Turani, *Razza padrona*, pp. 45–48.
38  Rosi and Scalfari, *Il caso Mattei*, p. 52.
39  F.R. Willis, *Italy Chooses Europe* (New York: Oxford University Press, 1971), p. 36.
40  For typical statements of this perspective, see Alain Lipietz, *Mirages and Miracles* (London: Verso, 1987), especially Chapters 1 and 2, and Michel Aglietta, *A Theory of Capitalist Regulation* (London: NLB, 1979). For a discussion of the regulation school, see p. 22 and, more fully, pp. 64–66, below.
41  See Grant Amyot, 'La ripresa e la battaglia contro il neocapitalismo (1955–1966)', in *I comunisti a Torino 1919–1972* (Rome: Editori Riuniti, 1974), pp. 239–240, and Castronuovo, 'La storia economica', p. 430.
42  Martinelli, 'Organised Business', p. 76.
43  See Augusto Graziani, 'La strategia della divisione', *Quaderni piacentini*, 56 (July 1975), pp. 41 ff.
44  M. Salvati, 'May 1968 and the Hot Autumn of 1969: the responses of two ruling classes', in Suzanne Berger, ed., *Organizing Interests in Western Europe* (Cambridge: Cambridge University Press, 1981), pp. 340–341.
45  See Lucio Magri, 'Spazio e ruolo del riformismo', in V. Parlato, ed., *Spazio e ruolo del riformismo* (Bologna: Il Mulino, 1974).

**3  Wealth and power in contemporary Italian business**

1  See below, pp. 56–57 and Chapter 4, pp. 66–67 and 77.
2  'Sectoral patterns of technical change: towards a taxonomy and a theory', *Research Policy*, 6 (1984), quoted in F. Onida and G. Viesti, eds, *The Italian Multinationals* (London: Croom Helm, 1988), p. 17.
3  One of the first of this large series of studies was Michael Piore and Charles Sabel, *The Second Industrial Divide* (New York: Basic Books, 1984). For a summary of some of this work, see P. Hirst and J. Zeitlin, 'Flexible Specialization: Theory and Evidence in the Analysis of Industrial Change', in J. Hollingworth and R. Boyer, eds, *Contemporary Capitalism: the Embeddedness of Institutions* (Cambridge: Cambridge University Press, 1997), pp. 234–239.
4  See Augusto Graziani, *I conti senza l'oste* (Turin: Bollati Boringhieri, 1997), p. 49.
5  See Table 3.3.
6  Ricerche e Studi, *R&S 1999* (Milan: 1999), vol. II, pp. 59–136 and 544–545, and *La Repubblica*, 21 Dec. 1996, p. 33.
7  Alan Friedman, *Tutto in famiglia* (Milan: Longanesi, 1988), pp. 373–374 and 388–389.
8  See, for example, Alan Friedman, *Il bivio* (Milan: Longanesi, 1996), for the contraposition between 'old' and 'new' in Italian capitalism; see especially pp. 199–201.
9  See Marco Revelli, *Le due destre*, pp. 9–10.
10  Friedman, *Il bivio*, p. 196.
11  *R&S 1995*, vol. I, p. 65.
12  Giuseppe Turani, 'Col cambio in salita la Fiat non va', *La Repubblica – Affari & Finanza*, 3 Feb. 1997, p. 9.
13  *Corriere della Sera*, 26 Oct. 1996.
14  *R&S 1995*, vol. I, p. 65.
15  Cf. Jeffry A. Frieden, 'National Economic Policies in a World of Global Finance', *International Organization*, 45, 4 (Autumn 1991), pp. 444–446.
16  *La Repubblica*, 11 Oct. 2002.

17  *R&S 1995*, vol. III, p. 201.
18  *L'Espresso*, 23 Oct. 1988, pp. 259–263.
19  Jeffry A. Frieden, 'National Economic Policies in a World of Global Finance', pp. 444–446.
20  *La Repubblica*, 28 July 2001.
21  *R&S 1999*, vol. II, pp. 197–232.
22  Law of 6 Aug. 1990, no. 223.
23  Friedman, *Il bivio*, p. 94. Cf. Friedman, 'The Economic Elites and the Political System', in S. Gundle and S. Parker, eds, *The New Italian Republic* (London: Routledge, 1996).
24  Cf. Turani, *I sogni del Grande Nord*, pp. 27–31.
25  The SuperGemina operation is described in Friedman, *Il bivio*, Chapters 3 and 4, and in Turani, *I sogni*, pp. 56–72.
26  *R&S 1999*, vol. I, pp. 1083–1105.
27  Giuseppe Turani, *L'Ingegnere* (Milan: Sperling & Kupfer, 1988) Chapter 1.
28  *La Repubblica*, 11 Mar. 1997, p. 25 and 9 Mar. 1997, p. 34.
29  See *La Repubblica*, 4 Oct. 1996, pp. 6–7, for the state of De Benedetti's holdings and a summary of Olivetti's losses.
30  *La Repubblica: Affari & Finanza*, 6 May 1999.
31  Friedman, *Il bivio*, p. 88.
32  *Ibid.*, p. 94. Cf. also Turani, *I sogni del Grande Nord*, pp. 32–35.
33  *Il bivio*, p. 87.
34  *Dati cumulativi di 1640 società italiane (1988)* (Milan: Mediobanca, 1988), pp. 31 and 37.
35  Franco Grassini, 'Molteplicità di obiettivi e governo delle partecipazioni statali', *L'industria*, n.s., IV, 4 (Oct.–Dec. 1983).
36  Laura Pennacchi, 'Ruolo, decisionalità e autonomia dei managers nelle partecipazioni statali', unpublished, n.d., pp. 15 ff.
37  Grassini, p. 646.
38  *La Repubblica*, 10 Nov. 1988, p. 44.
39  Cf. Giuseppe Turani in *La Repubblica*, 26 June 2000, p. 17, who agrees the managers could not be controlled because they had political protectors.
40  Laura Pennacchi, 'Ruolo, decisionalità e autonomia dei managers nelle partecipazioni statali'.
41  See G. Galli and A. Nannei, *Il mercato di stato* (Milan: Sugarco, 1984), Chapter 1 and pp. 97–110, and Augusto Graziani, 'La strategia della divisione', *Quaderni Piacentini*, a. XIV, n. 56 (July 1975), pp. 40–43.
42  As was the case with Mattei and Lanerossi. See also Laura Pennacchi, 'Valori e cultura dei manager pubblici', *Politica ed economia*, 3rd s., XIX, 3 (Mar. 1988), R. Prodi quoted in Alan Friedman, *Ce la farà il capitalismo italiano?* (Milan: Longanesi, 1989), pp. 88–89, and Franco Reviglio quoted in *ibid.*, pp. 99–100.
43  See Patrizio Bianchi, 'The IRI in Italy: Strategic Role and Political Constraints', *West European Politics*, 10, 2 (April 1987), pp. 285–287.
44  *La Repubblica – Affari & Finanza*, 14 Oct. 1988, p. 10.
45  Silvio Berlusconi, the Prime Minister, is currently (May 2003) standing trial for his role as Craxi's associate in blocking this sale; it is alleged that he ordered the bribing of judges.
46  *La Repubblica*, 18 Feb. 1990.
47  *R&S 1999, passim.*
48  As a senior manager of the Paribas bank, one of the Banca Commerciale shareholders, said about another operation: 'Well, the operation in itself is not so important to us as having the patronage of Monsieur Cuccia. You know, when you go to Rome . . .' (Friedman, *Il bivio*, p. 58).

49 For the 1997 controlling group of the Banca Commerciale, see *La Repubblica – Affari & Finanza*, 17 Mar. 1997, p. 4; for the same group just after privatization, see Magda Bianco and Sandro Trento, 'Capitalismi a confronto: i modelli di controllo delle imprese', *Stato e mercato*, 43 (April 1995), p. 87.
50 Magda Bianco and Sandro Trento, 'Capitalismi a confronto', pp. 86–87.
51 *La Repubblica – Affari & Finanza*, 17 Feb. 1997, p. 5.
52 *La Repubblica*, 9 Mar. 1997, p. 11.
53 *Il Mondo*, 13 Feb. 1998 and 5 June 1998.
54 *La Repubblica – Affari & Finanza*, 29 Sept. 1998; *Il Mondo*, 22 Jan. 1999; *ibid.*, 23 June 1999.
55 See John Zysman, *Governments, Markets, and Growth* (Ithaca, New York: Cornell University Press, 1983), pp. 69–75. Cf. also G. Nardozzi, *Tre sistemi creditizi: Banche ed economia in Francia, Germania e Italia* (Bologna: Il Mulino, 1983) and C. Scognamiglio, 'Le recenti tendenze del mercato mobiliare e la concentrazione finanziaria dell'industria italiana', *L'industria*, n.s., V, 1 (Jan.–Mar. 1986).
56 See Turani, *I sogni*, pp. 125–130.
57 See *La Repubblica*, 7 Jan. 1997.
58 Speech by Diego della Valle at PDS Congress: live broadcast on Radio Radicale, 22 Feb. 1997.
59 *La Repubblica – Affari & Finanza*, 17 Feb. 1997, p. 5.
60 A classic statement of this view is in Suzanne Berger, 'Introduction', to S. Berger, ed., *Organizing Interests in Western Europe* (Cambridge: Cambridge University Press, 1981), especially pp. 14–16.
61 A classic example is C. Wright Mills, *The Power Elite* (London: Oxford University Press, 1956), pp. 57–68; cf. Tom Bottomore, *Elites and Society* (Harmondsworth: Penguin, 1964), pp. 32–38, for a critique of this strand of elite theory.
62 Cf. Giulio Sapelli, *L'Italia di fine secolo* (Venice: Marsilio, 1998), pp. 142–143.
63 See note 66 below.
64 On the regional character of the Italian bourgeoisie, see Sapelli, *Sul capitalismo italiano*, pp. 24–29.
65 N. Abercrombie, S. Hill, and B. Turner, *The Dominant Ideology Thesis* (London, 1980), pp. 138–140.
66 A. Martinelli, A. Chiesi, and N. Dalla Chiesa, *I grandi imprenditori italiani* (Milan: Feltrinelli, 1981), p. 134.
67 *La Repubblica*, 6 Mar. 1997, p. 26.
68 *La Repubblica*, 25 June 2000 and 6 May 1999.
69 *Ibid.*, 15 Sept. 1999.
70 *I conti senza l'oste*, pp. 48–50, 71–73.
71 *Le due destre*, pp. 8–10.
72 *Ibid.*, p. 53; cf. Chapter 6, for the reflection of this division at the political party level.
73 *La Repubblica – Affari & Finanza*, 10 Mar. 1997, p. 4.

**4 Italian capitalism in comparative perspective**

1 Among many others, Michel Albert, *Capitalism against Capitalism* (London: Whurr, 1993), Lester Thurow, *Head to Head* (London: Nicholas Brealey, 1994), and the summary in Will Hutton, *The State We're In*, revised ed. (London: Vintage, 1996), Chapter 10.
2 See John Zysman, *Governments, Markets, and Growth* (Ithaca, New York: Cornell University Press, 1983), Chapter 6.

3 For an overview of some of the models of 'post-Fordism', see Mario Regini, 'La varietà italiana del capitalismo', *Stato e mercato*, 43 (April 1995), 'Social Institutions and Production Structure: the Italian Variety of Capitalism in the 1980s', in C. Crouch and W. Streeck, eds, *Political Economy of Modern Capitalism* (London: Sage, 1997), and *Modelli di capitalismo: Le risposte europee alla sfida della globalizzazione* (Rome-Bari: Laterza, 2000).

4 See previous note and Richard Locke, *Remaking the Italian Economy* (Ithaca, New York: Cornell University Press, 1995), for two of the major attempts to do so by scholars in the field. Of course, the strengths and weaknesses of Italian capitalism, as revealed by comparisons with other countries, are the daily bread of journalistic comment and polemic in Italy, but these discussions too often present Italy as *sui generis* or anomalous, rather than trying to set it *sine ira ac studio* in a truly comparative framework.

5 Letter to *Otechestvenniye Zapiski*, in Karl Marx and Friedrich Engels, *Collected Works*, vol. 24 (New York: International Publishers, 1989). On England, see Louis Althusser, 'The Object of *Capital*', in L. Althusser and Etienne Balibar, *Reading Capital* (London: NLB, 1970), pp. 194–198.

6 *Capital*, vol. III, 3rd ed. (Moscow: Progress, 1966), Chapter 14, 'Counteracting Influences'.

7 *Ibid.*, Chapter 48, pp. 820–821.

8 'The Eighteenth Brumaire of Louis Bonaparte', in *Surveys from Exile* (Harmondsworth: Penguin, 1973), pp. 172–174.

9 See Chapter 1, note 10.

10 *Ibid.*, pp. 326–327.

11 See V.I. Lenin, 'Imperialism, the Highest Stage of Capitalism' in *Selected Works*, vol. I (Moscow: Foreign Languages, 1952).

12 *Pouvoir politique et classes sociales*, p. 166 [English ed.: pp. 154–155].

13 See Alain Lipietz, *Mirages and Miracles* (London: Verso, 1987), Chapter 2, and the other works cited at Chapter 2, note 40, for a good outline of the regulation school approach.

14 See Regini, 'La varietà italiana del capitalismo', and P. Hirst and J. Zeitlin, 'Flexible Specialization: Theory and Evidence in the Analysis of Industrial Change', and R. Hollingsworth, 'Continuities and Changes in Social Systems of Production', both in J.R. Hollingsworth and R. Boyer, eds, *Contemporary Capitalism* (Cambridge: Cambridge University Press, 1997).

15 See Mike Davis, *Prisoners of the American Dream* (London: Verso, 1986), especially Chapter 5, and Alain Lipietz, 'The Globalisation of the Fordist Regime of Accumulation', in J. Holmes and C. Leys, eds, *Frontyard, Backyard: the Americas in the Global Crisis* (Toronto: Between the Lines, 1987), and 'The Fortunes and Misfortunes of Post-Fordism', in Robert Albritton, *et al.*, eds, *Phases of Capitalist Development* (Basingstoke: Palgrave, 2001).

16 Cf., for a particularly lucid attempt to apply the traditional analysis, Napoleone Colajanni, *Il capitalismo senza capitale* (Milan: Sperling & Kupfer, 1991), pp. 249–254 (see p. 72 below).

17 *Production, Power, and World Order* (New York: Columbia University Press, 1987), pp. 285–298.

18 *Ibid.*, p. 7.

19 *Scale and Scope* (with T. Hikino) (Cambridge, Massachusetts: Harvard University Press, 1990).

20 E.g. Giulio Sapelli, *Sul capitalismo italiano* (Milan: Feltrinelli, 1993), p. 49.

21 New York: William Morrow, 1992.

22 *The State We're In*, Chapter 10.

23 *Ibid.*, p. 272.

24  John Zysman, *Governments, Markets, and Growth*; see also Richard Locke, *Remaking the Italian Economy*, pp. 13–15.
25  G. Gallarotti, *The Anatomy of an International Monetary Regime: the Classical Gold Standard, 1880–1914* (New York: Oxford University Press, 1995), pp. 19–21 and 165–180.
26  G.A. Epstein and J. Schor, 'Macropolicy in the Golden Age', in S. Marglin and J. Schor, eds, *The Golden Age of Capitalism* (Oxford: Clarendon Press, 1990).
27  Peter Hall, in his excellent review article ('La "political economy" europea oggi', *Stato e mercato*, 44 (August 1995)), states that all the models in political economy he discusses, including most of those under discussion here, aim at explaining economic performance (p. 269).
28  See, for a stimulating contribution including a survey of the debate, Steven Lukes, *Power: a radical view* (London: Macmillan, 1974). See also William Connolly, *The Terms of Political Discourse*, 2nd ed. (Princeton, New Jersey: Princeton University Press, 1983)), Chapter 3.
29  Cf. Martin Carnoy, *The State and Political Theory* (Princeton, New Jersey: Princeton University Press, 1984), pp. 130–135.
30  *What Does the Ruling Class Do When It Rules?* (London: Verso, 1980), pp. 129 ff.
31  Cf. the work of e.g. Adam Przeworski, who assumes the working class may have interests which are coincident with those of capital. See for example, 'Material Interests, Class Compromise, and the State', in *Capitalism and Social Democracy* (Cambridge: Cambridge University Press, 1985).
32  Therborn's perspective seems to complement the 'derivationist' theory of the state (see above, Chapter 1), in that it sets an ideal path for the capitalist state as the promoter of accumulation, but in fact he recognizes that capital also has a tendency to seek political dominance. This conflict between economic and political goals was a central theme of Poulantzas' *Political Power and Social Classes*, though he assumes the political goals will take priority.
33  *Production, Power, and World Order*, p. 197. However, on pp. 226–228 he writes as if Italy, at least from 1968–69, fell within the category of the 'neo-liberal' state.
34  See A. Pizzorno, 'Le difficoltà del consociativismo', in *Le radici della politica assoluta e altri saggi* (Milan: Feltrinelli, 1993).
35  'La varietà italiana del capitalismo'.
36  *Remaking the Italian Economy*, Chapters 1 and 6.
37  N. Colajanni, *Il capitalismo senza capitale*, pp. 249–254; Pietro Grifone, *Il capitale finanziario in Italia* (Turin: Einaudi, 1945).
38  *Sul capitalismo italiano*, p. 48.
39  Cf. *ibid.*, pp. 144–145.
40  See e.g. Mario Regini, 'The Conditions for Political Exchange: How Concertation Emerged and Collapsed in Italy and Great Britain', in John Goldthorpe, ed., *Order and Conflict in Contemporary Capitalism* (Oxford: Oxford University Press, 1984).
41  See Marco Revelli, *Le due destre* (Turin: Bollati Boringhieri, 1996), Part II, Chapter 5, and, in the same sense, R. Mehl, 'Fiat Auto e Volkswagen: due strategie a confronto', *Economia e politica industriale*, 89 (March 1996).
42  See below, pp. 173–174, and Banca d'Italia, *Bollettino economico*, 21 (Oct. 1993), pp. 32–33, for a good summary of the agreement. For discussion and commentary, see Franca Alacevich, *Le relazioni industriali in Italia* (Rome: Nuova Italia Scientifica, 1996), Chapter 6, and Michele Salvati, 'Crisi politica, risanamento finanziario e ruolo della concertazione', *Il Mulino*, 359 (May–June 1995).
43  Ithaca, New York: Cornell University Press, 1985.
44  P. Kurzer, *Business and Banking* (Ithaca, New York: Cornell University Press, 1993), pp. 15–20.

45 For an interesting analysis, see S. Perez, 'Monetary Union and Wage Bargaining Institutions in the EU', *Comparative Political Studies*, 35, 10 (Dec. 2002).
46 See e.g. G. Vaciago, 'Maggior precisione in tema di finanziarizzazione: un commento a De Cecco', *L'industria*, IX, 2 (April–June 1988).
47 Giuseppe Turani, *I sogni del Grande Nord* (Bologna: Il Mulino, 1996), p. 122.
48 Colajanni, *Il capitalismo senza capitale*, pp. 229–249.
49 See Linda Weiss, *Creating Capitalism: the State and Small Business since 1945* (Oxford: Blackwell, 1988) and Regini, 'La varietà italiana del capitalismo'.
50 See Banca d'Italia, *Bollettino economico*, 27 (Oct. 1996), p. 21.
51 Hutton, *The State We're In*, pp. 266–267.
52 See M. Ferrera, 'Il modello sud-europeo di Welfare State', *Rivista italiana di scienza politica*, XXVI, 1 (April 1996).
53 See Michele Salvati, 'The Impasse of Italian Capitalism'.
54 I. Cipolletta, 'L'industria italiana negli ultimi 15 anni: il ciclo delle interpretazioni', in I. Cipolletta, ed., *Struttura industriale e politiche macroeconomiche in Italia* (Bologna: Il Mulino, 1986).
55 Colajanni, *Il capitalismo senza capitale*, pp. 229 ff.

## 5 Italian capital in the global economy

1 For an overview of much of the first wave of literature, see Peter Hall, 'La "political economy" europea oggi', *Stato e mercato*, 44 (Aug. 1995). For a particularly pessimistic view, see P. Kurzer, *Business and Banking* (Ithaca, New York: Cornell University Press, 1993). Note also Jeffry Frieden, 'National Economic Policies in a World of Global Finance', *International Organization*, 45, 4 (Autumn 1991); G. Garrett, *Partisan Politics in the Global Economy* (Cambridge: Cambridge University Press, 1998), and 'Global Markets and National Politics: Collision Course or Virtuous Circle?' *International Organization*, 52, 4 (Autumn 1998); E. Huber and John Stephens, 'Internationalization and the Social Democratic Model', *Comparative Political Studies*, 31, 3 (June 1998); T. Iversen, *Contested Economic Institutions* (Cambridge: Cambridge University Press, 1999).
2 P. Hirst and G. Thompson, 'The problem of "globalization": international economic relations, national economic management, and the formation of trading blocs', *Economy and Society*, 21, 4 (Nov. 1992).
3 L. Panitch, 'Globalisation and the State', *The Socialist Register 1994*, ed. R. Miliband and L. Panitch (London: Merlin, 1994). Cf. also G. Garrett, 'The Causes of Globalization', *Comparative Political Studies*, 33, 6/7 (Aug.–Sept. 2000), especially pp. 967–970.
4 Alan Milward, *The European Rescue of the Nation-State*, 2nd ed. (London: Routledge, 2000), and 'Approaching Reality: Euro-Money and the Left', *New Left Review*, 216 (Mar.–April 1996), p. 58.
5 G. Garrett, 'Capital Mobility, Trade, and the Domestic Politics of Economic Policy', *International Organization*, 49, 4 (Autumn 1995).
6 Peter Katzenstein, *Small States in World Markets* (Ithaca, New York: Cornell University Press, 1985).
7 Source: see Table 5.2.
8 *Previsioni dell'economia italiana*, IX, 1 (June 1995), p. 161.
9 *Ibid.*, p. 137.
10 *Ibid.*, p. 144.
11 *Ibid.*, p. 149.
12 *Ibid.*, pp. 134 and 153 (controlled subsidiaries only).

13  US Department of State, *FY2001 Country Commercial Guide: Italy*, Table 7: outward FDI was US$165,564 m., and inward FDI was US$105,598 m.
14  *Previsioni dell'economia italiana*, IX, 1 (June 1995), pp. 157 and 159.
15  *Previsioni dell'economia italiana*, IX, 1 (June 1995), p. 65.
16  Interview, 9 Dec. 1996.
17  *La Repubblica*, 15 Dec. 1996, for the most critical speech by Giorgio Fossa, president of Confindustria.
18  Istituto Nazionale di Statistica, *Gli stranieri in Italia*, note e relazioni no. 1 (Rome: ISTAT, 1995), p. 52.
19  A credible estimate for the end of 1996 was 350,000–400,000 illegal immigrants in addition to the 1,086,000 legal ones; these figures include both economically active and inactive immigrants ('Venti d'Europa', Radio RAI 1, 24 Mar. 1997). The ISTAT data for 1989 gave a total number of immigrants between 1.1 and 1.2 million.
20  Cf. P. Gourevitch, *Politics in Hard Times* (Ithaca, New York: Cornell University Press, 1986), pp. 65–66.
21  See F. Willis, *Italy Chooses Europe* (New York: Oxford University Press, 1971).
22  European Commission, *Eurobarometer*, 53 (Oct. 2000), pp. 26 and 82.
23  See e.g. K. Dyson and K. Featherstone, *The Road to Maastricht* (Oxford: Oxford University Press, 1999), pp. 510–512 and 530–531. The authors also discuss the economic policy considerations that led the Italian government to seek membership.
24  There is a large literature on Maastricht (see discussion below, pp. 125–126. Besides Dyson and Featherstone, *ibid.*, see J. Walsh, *European Monetary Integration and Domestic Politics* (Boulder, Colorado: Lynn Rienner, 2000), J. Frieden, D. Gros, and E. Jones, eds, *The New Political Economy of EMU* (Lanham, Maryland: Rowman and Littlefield, 1998), B. Eichengreen and J. Frieden, eds, *Forging an Integrated Europe* (Ann Arbor: University of Michigan Press, 1998), and A. Watson, *Aspects of European Monetary Integration* (Basingstoke: Macmillan, 1997).
25  R. Masera, 'Single market, exchange rates and monetary unification', in A. Steinherr, ed., *30 Years of European Monetary Integration from the Werner Plan to EMU* (London: Longman, 1994).
26  *Previsioni dell'economia italiana*, X, 2 (Dec. 1996), pp. 30–33.
27  *Ibid.*, p. 32.
28  Interview with I. Cipolletta, 15 Nov. 1988.
29  See e.g. *Corriere della Sera*, 26 Oct. and 30 Nov. 1996.
30  See J.A. Frieden and R. Rogowski, 'The Impact of the International Economy on National Policies: An Analytical Overview', in R.O. Keohane and H.V. Milner, *Internationalization and Domestic Politics* (Cambridge: Cambridge University Press, 1996), pp. 36 ff.
31  *Ibid.*

## 6  Business and the political system

1  See e.g. R.O. Keohane and H.V. Milner, 'Introduction', in *Internationalization and Domestic Politics* (New York: Cambridge University Press, 1996), p. 10.
2  See above, Chapter 2.
3  See G. Amyot, 'Italy: The Long Twilight of the DC Regime', in Steven Wolinetz, ed., *Liberal Democracies: Parties and Party Systems* (London: Routledge, 1988).
4  Antonio Gramsci, *Selections from the Prison Notebooks*, ed. Q. Hoare and G. Nowell Smith (London: Lawrence and Wishart, 1971), p. 155; cf. *ibid.*, pp. 269–270.
5  *Ibid.*, p. 156.

6 Antonio Gramsci, *Quaderni del carcere*, ed. V. Gerratana, vol. III (Turin: Einaudi, 1975), p. 1712.
7 *Selections from the Prison Notebooks*, pp. 269–270.
8 *Ibid.*, p. 227.
9 Judith Chubb, *Patronage, Power and Poverty in Southern Italy* (Cambridge: Cambridge University Press, 1982), pp. 122–127.
10 Cf. Nicos Poulantzas, 'On Social Classes', *New Left Review*, 78 (Mar.–April 1973), pp. 37–39, and Gramsci, *Selections from the Prison Notebooks*, pp. 212 ff.
11 Chubb, pp. 111 ff.
12 See Alan Zuckerman, *The Politics of Faction: Christian Democratic Rule in Italy* (New Haven: Yale University Press, 1979), pp. 119 ff., and Marco Follini, *L'arcipelago democristiano* (Bari: Laterza, 1990), pp. 37 ff., for a more indulgent view from inside the party.
13 *Ibid.*, p. 38.
14 Interview, 26 Nov. 1988.
15 Franco Cazzola, in G. Pasquino, ed., *Il sistema politico italiano*, p. 195. See pp. 195–205 on the presence of the PSI in this period.
16 Cf. Leonardo Paggi and Massimo D'Angelillo, *I comunisti italiani e il riformismo* (Turin: Einaudi, 1986), p. xiii and *passim*. Paggi and D'Angelillo's thesis is that the PCI remained subordinate to the dominant pre-Keynesian liberal orthodoxy in economic thought: cf. pp. 127–129. See also below.
17 A. Martinelli *et al.*, *I grandi imprenditori italiani* (Milan: Feltrinelli, 1981), p. 114.
18 Cesare Romiti, *Questi anni alla Fiat*, interviewed by G. Pansa (Milan: Rizzoli, 1988), p. 293.
19 On the fall of the DC regime, see, for a synthetic overview, Paul Ginsborg, 'Explaining Italy's Crisis', in S. Gundle and S. Parker, eds, *The New Italian Republic* (London: Routledge, 1996). Of the fairly large literature, see also M. Salvati, 'L'imprevista ma prevedibile caduta di un regime', *Il Mulino*, 43, 2 (Mar.–April 1994), Stefano Guzzini, 'The "Long Night of the First Republic": years of clientelistic implosion in Italy', *Review of International Political Economy*, 2, 1 (Winter 1995), Mark Gilbert, *The Italian Revolution: the End of Politics, Italian Style* (Boulder: Westview, 1995), and Patrick McCarthy, *The Crisis of the Italian State* (New York: St. Martin's, 1995).
20 Cf. Turani, *I sogni del Grande Nord*, pp. 102–116.
21 Cf. Graziani, *I conti senza l'oste*, p. 46. In the same vein as we do, Michele Salvati does not consider the 'external' explanations, the end of the Cold War and Italy's position in the EU, decisive because of their timing, and instead believes the decay of the political system itself was the prime cause of the crisis ('L'imprevista ma prevedibile caduta di un regime').
22 See Paul Furlong, 'Political Catholicism and the Strange Death of the Christian Democrats', in Gundle and Parker, eds, *The New Italian Republic*.
23 Piergiorgio Corbetta and Arturo Parisi, *A Domanda Risponde* (Bologna: Il Mulino, 1997), pp. 227 and 279.
24 See Maurice Duverger, *Political Parties* (New York: Wiley Science Editions, 1963), pp. 63–71, for this classic distinction.
25 See Ken Carty, 'Three Canadian Party Systems', in George Perlin, ed., *Party Democracy in Canada* (Scarborough: Prentice-Hall, 1988) and Grant Amyot, 'Democracy Without Parties: A New Politics?' in B. Tanguay and A.G. Gagnon, eds, *Canadian Parties in Transition* (Scarborough: Nelson, 1996), pp. 525–526. This seems to be a different development from Katz and Mair's 'cartel party', which relies on state financing and support ('Party Organization, Party Democracy, and the Emergence of the Cartel Party', in Peter Mair, *Party System Change* (Oxford: Clarendon, 1997), pp. 107–116).

26  Nicos Poulantzas, *Political Power and Social Classes* (London: NLB, 1975), pp. 283–286.
27  See Paolo Segatti, 'I programmi elettorali e il ruolo dei mass media', in S. Bartolini and R. D'Alimonte, *Maggoritario ma non troppo* (Bologna: Il Mulino, 1995), pp. 150–159.
28  Corbetta and Parisi, eds, *A Domanda Risponde*, pp. 153 and 170–171.
29  Carlo Callieri, quoted in *La Stampa*, 20 April 1996, p. 5.
30  Revelli, *Le due destre*, p. 53.
31  Cf. Liborio Mattina, 'Gli attori economici. Vincitori e vinti', in I. Diamanti and R. Mannheimer, eds, *Milano a Roma. Guida all'Italia elettorale del 1994* (Rome: Donzelli, 1994), p. 157. See also Suzanne Berger, 'The Uses of the Traditional Sector in Italy: Why Declining Classes Survive', in Frank Bechhofer, ed., *The Petite Bourgeoisie: Comparative Studies of the Uneasy Stratum* (London: Macmillan, 1981) and 'Regime and interest representation: the French traditional middle classes', in Suzanne Berger, ed., *Organizing Interests in Western Europe* (Cambridge: Cambridge University Press, 1981), p. 86.
32  See S. Gundle and S. Parker, 'Introduction', *The New Italian Republic*, p. 14.
33  Cf. note 16 above.
34  Cf. Grant Amyot, *The Italian Communist Party: the Crisis of the Popular Front Strategy* (London: Croom Helm, 1981), p. 217.
35  Cf. Enrico Berlinguer, *Austerità, occasione per cambiare l'Italia* (Rome: Editori Riuniti, 1977) and Mario Regini, 'The Conditions for Political Exchange: How Concertation Emerged and Collapsed in Italy and Great Britain', in John Goldthorpe, ed., *Order and Conflict in Contemporary Capitalism* (Oxford: Clarendon Press, 1984), pp. 139–142.
36  'La nostra politica nazionale' (report to the cadres of the Naples organization, 11 April 1944), in *La via italiana al socialismo*, 2nd ed., ed. L. Gruppi and P. Zanini (Rome: Editori Riuniti, 1972), p. 43; see Amyot, pp. 42–43.
37  See note 16 above.
38  See below, p. 130.
39  Cf. Gramsci's characterization of the Ramsay MacDonald Labour governments as 'Caesarist' (*Selections from the Prison Notebooks*, p. 220).
40  *Le relazioni sindacali in Italia: Rapporto 1996–97*, ed. G. Baglioni, S. Negrelli, and D. Paparella (Rome: Edizioni Lavoro, 1997), p. 340.
41  See A. Martinelli, 'Borghesia industriale e potere politico', in *I grandi imprenditori italiani*, pp. 271–272.
42  Massimo Giannini, 'Confindustria gregaria del governo', *La Repubblica*, 11 Jan. 2002, pp. 1, 16.
43  See *Corriere della Sera*, 7 Sept. 2001 and 18 Oct. 2001; the Confcommercio was concerned to maintain consumers' purchasing power and to preserve the method of concertation with the unions in matters of social and labour policy.
44  See Luca Lanzalaco, 'L'elezione di Pininfarina alla presidenza della Confindustria e i problemi dell'associazionismo imprenditoriale', in R. Catanzaro and R. Nanetti, eds, *Politica in Italia: Edizione 1989* (Bologna: Il Mulino, 1989).
45  Maurizio Ricci, *Anni di ferro: Merloni alla Confindustria* (Rome: Ediesse, 1984), p. 12.
46  *La Repubblica*, 2 Feb. 1988.
47  *Panorama*, 13 Mar. 1988 and *La Repubblica*, 4 Mar. 1988.
48  *Corriere della Sera*, 7 and 9 April, 1992.
49  M. Me.[rlini], 'La Confindustria non studia più', *Politica ed economia*, 3rd series, XIII, 12 (Dec. 1982).
50  Cf. Joseph LaPalombara, *Interest Groups in Italian Politics* (Princeton, New Jersey: Princeton University Press, 1964), pp. 267–271.

51  *Le relazioni sindacali in Italia: Rapporto 1988–89,* eds G. Baglioni, P. Fetrin, and G. Pisu (Rome: Edizioni Lavoro, 1990), pp. 236 and 240.
52  Mirella Baglioni, 'Le associazioni nel settore della piccola e media impresa', *Quaderni di Diritto del Lavoro e Relazioni Industriali,* n. 8 (1990).
53  M. D'Antonio and G. Negri, *Il partito politico di fronte allo Stato di fronte a se stesso* (Milan: Giuffrè, 1983), p. 131.
54  Gianfranco Pasquino, *Istituzioni, partiti, lobbies* (Bari, Laterza, 1988), pp. 98 and 140.
55  Interview, 26 Nov. 1988.
56  *L'Espresso,* 10 May 1992.
57  *La Repubblica,* 25 April 1992.
58  *Ibid.,* 3/4 May 1992.
59  *La Repubblica,* 25 April 1992 and *L'Espresso,* 10 May 1992.
60  *La Repubblica,* 28 April 1992.
61  *Ibid.*
62  See A. Graziani, *I conti senza l'oste,* p. 45.
63  Interview, 31 Jan. 1990.
64  Cf. Pasquino, pp. 101 ff.
65  Interviews, 8 Nov., 9 Nov., and 18 Nov. 1988.
66  Interview, 26 Nov. 1988.
67  Theodore Lowi, 'The Public Philosophy: Interest-Group Liberalism', *American Political Science Review,* 61, 1 (March 1967).

## 7 Making Italian macroeconomic policy

 1  Kenneth Dyson and Kevin Featherstone, *The Road to Maastricht* (Oxford: Oxford University Press, 1999); see especially pp. 14 and 772.
 2  *Monetary Politics* (Ann Arbor: University of Michigan Press, 1997), pp. 67 and 110.
 3  'Invested interests: the politics of national economic policies in a world of global finance', *International Organization,* 45, 4 (Autumn 1991), pp. 444–446.
 4  E.g. Jeffry Frieden and Erik Jones, 'The Political Economy of European Monetary Union: A Conceptual Overview', in J. Frieden, D. Gros, and E. Jones, eds, *The New Political Economy of EMU* (Lanham, Maryland: Rowman & Littlefield, 1998), pp. 175 ff.
 5  James Walsh, *European Monetary Integration and Domestic Politics* (Boulder: Lynne Rienner, 2000), pp. 147–154.
 6  V. Chiorazzo and L. Spaventa, 'The Prodigal Son or a Confidence Trickster? How Italy got into the EMU', in D. Cobham and G. Zis, eds, *From EMS to EMU* (Basingstoke: Macmillan, 1999).
 7  Cf. Suzanne Berger, ed., *Organizing Interests in Western Europe* (Cambridge: Cambridge University Press, 1981).
 8  Interview, 8 Nov. 1988.
 9  G.A. Epstein and J. Schor, 'Il divorzio fra Banca d'Italia e Tesoro: un caso di indipendenza delle banche centrali', in P. Lange and M. Regini, eds, *Stato e regolazione sociale* (Bologna: Il Mulino, 1987).
10  Eugenio Peggio, 'La Banca d'Italia e le idee di Baffi', *Rinascita,* 8 (June 1979).
11  Giorgio La Malfa, 'Autonomia difficile', *La Stampa,* 20 Feb. 1986.
12  See Dyson and Featherstone, p. 462 note 18. Padoa Schioppa was vindicated a few years later when he was chosen to the Executive Committee of the new European Central Bank.
13  Marcello De Cecco, 'Una politica monetaria per gli anni '80', *Note economiche,* XV, 5–6 (Sept.–Dec. 1982).

14 Elisabetta Addis, 'Banca d'Italia e politica monetaria: la riallocazione del potere fra Stato, mercato e Banca centrale', *Stato e mercato*, 19 (April 1987).
15 Cf. Dyson and Featherstone, pp. 474–479.
16 P.C. Padoan, 'Sistema Monetario Europeo e politiche nazionali', in P.C. Padoan, ed., *Poltiche monetarie e politiche di bilancio nella Comunità Europea* (Bologna: Il Mulino, 1988), pp. 23–25.
17 *Ibid.*, pp. 45 ff.
18 Augusto Graziani, introduction to A. Graziani, ed., *La spirale del debito pubblico* (Bologna: Il Mulino, 1988).
19 See Martin Carnoy, *The State and Political Theory* (Princeton, New Jersey: Princeton University Press, 1984), p. 132.
20 Cipolletta, 'L'industria italiana negli ultimi 15 anni'; cf. note 1 above.
21 Interview, 16 Nov. 1988.
22 Interview, 15 Nov. 1988.
23 Augusto Graziani, 'Il privilegio della doppia valuta', *Politica ed economia*, 3rd series, XVIII, 10 (Oct. 1987).
24 *La Repubblica*, 21 June 1980.
25 Cesare Romiti, *Questi anni alla Fiat* , pp. 108–109.
26 *L'Unità*, 25 Mar. 1981.
27 *Paese Sera*, 5 Oct. 1981.
28 'Più competitività per le imprese italiane', July 1985.
29 Walsh, p. 12.
30 V. Conti and R. Hamaui, eds, *Il mercato dei titoli di Stato in Italia* (Bologna: Il Mulino, 1993), p. 316.
31 M. Kalecki, 'Political Aspects of Full Employment', in *Selected Essays on the Dynamics of the Capitalist Economy* (Cambridge: Cambridge University Press, 1971), pp. 138–145.
32 'Più competitività'.
33 F. Cavazzuti, *Debito pubblico Richezza privata* (Bologna: Il Mulino, 1986), pp. 26 ff.
34 S. Pérez, 'Monetary Union and Wage Bargaining Institutions in the EU', pp. 1215–1216.
35 See *Previsioni dell'economia italiana*, IX, 2 (Dec. 1995), fig. 20, p. 67.
36 Enrico Marro and Edoardo Vigna, *Sette mesi di Berlusconi* (Rome: Ediesse, 1995), pp. 109–110.
37 Cf. p. 130 above.

## 8  The politics of budgets and public debt

1 V. Tanzi and D. Fanizza, 'Fiscal Deficit and Public Debt in the Industrial Countries, 1970–1994', IMF Working Paper (May 1995).
2 Robert A. Mundell, 'Debts and Deficits in Alternative Economic Models', in M. Baldassari, R. Mundell, and J. McCallum, eds, *Debt, Deficit, and Economic Performance* (Basingstoke: Macmillan, 1993), pp. 90–92: e.g. 'A very expansive fiscal policy, for example, cannot cause much inflation if it is financed by bonds, and it might conceivably cause an appreciation of the currency' (p. 90).
3 Tanzi and Fanizza, p. 12. I am indebted to this paper for parts of the following discussion of the negative effects of debt.
4 *Ibid.*, p. 12. The authors calculate that each 1 per cent increase in the debt–GDP ratio increases the real interest rate in Italy by 7 basis points (0.07 per cent).
5 Calculated from Table 46 in Daniele Franco, *L'espansione della spesa pubblica in Italia* (Bologna: Il Mulino, 1993), pp. 165–166.
6 See, among the vast literature, Ian Gough, *The Political Economy of the Welfare*

*State* (London: Macmillan, 1979), and Göran Therborn, 'Classes and States: Welfare State Developments, 1881–1981', *Studies in Political Economy*, 14 (Summer 1984); more recently, E. Huber and J.D. Stephens, *Development and Crisis of the Welfare State: Parties and Policies in Global Markets* (Chicago: University of Chicago Press, 2001). Gough also points out that a centralized state is more conducive to the expansion of the welfare state than a decentralized one.

7 See Franco, pp. 24–26.
8 Calculated from *ibid.*, pp. 60–61 and 70.
9 *Ibid.*, pp. 60–61.
10 *Ibid.*, pp. 100–101.
11 Franco, Table 26, pp. 119–120.
12 See Franco, Table 30, pp. 136–137.
13 E.g. Alan Peacock, *The Economic Analysis of Government and Related Themes* (Oxford: Martin Robertson, 1979), pp. 109–112, on this so-called 'Baumol thesis'.
14 Gianfranco Pasquino, *Istituzioni, partiti, lobbies* (Bari: Laterza, 1988), p. 143.
15 *Democracy, Italian Style* (New Haven: Yale University Press, 1987), pp. 159–160; La Palombara in the end rejects this term.
16 See Giuseppe Di Palma, *Surviving Without Governing* (Berkeley: University of California Press, 1977), pp. 54–64.
17 See T. Lowi, 'The Public Philosophy: Interest Group Liberalism', *American Political Science Review*, 61, 1 (March 1967), for the seminal article in this vein.
18 *Creating Capitalism* (Oxford: Blackwell, 1988), pp. 3, 9, and *passim*.
19 Innocenzo Cipolletta, 'Le politiche congiunturali e la ristrutturazione produttiva', in I. Cipolletta, ed., *Struttura industriale e politiche macroeconomiche in Italia* (Bologna: Il Mulino, 1986), p. 68.
20 R. Artoni and E. Pontarollo, eds, *Trasferimenti, domanda pubblica, e sistema industriale* (Bologna: Il Mulino, 1986), editors' introduction, p. 25, and Centro Europa Ricerche (CER), *3° rapporto: Mercato e politica industriale* (Bologna: Il Mulino, 1989), p. 293.
21 Artoni and Pontarollo, p. 77.
22 Centro Europa Ricerche, p. 204.
23 R. Artoni and P. Ravazzi, 'I trasferimenti statali all'industria', in Artoni and Pontarollo, p. 37.
24 Centro Europa Ricerche, p. 204.
25 Senato della Repubblica, VIII[a] Legislatura, 321[a] e 322[a] sedute pubbliche, martedì 27 ottobre 1981, and Senato della Repubblica, Giunte e Commissioni parlamentari, 304[o] resoconto, 10[a] Commissione, seduta di giovedì 24 settembre 1981, p. 6.
26 E. Pontarollo and L. Solimene, 'Domanda pubblica e struttura di mercato', in Artoni and Pontarollo, especially pp. 127–128.
27 *Ibid.*
28 'Una politica per lo sviluppo. Vademecum per il confronto elettorale', in *Confindustria per la modernizzazione: Proposte e intese 1992–1995* (Rome: SIPI, 1995), p. 37.
29 P. Bellucci, 'Classi, identità politiche e interessi', in P. Corbetta and A.M.L. Parisi eds, *A domanda risponde* (Bologna: Il Mulino, 1997), p. 279.
30 See G. Amyot, *The Italian Communist Party: the Crisis of the Popular Front Strategy* (London: Croom Helm, 1981), pp. 42–43.
31 Data compiled from Banca d'Italia, *Bollettino economico*, Oct. 1992, pp. 46–47; Feb. 1993, pp. 72–73; Feb. 1994, pp. 68–69; Feb. 1995, pp. 76–78; Feb. 1996, pp. 68–69; Feb. 1997, pp. 78–79, and Dino Pesole, *I debiti degli italiani* (Rome:

Editori Riuniti, 1996), Chapters 6 and 7, *passim*, and *La Repubblica*, 12 July 1996.

32  The distinction between temporary and permanent measures is not, of course, completely clear-cut, since some temporary changes may never be repealed, while others intended to be permanent may in fact be reversed. Permanent changes have been valued, for the purpose of the totals, at their annual effect.

33  Enrico Marro and Edoardo Vigna, *Sette mesi di Berlusconi* (Rome: Ediesse, 1995), p. 142.

## 9  The state and industrial relations

1  *Pouvoir politique et classes sociales de l'état capitaliste* (Paris: Maspéro, 1968), pp. 202–203. Cf. pp. 205–209 on economic concessions (English ed. pp. 188–194].

2  Cf. Theda Skocpol, 'Political Response to Capitalist Crisis: Neo-Marxist Theories of the State and the Case of the New Deal', *Politics and Society*, 10, 2 (1980), pp. 194–196, on the role that the structure of the Democratic Party played in inhibiting a radicalization of the New Deal.

3  As Göran Therborn has pointed out, there is little point in identifying the subjective interests of capitalists; it is useful only to speak of policies favourable to an objective process, such as capital accumulation (*What Does the Ruling Class Do When It Rules?* London: Verso, 1980, pp. 131–132). Even these policies are difficult to identify, especially *ex ante* (Martin Carnoy, *The State and Political Theory*, Princeton: Princeton University Press, 1984, pp. 132 ff.).

4  G. Baglioni, S. Negrelli, and D. Paparella, eds, *Le relazioni sindacali in Italia: Rapporto 1994–95* (Rome: Cesos-Edizioni Lavoro, 1998), p. 249.

5  Even employers who do not belong to the association that signed the contract are generally held to be legally bound to follow it: see Gino Giugni, *Diritto sindacale* (Bari: Cacucci, 1981), pp. 165–171; Giugni also provides the legal background to this approach taken by the courts (pp. 145–165). Note that, even in the absence of a clear legal obligation, many employers regard applying the national contract as a 'norm of correct management' (p. 166).

6  Data calculated from figures in Colin Crouch and Alessandro Pizzorno, *Conflitti in Europa* (Milan: Etas Libri, 1977), pp. 71 and 73. Union membership figures are for CGIL and CISL only.

7  For the company president's version of these events, see Cesare Romiti, *Questi anni alla Fiat*, pp. 106–130.

8  G. Baglioni, S. Negrelli, and D. Paparella, eds, *Le relazioni sindacali in Italia: Rapporto 1996–97* (Rome: Cesos-Edizioni Lavoro, 1998), Tav. 3, p. 143.

9  See e.g. Mimmo Carrieri, *Seconda Repubblica. Senza sindacati?* (Rome: Ediesse, 1997), pp. 80 ff.

10  Romiti, *Questi anni alla Fiat*, p. 229.

11  Marco Revelli, 'Fiat: la via italiana al "postfordismo"' in *Le due destre* (Turin: Bollati Boringhieri, 1996), p. 129. Cf. Richard Locke, *Remaking the Italian Economy* (Ithaca, New York: Cornell University Press, 1995), pp. 109–113.

12  Cf. Miriam Golden, *Labor Divided* (Ithaca, New York: Cornell University Press, 1988), pp. 233–234: the national leadership tried to moderate the Fiat Factory Council's tactics during the 1980 strike.

13  This distinction between the two positions of Italian business is a development of the one suggested by Revelli in *Le due destre*, pp. 7–10. Cf. Locke, *Remaking the Italian Economy*, which suggests that those districts with locally focussed ('polycentric') industrial relations were most successful economically: e.g. pp. 122 ff. (Turin vs. Milan).

14 As pointed out above (p. 116), in 2000, for the first time, Confindustria elected a president who had been opposed by Fiat: Antonio D'Amato initiated a more sharply neo-liberal course and a rapprochement with Silvio Berlusconi and the right-wing opposition.

15 See Dyson and Featherstone, pp. 524–525.

16 See G. Baglioni, A. De Sanctis, and S. Negrelli, eds, *Le relazioni sindacali in Italia: Rapporto 1989–90* (Rome: Cesos-Edizioni Lavoro, 1991) Tav. 3, p. 31. The detailed mechanism involved 100 per cent indexation of a minimum monthly wage, and 25 per cent inflation protection for the portion of a worker's income above that.

17 G. Baglioni, B. Liverani, and S. Negrelli, eds, *Le relazioni sindacali in Italia: Rapporto 1992–93* (Rome: Cesos-Edizioni Lavoro, 1994), p. 88.

18 *Ibid.*

19 Mario Regini, 'Still Engaging in Corporatism? Recent Italian Experience in Comparative Perspective', *European Journal of Industrial Relations*, 3, 3 (1997), and M. Regini and Ida Regalìa, 'Employers, Unions, and the State: The Resurgence of Concertation in Italy', *West European Politics*, 20, 1 (Jan. 1997).

20 Roberto Mania and Alberto Oriolo, *L'accordo di San Tommaso* (Rome: Ediesse, 1993), p. 43. The full text of the agreement is reproduced here, including details not discussed in this chapter.

21 *Ibid.*, p. 50.

22 The mechanism for the choice of this third is variable and complex: see *ibid.*, pp. 62–63.

23 G. Baglioni, S. Negrelli, and D. Paparella, eds, *Le relazioni sindacali in Italia: Rapporto 1993–94* (Rome: Cesos-Edizioni Lavoro, 1995) Tav. 1, p. 119.

24 *L'accordo di San Tommaso*, pp. 48–49.

25 *Previsioni dell'economia italiana*, X, 2 (Dec. 1996), pp. 80–81. This is the semi-annual publication of Confindustria's research centre.

26 See e.g. 'Riello va controcorrente', *La Repubblica*, 24 Dec. 1996, and 'Maratona sulle tute blu', *ibid.*, 7 Jan. 1997.

27 See Sergio Cofferati (with G. Sateriale), *A ciascuno il suo mestiere*, Milan, Mondadori, 1997, p. 45.

28 'Metalmeccanici, Treu interviene', *La Repubblica*, 17 Nov. 1996.

29 'Metalmeccanici, non potete recuperare tutta l'inflazione', *ibid.*, 27 Nov. 1996.

30 'Metalmeccanici, è fatta', *ibid.*, 5 Feb. 1997.

31 '200 mila lire alle tute blu', *ibid.*, 22 Dec. 1996.

32 'Prodi: "Romiti teme un governo che dura" ', *ibid.*, 14 Dec. 1996.

33 *Ibid.*

34 'Metalmeccanici, è fatta', and 'Quel sì sofferto dei "duri" Fiom', *ibid.*

35 Carrieri, pp. 48–50 and 55.

36 Cf. ' "E l'accordo del '93 che dà frutti in busta" ', *La Repubblica*, 30 Aug. 1996, 'Lavoro più flessibile per sconfiggere la crisi', *ibid.*, 7 Sept. 1996, and *Le relazioni sindacali in Italia: Rapporto 1996–97*, p. 170.

37 *L'accordo di San Tommaso*, pp. 118–123.

38 *Le relazioni sindacali in Italia: Rapporto 1996–97*, pp. 164–170.

## 10 Conclusion: the limits of the state's autonomy

1 See Chapter 1, note 6, and Holloway and Picciotto, 'Introduction', in *State and Capital*, pp. 24–28.

2 'The State Apparatus and Social Reproduction: Elements of a Theory of the Bourgeois State', in *ibid.*, p. 82.

3 *Ibid.*, p. 90.

4  *Ibid.*, pp. 100–101.
5  See above, pp. 1–2.
6  See Ellen Meiksins Wood, 'The Separation of the Economic and the Political in Capitalism', *New Left Review*, 127 (May–June 1981), especially pp. 91–92.
7  John Ashworth, *Slavery, Capitalism, and Politics in the Antebellum Republic*, vol. 1: *Commerce and Compromise, 1820–1850* (Cambridge: Cambridge University Press, 1995), pp. 95–101 and 119–121.
8  Cf. Gramsci's comments on the modern form of Caesarism, which depends more on state and private organizations – especially economic ones – than on military force (*Selections from the Prison Notebooks*, pp. 220–221).
9  Cf. Gramsci, *ibid.*, p. 221.
10  McNamara, *The Currency of Ideas*, Chapter 6.
11  Cf. Peter Hall, *Governing the Economy*, Chapter 1, for a summary of different approaches; cf. also Theda Skocpol, 'Political Response to Capitalist Crisis: Neo-Marxist Theories of the State and the Case of the New Deal', *Politics and Society*, 10, 2 (June 1980).
12  Cf. Skocpol, pp. 160–169, and Hall, pp. 13–14.
13  Cf. Hall, pp. 13–15 and Skocpol, p. 157.
14  Cf. Hall, pp. 10–13.
15  Cf. Hall, pp. 15–17 and Skocpol, especially pp. 192–201. Note that Dyson and Featherstone lay much stress on the role of a threesome of 'policy entrepreneurs'.
16  'The Ruling Class Does Not Rule: Notes on the Marxist Theory of the State', *Socialist Revolution*, 33 (May–June 1977), and Skocpol, pp. 182–192.
17  Hall, pp. 17–20 and *passim*.
18  *Ibid.*, p. 19.
19  *Politics in Hard Times*, p. 65.
20  See Marcus Pistor, 'European Integration as Accumulation Strategy: The European Integration Strategy of the Federation of German Industries (BDI) from Eurosclerosis to Economic and Monetary Union', Ph.D. thesis, Queen's University (2002), pp. 177 ff.

# Index

For Product Safety Concerns and Information please contact our EU
representative  GPSR@taylorandfrancis.com
Taylor & Francis Verlag GmbH, Kaufingerstraße 24, 80331 München, Germany

www.ingramcontent.com/pod-product-compliance
Ingram Content Group UK Ltd.
Pitfield, Milton Keynes, MK11 3LW, UK
UKHW020957180425
457613UK00019B/723